FRESH
ENCOUNTER

FRESH

REVISED &
EXPANDED

ENCOUNTER

GOD'S PATTERN *for* SPIRITUAL AWAKENING

HENRY & RICHARD
BLACKABY

CLAUDE KING

NASHVILLE, TENNESSEE

978-0-8054-4780-4

Published by B&H Publishing Group,
Nashville, Tennessee

Henry and Richard Blackaby are represented by the literary agency
of Wolgemuth & Associates, Inc.

Dewey Decimal Classification: 269.24
Subject Heading: REVIVALS \ CHRISTIAN LIFE \ SPIRITUAL LIFE

All Scripture references are taken from the New King James Version (NKJV),
copyright © 1979, 1980, 1982, Thomas Nelson, Inc., Publishers.

8 9 10 11 12 • 18 17 16 15 14

CONTENTS

FOREWORD

I am a committed Christian, actively involved in serving Christ inside and outside my home, the second daughter of Billy and Ruth Graham. I am not just a nominal churchgoer but am presently engaged in a ministry of my own through which I call others to repentance of sin. Yet I have discovered that this shepherd is also a sheep, this teacher is also a disciple, and this "saint" is also a sinner. Therefore, I know the cross isn't just for "them"; it's for me.

The cross is for you, too. Whoever you are—whether your parents were Christians or of some other religion, whether you were raised inside or outside the church, regardless how successful you are or how miserably you've failed—I guarantee that you need repentance from sin. You may well be unaware of the specific sin in your life, yet the symptoms are there because sin diminishes your joy, hinders your fellowship with God, dilutes the power of your prayers and witness, and dulls the sharp edge of your commitment. It robs you of the vitality of your Christian faith.

Every time I read *Fresh Encounter*, I am convicted. Some sin that has been lurking in the shadows of my heart is exposed in the light of the truth contained in this volume. As uncomfortable as it makes me, I praise God for the revelation that leads me once again to the foot of the cross, where I repent of that sin in particular and ask for cleansing and a refilling of the Holy Spirit.

The beauty of *Fresh Encounter* is that it will enable you to search your own heart, too, and see if anything there is offensive to God (Ps. 139:23–24). I have found it effective not only in my own life but also in the life of my ministry staff as they delved into this study together. As my staff works with me to bring revival to the hearts of God's people, they must not miss out on it for themselves. This book has had a crucial role in helping all of us at Angel Ministries maintain revival in our own lives.

Fresh Encounter has also been a strategic tool in preparing for our "Just Give Me Jesus" revivals, which we hold in arenas throughout the world. When a team of women indicates they are praying about inviting me to hold a revival in their area, I ask them to go through this study as a way of preparing their hearts as well as focusing their minds on genuine revival. As they complete this book, they understand that real revival includes evangelism but is not limited to it. And as they work for revival, they do so not only with willing hands but also with clean hearts.

In my book *I Saw the LORD,* I describe revival in the following way:

For some, revival provokes images of sawdust trails, emotional outbursts, off-key singing, finger-pointing preaching, and hell-fire praying. But the revival I'm talking about—the revival God is calling you and me to experience—is something completely different. It's authentic, personal revival.

Personal revival is . . .
Jesus in you
And Jesus around you
And Jesus through you
And Jesus under you
And Jesus over you
And Jesus before you
And Jesus behind you.
Personal revival is just Jesus . . .
Jesus on your mind,
Jesus filling your heart,
Jesus overflowing from your lips.[1]

As you begin this book, my prayer is that you will have a *Fresh Encounter* with Him.

—Anne Graham Lotz

PREFACE

evival has been one of the most mysterious, compelling, sublime, and desperately needed phenomenon in human history. You cannot remain indifferent to it although it produces a wide variety of responses. Over the centuries revival has produced massive influxes of converts into the churches, yet ecclesiastical leaders are often bewildered at how to respond to it or even whether or not they are in favor of it. Revival quickens the human spirit and enlivens worship. It makes prayer exciting, preaching dynamic, and Christian service fervent. Yet churches are as prone to resist revival when it comes as they are to embrace it. Revival seems to defy a simple explanation, let alone a means to control it.

Revivals are God initiated, and God has laid down explicit prerequisites for them (2 Chron. 7:14). Even when God's people are longing and praying for revival, it comes suddenly and unexpectedly. Just as inexplicably, revival can dissipate or end abruptly.

Revival has always met resistance, even within the church, which may seem surprising since revivals have been responsible for many significant advances for God's kingdom. Yet revival also exposes the sin and morbidity of congregations. Numerous accounts of revival testify to the profound sense of God's presence during worship services. This keen awareness of God's nearness was noticeably missing in services preceding the revival. The dynamic preaching often experienced in revival contrasts the anemic and ineffective exhortation of earlier days. The electric singing during revivals eclipses the lifeless music that was the norm. The testimonies of radically changed lives in revival exposes the absence of personal transformation before revival. The fervent and extended prayer times throughout the day and night replace previously forsaken prayer meetings. Most notable is the profound conviction of sin during revival compared to the heretofore complacent and indulgent attitude toward sin before revival. While this book is intended both to explain and to promote revival, Brian Edwards was correct in claiming: "Revival does not need a defense; it needs to be experienced."[1]

Revival amplifies the Christian experience, making the Holy Spirit's work in a person's life unmistakable. Revival demonstrates what is important to God, and it exposes how far God's people have departed from His intention. Revival is not for those who enjoy the status quo. It will disconcert those who rationalize and accommodate their sin. It will unsettle stoic Christians with its fervency. But for those who cannot bear to continue their Christian experience at the same low level to which they have grown accustomed, revival is their deliverance. When churches realize that if the Spirit does not breathe fresh life into their midst they will continue to suffer spiritual powerlessness and cultural irrelevance, then revival is the answer to their desperate prayers.

Contemporary Hearts Cry for Revival

Across America and around the world, God's people are crying out for a fresh encounter with Him. Everywhere we travel we hear churches pleading with God to revive them, their nation, and their world. There is widespread dissatisfaction with today's church. Numerous efforts have been attempted to make the church more relevant, seeker friendly, contemporary, or cutting edge. Yet despite millions of dollars, hundreds of best-selling books, countless church growth conferences, and an endless stream of Christian trends, the church displays a powerlessness that cannot even evangelize people today at the same rate as society's population growth.

Contemporary believers wonder why the mighty movements of God recorded in Scripture and Christian history are noticeably absent today. Modern pastors are burning out at epidemic levels as they experience the demoralizing futility of attempting to lift their church members out of their spiritual lethargy. While some individuals and churches are experiencing a fresh wind of God's Spirit blowing upon them, many others are asking, "Is there a Word from the Lord? What does God want us to do?" Throughout history God has always had a response to those who seek Him (Jer. 33:3).

Just as it was in biblical times, standing in Holy God's presence is an awesome, life-changing experience. While God is always present in a believer's life, revival is a sacred moment when the Holy Spirit draws powerfully, unmistakably near to His people. Revival involves a fresh encounter with Almighty God. Any meeting with God entails a serious, irrevocable accountability. Revival does not merely call for minor adjustments in our schedule. It elicits a humble, on-our-face response to our

Creator. Revival does not result from an encounter with a doctrine but a response to a Person.

This book will examine what Scripture says about Almighty, Hallowed God's requirements for fellowship with Him. As you read Scripture, the Holy Spirit will assist you to understand and apply what it says. You will not merely encounter Bible verses; you will also come face-to-face with the living God because every encounter with God's Word is a meeting with Him.

To obtain the maximum benefit from this book, we encourage you to do the following:

- Take your time. Don't rush through it. God's truths are life-changing and worth time spent meditating on them.
- Expect to encounter God as you read.
- Spend time with God in prayer after you read each chapter.
- Meet together with one or more believers to discuss what God is revealing to you.
- Immediately respond to Him with thorough obedience concerning everything He tells you.
- Encourage others who are seeking revival and share with them what God is teaching you.
- Continue praying, studying, and responding to Him until you and your church experience revival.

This book is designed to help you encounter God through His Word in such a manner that you experience true, deep, and lasting renewal in your life and church. Once God has revived His people, evangelizing others is inevitable.

Warning!

Whenever God speaks, it is never merely for observation or discussion. It is always intended for obedience. God does not make suggestions. He speaks commands. Do you want God to speak to you, your family, and your church? Then be prepared to obey Him. To hear the Creator of the universe communicate with you and then refuse to do what He says is an unmitigated offense. He is your Lord. Christ is Head of the church. He is the sovereign Ruler of the universe. He has every right to ask you whatever He pleases.

Do not read this book unless you mean business with God. If the Holy Spirit takes Scripture and brings you face-to-face with God, you are accountable to respond to what you read. When you hear from God, you must either reject Him or obey Him. To sin in ignorance is one thing, but God holds people accountable who sin with knowledge of the truth (2 Pet. 2:20–21). Jesus asked His followers this troubling question: "But why do you call Me 'Lord, Lord,' and not do the things which I say?" (Luke 6:46).

If you choose to study this material, you will learn what God requires of His people. Then you will face a choice: to do as He says or to carry on business as usual. Be careful to count both costs. Don't merely evaluate the price to obey what God tells you. Be sure to consider the profound loss in not returning to Him. What will it mean to your family or your church if you refuse to follow God's directions? What will happen if you fail to do what He says? Moses warned God's people that the Word of God "is not a futile thing for you, because it is your life" (Deut. 32:47).

Jeremiah and Israel

Jeremiah 41–42 recounts a tragic story from Israel's history. Jerusalem had fallen to the invincible Babylonian army. The Jewish leaders gathered a remnant of the people and prepared to flee to Egypt for safety. As they prepared to depart, they sought God's counsel.

> Now all the captains of the forces . . . and all the people, from the least to the greatest, came near and said to Jeremiah the prophet, "Please, let our petition be acceptable to you, and pray for us to the LORD your God, for all this remnant (since we are left but a few of many, as you can see), that the LORD your God may show us the way in which we should walk and the thing we should do."
>
> Then Jeremiah the prophet said to them, "I have heard. Indeed, I will pray to the LORD your God according to your words, and it shall be, that whatever the LORD answers you, I will declare it to you. I will keep nothing back from you."
>
> So they said to Jeremiah, "Let the LORD be a true and faithful witness between us, if we do not do according to everything which the LORD your

God sends us by you. Whether it is pleasing or displeasing, we will obey the voice of the Lord our God to whom we send you, that it may be well with us when we obey the voice of the Lord our God." (Jer. 42:1–6)

The people vowed to obey whatever God directed. This moment was critical. It involved life and death. After ten days the Lord sent word that the people were to remain in the land He had given them. God also sent this warning:

"Then hear now the word of the Lord, O remnant of Judah! Thus says the Lord of hosts, the God of Israel: 'If you wholly set your faces to enter Egypt, and go to dwell there, then it shall be that the sword which you feared shall overtake you there in the land of Egypt; the famine of which you were afraid shall follow close after you there in Egypt; and there you shall die.'" (Jer. 42:15–16)

The people knew they were in a desperate condition. Their lives were intolerable. But they despised God's remedy. They heard God's Word, but they chose to ignore it. God knew the people were bent on going their own way. They went through the perfunctory motions of seeking His guidance, but they had already made up their minds to go to Egypt. Jeremiah exhorted the people:

"The Lord has said concerning you, O remnant of Judah, 'Do not go to Egypt!' Know certainly that I have admonished you this day. For you were hypocrites in your hearts when you sent me to the Lord your God, saying, 'Pray for us to the Lord our God, and according to all that the Lord your God says, so declare to us and we will do it.' And I have this day declared it to you, but you have not obeyed the voice of the Lord your God, or anything which He has sent you by me. Now therefore, know certainly that you shall die by the sword, by famine, and by pestilence in the place where you desire to go to dwell." (Jer. 42:19–22)

The people made a show of asking for God's directions, but they had no intention of adjusting their plans. That fatal mistake would cost them dearly. Generations of Christians have perpetuated this foolhardy approach to relating to God.

Studying this material will bring you face-to-face with God's requirements for revival. Make sure you, your family, and your church are prepared to do whatever God tells you. Remember that God will respond to you based on what you do and not merely what you promise to do.

God Is at Work!

When the world seems darkest, God's light shines brightest. God knows how to use people in every age to accomplish His purposes. While the spiritual condition of our world may appear extremely bleak, the reality is we are living in a most exciting time! God is moving mightily worldwide to break down long-standing barriers to the gospel. Modern technology is making the preaching of the gospel to all the nations a real possibility. People worldwide are demonstrating a profound spiritual hunger. Nations once closed to Christian witness are now requesting Bibles and asking people to teach them about Christ. The question is this: Will we submit to God's refining fire so He will purify us and work through us to redeem a lost world? We hope your answer is yes!

Henry Blackaby and Claude King wrote the original version of *Fresh Encounter* in 1995. Since that publication, much has happened in the Christian community and around the world. This new edition is greatly revised and expanded. Richard Blackaby took the lead in revising and expanding the 2009 edition. God has granted each of us the enormous privilege of traveling around the world and visiting Christians and churches that have experienced a fresh touch of the Holy Spirit. We have seen what God can do through one individual or church that is wholly yielded to Him. We believe God has enough Christians and churches on the earth today to reach the world for Christ if only each Christian and every church would surrender themselves fully to God. For that to happen, a mighty revival must sweep through our churches. That is the focus of much of our ministry today, and that is why we wrote this book.

May we continue to tremble with holy fear when God speaks (Isa. 66:2), and may we be filled with hope and anticipation for what God is going to do among His people for His glory.

—Henry and Richard Blackaby, Claude V. King
2009

CHAPTER I

The Normal Christian Life:
How Far Have You Fallen?

The aged apostle was banished to the desolate isle of Patmos, exiled for the crime of spreading Christianity. The powerful Roman Empire was seeking to obliterate the Christian movement. The apostles Paul and Peter had already met violent deaths under the sadistic emperor Nero. The seemingly invincible Roman Empire appeared poised to triumph over the fledgling church. Isolated from his fellow believers, hardened convicts his only companions, John prayed for his Christian brethren.

One Lord's Day as he prayed, John heard a loud voice. He turned toward the sound and saw something so terrifying and awesome he fell to the ground as if he were dead. In that moment he beheld the risen Christ standing triumphant among His churches. The book of Revelation relates the details of this transfixing event. Christ revealed His keen awareness of the condition of the churches during John's day. He knew how each congregation was coping with the pressures and temptations the world was pressing upon them. The church at Ephesus enjoyed an especially noble heritage, having been founded by the apostle Paul (Acts 19). The Ephesian church had witnessed amazing miracles. The risen Christ commended them for their discernment and their forbearance: "I know your works, your labor, your patience, and that you cannot bear those who are evil. And you have tested those who say they are apostles and are not, and have found them liars; and you have persevered and have patience, and have labored for My name's sake and have not become weary" (Rev. 2:2–3). John wrote to the believers at Ephesus, relaying the Lord's pleasure with them. Surely it encouraged them to know that the Head of the church declared them to be orthodox and discerners of true and false teaching.

But then those unsettling words: "Nevertheless I have this against you, that you have left your first love" (Rev. 2:4). The Ephesians were orthodox, but they had neglected their love relationship with their risen Savior. The Lord gave this strong directive: "Remember therefore from where you have fallen; repent and do the first works, or else I will come to you quickly and remove your lampstand from its place—unless you repent" (Rev. 2:5).

People are generally unaware of how far they have drifted from God. When God told His people to return to Him in the prophet Malachi's time, they responded by asking, "In what way shall we return?" (Mal. 3:7). They were tragically unaware of how spiritually disoriented they had become. They dutifully performed their religious rituals and regularly attended weekly worship services, assuming this evoked God's pleasure. But God's appraisal of such behavior was pronounced by the prophet Isaiah: "Inasmuch as these people draw near with their mouths and honor Me with their lips, but have removed their hearts far from Me" (Isa. 29:13). Allowing your heart to shift from God is dangerous: living in a state of misguided complacency can be fatal. One of the key steps to revival is having your eyes opened to see the spiritual height from which you have fallen.

Martin Lloyd-Jones lamented the fact that "the greatest problem confronting us in the church today is that the vast majority of professing Christians are not convinced of the 'reality and the desirableness of revivals.'"[1] Church leaders may document their growing attendance and increased contributions. Congregations can point to their spacious modern facilities and a wide array of church programming. Surely God is pleased with them. But God insists we look deeper. He asks us to consider what our walk with Him was once like. We must review what Scripture says pleases God. Looking back over our spiritual pilgrimage will reveal if we have wandered away from a relationship *with* God into service *for* God.

You may feel unsure of how needy you are for renewal or whether your church needs revival. Let's review what God intends for our walk with Him to be like. Examine your life and your church against the following scriptural backdrop to see if you have departed from God and from His ideal.

Your Personal Walk with God

A believer's walk with God is multifaceted and constantly susceptible to change. God has the power and intent to radically permeate every aspect of your life. The following eight points are merely a summary of what a Christian should experience.

Words on paper cannot capture the immeasurable essence of a life lived closely to the Creator and Savior. Work prayerfully through these eight characteristics with an attitude of humility and a willingness to acknowledge and repent from any point where you have departed from Him.

CHARACTERISTICS OF A NORMAL CHRISTIAN LIFE

1. Intimate Fellowship with God
2. Joy in God's Presence
3. A Sense of Peace
4. A Holy Life
5. A Spirit-Filled Life
6. Recognizing God's Voice
7. Filled with the Fruit of the Spirit
8. Experiencing God's Power

---

1. Intimate Fellowship with God

God created you to have a close, personal relationship with Him. Scripture describes God as walking in the garden in the cool of the day seeking Adam and Eve to converse with them (Gen. 3:8). When the first couple hid themselves because of their sin, God called out to them, "Where are you?" (Gen. 3:9). In this beautiful passage we see God seeking fellowship with His people and pursuing them while they sin and try to avoid Him. Does it matter to God whether we choose to spend time with Him? Through His prophet Jeremiah, the Lord declared: "And I spoke to you, rising up early and speaking, but you did not hear, and I called you, but you did not answer" (Jer. 7:13). God did not create people in order to watch us perform religious rituals and scurry busily about accomplishing religious tasks on His behalf. He made us for a relationship, so we could commune with Him and enjoy His presence. As astounding as it may seem, He seeks fellowship with us. When intimate fellowship with God is broken, it is never because He wanted it that way. It is always a result of our choice.

2. Joy in God's Presence

The psalmist declared, "In Your presence is fullness of joy" (Ps. 16:11). To walk closely with God is to experience complete, divine joy. Jesus promised that those who abide in Him will experience His joy overflowing within them (John 15:11). God is worthy of our fear and our reverence, but He is also someone in whom we delight (Ps. 37:4). The soul that enjoys the Lord's presence will not consider time spent with Him in His Word and prayer to be drudgery or monotonous. Time spent in His presence will be a delight. Communing with God satisfies the soul like no other activity. Many Christians have "quiet times" out of duty, discipline, or guilt. But those who experience true fellowship with God long for those moments of joyful communion with Him.

3. A Sense of Peace

Jesus said that when we walk closely with Him, the concerns of this world will not weigh us down or discourage us (Matt. 11:28–30). Scripture commands us to cast our anxieties upon Christ because He cares for us (1 Pet. 5:7). Everyone experiences trials and hardships, but these adversities should not defeat or derail those walking closely with Christ. We must learn to allow Christ to carry the burden of concern for us (Matt. 11:28–30). To shift the weight of our problems, which is far too heavy for us, onto the shoulders of the One who can decisively deal with them is an incredibly freeing experience. By trusting Christ in all circumstances, we become enveloped in an absolute sense of peace, unexplainable except that the Holy Spirit has set a guard over us (Phil. 4:6–7).

4. A Holy Life

God not only wants His people to be holy; He commands it (Lev. 11:44; 1 Pet. 1:15–17). To be holy means to be set apart for God's purposes, to be pure and uncontaminated by sin. It includes being thoroughly righteous in thought and action. Holiness never compromises with sin but recoils from it. We align ourselves with either God or sin. Scripture is clear: "Whoever abides in Him does not sin. Whoever sins has neither seen Him nor known Him" (1 John 3:6). We cannot be in close fellowship with Christ and habitually sin. If you are knowingly sinning yet claiming to abide in Christ, you are lying. God knows it. Others probably see it too.

5. A Spirit-Filled Life

When you became a Christian, Christ, by His Holy Spirit, permanently entered your life (Rom. 8:14–17). The Christian life is not about trying to do your best for God. It is Christ living out His holy life through you (Gal. 2:20). Duncan Campbell said:

"A Christian is a supernatural being who has had a supernatural experience, and that is something more than singing choruses; that is something more than making a decision; that is something more than becoming a member of a church; that is something more than enjoying conventions. It is Christ at the center of my life."[2]

While all Christians have the Holy Spirit residing within them, every area of a Christian's life is not necessarily surrendered to the Spirit's control. We can restrict the Spirit's influence in our lives to the smallest corner of our lives. Nevertheless, the Holy Spirit is never content to be a mute, neglected guest in the upstairs guest room of our lives. He intends to be absolute Lord and to occupy and rule every dimension of our existence. Scripture exhorts believers to be *filled* with the Spirit (Eph. 5:18). This means our lives are completely and continually surrendered to Him. Every aspect of our lives is accessible and yielded to Christ. Often during revivals people spoke of God's presence being "real" to them or of God "entering the room." In reality this indicates that previously these believers had only yielded a portion of their lives to the Spirit's control. When they fully surrendered their lives to Christ, they suddenly experienced His presence to a degree they had heretofore never known. These people's souls had become so barren and parched that when the Holy Spirit filled them, it appeared to them as if Almighty God had walked into the room.

Christians can grow so accustomed to spiritual barrenness that we no longer realize how desperately we need fresh dewdrops from heaven. Octavius Winslow declared: "Oh, it is an alarming condition for a Christian man, when the heart contradicts the judgment, and the life belies the profession! When there is more knowledge of the truth than experience of its power,—more light in the understanding than grace in the affections,—more pretension in the profession than holiness and spirituality in the walk!"[3] When the Holy Spirit fills us, it will be obvious to us and to everyone around us.

6. Recognizing God's Voice

Through His prophet Jeremiah, God offered His people the amazing promise: "Call to Me, and I will answer you, and show you great and mighty things, which you do not know" (Jer. 33:3). God has countless thoughts toward us (Ps. 40:5). God intends to speak to His people. Moreover, Jesus said that those who were His sheep would recognize His voice (John 10:27). However, Scripture warns that if our heart hardens toward God, we will no longer hear His voice (Deut. 30:17). God intends for us to enjoy a two-way relationship with Him involving both speaking and listening. If you are not hearing from God, could it be you have already braced yourself to resist what He says? Over time your heart can grow stiffer until you are impervious to God's voice.

7. Filled with the Fruit of the Spirit

When the Holy Spirit is at work in a believer's life, He will produce spiritual fruit. Fundamentally, the fruit of the Spirit are the character traits of Christ. They include "love, joy, peace, longsuffering, kindness, goodness, faithfulness, gentleness, self-control" (Gal. 5:22–23). Believers who live in the fullness of the Holy Spirit will demonstrate each of these traits in their lives. An absence of any of these traits is a symptom that the believer is in some way quenching the Holy Spirit (I Thess. 5:19). Henry Scougal placed great weight on the reality of a Christlike character in a believer. He said, "I had rather see the real impressions of godlike nature upon my own soul, than have a vision from heaven, or angel sent to tell me that my name were enrolled in the book of life."[4] One of the greatest assurances you can receive of God's presence in your life is the sanctifying work of the Holy Spirit.

8. Experiencing God's Power

Duncan Campbell once asked, "How is it that while we make such great claims for the power of the Gospel, we see so little of the supernatural in operation?"[5] Orthodox Christians routinely affirm that God is almighty, yet rarely do they experience His powerful presence actively working in their lives. God promised His people in Old Testament times that if they observed His commandments they would regularly defeat their enemies (Deut. 28:7, 28). Likewise in the New Testament, the apostle Paul declared that if God is for us it matters not who is against us (Rom. 8:31). The Bible never promises an absence of opposition, but Scripture does indicate that believers who walk closely with Christ will experience spiritual victory. Just as God achieved triumph out of Jesus' brutal death on a cross, so there is no challenge we will face that can ultimately defeat us when we are experiencing intimate fellowship with our Savior.

Continual Defeat

Henry once met a despondent pastor whose life was in shambles. His wife left him. He was estranged from his two adult children. One daughter was in prison, the other in a drug rehabilitation center. His church released him as a result of the meltdown in his personal life. His health suffered from the constant stress. Without an income and facing bitter divorce proceedings, he reluctantly sold his house. Bills were mounting, and he felt abandoned by his friends, colleagues, and church. His analysis of his situation? Spiritual warfare. He believed Satan had specifically targeted him, much like Job, and robbed him of everything. Satan is indeed real and malicious, but it appeared to Henry that this man was experiencing humiliating defeat in every battle he entered. There was no victory in any sector of his life. God warned that when a life is displeasing to Him, He will surrender that person to his enemies (Deut. 28:25). Everyone endures hardship, but routine spiritual defeat is a telling sign that your life is displeasing to God.

Conclusion

The preceding is not an exhaustive list of what it means to be a Spirit-filled Christian. It does provide a benchmark, however, to identify what the normal Christian life ought to look like. If these qualities are not prevalent in your life, consider whether you have ever matured in your Christian life to the point you have experienced the life God saved you for. Or perhaps you, too, should consider the heights from which you have fallen.

Walking with God as a Church

Just as believers' lives reflect their intimacy with God, so the church is intended to be the image of the One who founded it. When a congregation pleases God, it will manifest the following characteristics:

THE NATURE OF THE CHURCH

1. Withstanding the Gates of Hell
2. Having Power to Make Disciples
3. Making a Habit of Praying
4. Accurately Teaching and Preaching God's Word
5. Loving One Another
6. Courageously Confronting Sin
7. Godly Leaders

---

1. Withstanding the Gates of Hell

Jesus clearly taught that any church He builds and over which He is Head cannot be defeated by Satan (Matt. 16:18). Churches will experience unavoidable hardship and challenges in this imperfect world. The fury of hell is being unleashed against today's churches, attacking marriages, families, teenagers, morality, integrity, and purity. Those congregations walking closely with Christ as their Head will feel the full wrath of our mortal enemy, but Satan's forces *will not* carry the day. What about congregations with a divorce rate that matches secular society or church teenagers who are indulging in drugs and promiscuity? In some churches suicides and corporate scandals and the church's ills are occurring with alarming frequency. Is it feasible to blame today's loose morals on the insidious influence of Hollywood, or the lack of statesmen in government for the church's ills? Jesus guaranteed that any church surrendered to Christ as Head would withstand the fiercest satanic onslaught. Clearly, though outside forces assail the body of Christ, the answer for the church's shortcomings lies within.

2. Having Power to Make Disciples

The risen Christ declared to His followers: "All authority has been given to Me in heaven and on earth. Go therefore and make disciples of all nations" (Matt. 28:18–19). When churches go in the name and authority of Christ, God's power is fully at their disposal as they share the gospel and make disciples. Churches have experienced that power and witnessed adamant atheists coming to faith in Christ. Hardened convicts have proven no match for God's might. Fractured marriages have been restored by the healing power of God extended through the church. Drug addicts and alcoholics have been marvelously set free. When the church is empowered by the Holy Spirit, the gates of hell tumble down around it.

Conversely, when a church is not experiencing God's power to set people free, it clearly is in need of revival. When congregations go year after year seeing few if any conversions; when they witness marriages dissolving in their midst into acrimonious divorce; when they observe their young people leaving church in droves; when carnality rages throughout the membership as well as the leadership; when they witness their neighborhood sinking into increasing immorality, crime, and brokenness, the church *must* ask itself, "How far have we fallen? Have we left our first love?" Making excuses is easy. The rising influence of secularism, consumerism, pluralism, tolerance, humanism, big government, and corporations can all become scapegoats for the church's powerlessness. But the truth is that none of these can thwart God's might when the Holy Spirit moves in the midst of a church. Duncan Campbell once observed: "It is fire we want. The best advertising campaign that any church or any mission can put up is fire in the pulpit and a blaze in the pew. Let us be honest. We say 'God send a revival,' but are we prepared for the fire?"[6]

3. Making a Habit of Praying

If there was a defining characteristic of the early church, it is that its people prayed. The book of Acts begins with the risen Christ instructing His followers not to leave Jerusalem or to undertake any ministry until they had been endued with power from on high (Acts 1:4–5). So the members met regularly and "all continued with one accord in prayer and supplication" (Acts 1:14). After these believers had prayed extensively, the Spirit fell upon them with such force that three thousand people were immediately converted.

After the early church faced persecution and threats, they met to pray. "And when they had prayed, the place where they were assembled together was shaken; and they were all filled with the Holy Spirit, and they spoke the word of God with boldness" (Acts 4:31). That's power!

Praying for Revival

When God came in revival at Asbury College in Kentucky, prayer groups had been fervently praying. When God brought revival to Wales, God's people had been praying. When Duncan Campbell arrived in the Hebrides, he found that God's people had been praying. Before Charles Finney went to a city to preach, he would send Father Nash ahead of him to pray for the upcoming meetings. Charles Spurgeon had a large group of people who prayed during every service. In every report from churches who have witnessed the mighty working of God, fervent prayer has always played a key role. Jesus Himself declared that His Father's house was to be a house of prayer (Matt. 21:13). A church that pleases God is a church that habitually and earnestly prays.

4. Accurately Teaching and Preaching God's Word

The Jerusalem church grew so large it required an increasing amount of administration, so the apostles appointed deacons to care for the widows, for they declared, "We will give ourselves continually to prayer and to the ministry of the word"

(Acts 6:4). As new converts entered the church, they "continued steadfastly in the apostles' doctrine and fellowship, in the breaking of bread, and in prayers" (Acts 2:42). Christians in the early church were avid students of God's Word. Church leaders exhibited wholehearted confidence in Scripture, and they preached it boldly and uncompromisingly.

David Matthews insists, "Nothing worthwhile has ever happened in the history of the Church since Pentecost but what is based upon an unshakable belief in the power of the eternal Word."[7] Clearly people used powerfully in revival had an unwavering conviction in the words of Scripture, and, though they varied in their oratorical ability, they pronounced biblical truths with a compelling earnestness. A church is never more in need of revival than when it is twisting and compromising God's Word to satisfy the popular trends and politically correct dogmas of the day. Yet tragically, such churches are also never farther from revival than when they treat God's Word carelessly or irreverently. To be pleasing to God, a church must teach its people to practice everything Christ commanded (Matt. 28:20).

5. Loving One Another

In a healthy church one member cannot suffer without other members of the body feeling the pain (1 Cor. 12:26). The early church was characterized by love and unity. Members freely gave their possessions to assist those in need (Acts 4:32–37). Jesus declared that the unity of His disciples would compel the world to believe in Him (John 17:21). As Christians love one another and carry each other's burdens, the world is convinced of the validity of the Christian message.

Love and a Theme Park

In a church where Richard was a member, there is a forty-six-year-old woman named Margaret who has an eighteen-year-old daughter named Kristie. Both women suffer from a debilitating condition that has left them mentally and physically impaired. Over the years Margaret's church has extended many acts of love to her. She regularly receives food supplements and financial gifts and is often invited into homes for meals and fellowship. Margaret cannot drive a car, but she tries to be as independent as possible. Last year her bike, which is her means of transportation, was stolen. The congregation acted immediately, taking up a collection and presenting her with a brand-new bike. Recently associate pastor Jonathan Chisholm and his wife Cathey took Margaret and Kristie with them to Disney World. Members of the church contributed money to help with the expenses. Margaret claims it was the highlight of her life. The secular paper in town ran a full-page story about the kind way Margaret's church has cared for her over the years. When church bodies are functioning in a healthy manner, no one is overlooked. Everyone is cared for. Everyone is loved.

6. Courageously Confronting Sin

In our efforts to be "tolerant" and our hesitation to be judgmental, today's Christians hardly know how to deal with sin in the church. But the media knows what to do and takes great delight in documenting the moral failures of church leaders. Biblical times were not free from impiety among God's people. However, when it occurred, God led His people to deal with sin immediately and decisively. When Achan sinned, all of God's people were adversely affected (Josh. 7:25). Joshua realized they could not move forward until the sin had been utterly exterminated from the camp.

Jesus gave clear instructions about how to deal with a fellow Christian who was sinning (Matt. 18:15–20). If a Christian sinned against someone, the offended person was to confront the sinner. If the transgressor did not repent, the person returned with one or two witnesses. If the matter remained unresolved, it was brought before the entire church. The final recourse, if the malefactor refused to repent, was for the church to expel that person from its membership. Jesus, who embodied love, understood that unchecked sin was lethal to a church's spiritual vitality. In the early church in Jerusalem, Ananias and Sapphira lied to fellow church members and to the Holy Spirit. The Holy Spirit took dramatic action and immediately put the dishonest couple to death (Acts 5:1–11). As a result, "great fear came upon all the church and upon all who heard these things" (Acts 5:11). Rather than turning people away from the church because of this decisive response to sin, Scripture reports: "And believers were increasingly added to the Lord, multitudes of both men and women" (Acts 5:14). When God and the church dealt forthrightly with sin, God's work was ultimately strengthened and the community felt the impact.

In today's pluralistic age, the popular mantra among God's people has become, "Who am I to judge?" Yet sin is an offense against Holy God. A church cannot tolerate or excuse sin and please God.

7. Godly Leaders

Jesus explained that His disciples had not chosen Him; He had selected them (John 15:16). More specifically, His Father gave them to Him (John 17:12). The heavenly

Father knew each disciple, and He understood how each one could participate in His divine work. Those who led the early church were chosen by God to lead. When the eleven disciples were determining who should replace Judas, they did not take a vote among themselves or place an advertisement on the church bulletin board. They sought the mind of the Lord (Acts 1:15–26). When the church needed people to serve as deacons, its members were told to "seek out from among you seven men of good reputation, full of the Holy Spirit and wisdom, whom we may appoint" (Acts 6:3). Those selected were not people who held influential positions in the marketplace or who had the largest personal incomes. These were individuals who were filled with the Holy Spirit. They included people like Stephen who was "full of faith and power" (Acts 6:8). They did not attain their ecclesiastical positions through political maneuvering or scheming but by God's clear appointment. As the church developed certain offices, it upheld strict standards (1 Tim. 3:1–13). The early church understood that as go the leaders so goes the church.

Conclusion

If you are presently experiencing God's ideal for your life personally and for your church, then you may not feel a need for revival. It could also be that you are not aware of how far you have fallen. If you simply compare yourself with other Christians or churches, you can mistakenly assume you are pleasing God. Always look to God's ideal. Never water down what God says in His Word. Do not assume revival is impossible in today's society. With God all things are possible! Refuse to settle for anything less than God's best for you and your church.

QUESTIONS FOR REFLECTION AND DISCUSSION

1. Review the signs of a vibrant walk with God. Are any of these characteristics lacking in your life? How do you sense God wants to draw you closer to Him?
2. Are you currently living a Christian life thoroughly pleasing to God? If not, in what way do you sense you are personally in need of revival?
3. What are you presently doing to prepare your life for revival?
4. What characteristics of God's ideal do you sense are lacking in your church? What can you do personally to bring needed change?
5. How are you presently praying for your church and its leaders?

CHAPTER 2

What Is Revival?: Definitions and Misconceptions

Seeking to understand revival is like attempting to comprehend the Trinity. We cannot fathom the triune nature of God because He is divine and we are not. People display supreme human arrogance when they insist they will not accept the gospel claims until they understand the nature and work of God to their satisfaction. Such a demand is ludicrous. To understand God completely we would have to be gods ourselves. The only truths we can ascertain about the divine with any certainty are those facts God chooses to reveal to us. An unsanctified mind cannot comprehend divine realities even though they are clearly written on the pages of Scripture.

Likewise we can never fully grasp the magnitude of what happens in revival because it is fundamentally a divine work. God has graciously spoken of it in His Word, and we have numerous accounts of it throughout history. We are wise to examine what Scripture declares concerning revival. Also helpful, to say nothing of deeply inspirational, is to review carefully the great moments of revival throughout history. Nevertheless, many aspects of spiritual renewal cannot be fully apprehended by our finite minds, and diverse opinions abound concerning its origin and nature. In this chapter we will consider several definitions revival experts have proposed. We will also examine common misconceptions concerning revival.

Suggested Definitions

To encapsulate the magnitude of revival in one succinct definition is impossible. People who have spent the greater part of their lives studying the workings of God have captured distinct aspects of revival that when, taken together, help us appreciate the multifaceted nature of God's powerful activity among His people. Notice the variety of definitions for revival:

> Revival is that strange and sovereign work of God in which He visits His own people—restoring, reanimating, and releasing them into the fullness of His blessing.[1] (Stephen Olford)

> Revival is God's invasion into the lives of one or more of His people in order to awaken them spiritually for kingdom ministry.[2] (Malcom McDow and Alvin Reid)

> Revival is a time when heaven comes closer to earth.[3] (Francois Carr)

> Revival is a community saturated with God.[4] (Duncan Campbell)

> Revival is an extraordinary movement of the Holy Spirit producing extraordinary results.[5] (Richard Owen Roberts)

> Revival, above everything else, is the glorification of the Lord Jesus Christ, the Son of God. It is the restoration of him to the center of the life of the church.[6] (Martin Lloyd Jones)

> A true Holy Spirit revival is a remarkable increase in the spiritual life of a large number of God's people, accompanied by an awesome awareness of the presence of God, intensity in prayer and praise, a deep conviction of sin with a passionate longing for holiness and unusual effectiveness in evangelism leading to the salvation of many unbelievers.[7] (Brian Edwards)

> Revival is a divine intervention in the normal course of spiritual things. It is God revealing Himself to man in awful holiness and irresistible power . . . It is man retiring into the background because God has taken the field.[8] (Arthur Wallis)

Each definition by these respected authors brings helpful focus to the complex nature of revival. You will notice that because revival is such a powerful phenomenon, people inevitably move from defining revival to describing it. It is easier to describe what revival *does* than to define what revival *is*. Having acknowledged this, we submit here our own definition of revival:

> Revival is a divinely initiated work in which God's people pray, repent of their sin, and return to a holy, Spirit-filled, obedient, love relationship with God.

We will spend the remainder of this book delving into this definition, but at this stage let us highlight its main points:

First and foremost, revival is a work of God. Spiritually dormant Christians cannot resuscitate themselves. Those in a coma cannot push the button beside their hospital bed to alert the nurse's station of their dire condition. They cannot give themselves medicine or go for a walk to get some fresh air. God is the Creator and Sustainer of life; only He can dispense it. Even when people begin to sense their need for revival and they start meeting with others to pray for it, they are simply responding to a divine initiative, convicting them of their sin and prompting them to return to God.

Second, the first thing God does with His people in revival is to take them to the place of repentance. There will be no revival where there is no repentance. Some writers on revival have spoken of a "repentance revival" as if this is one type out of many varieties of revival.[9] However, such a view is untenable. Scripture clearly teaches that sin brings spiritual death (Rom. 6:23). The only remedy for sin is repentance (1 John 1:9–10). Just as the first words of John the Baptist and Jesus in their earthly ministries was "repent," so the first place the Holy Spirit will always take people experiencing the spiritually deadening effects of sin is to the place of repentance (Matt. 4:17; Mark 1:4–5).[10]

Third, revival involves returning to God. When God seems distant from us, it is never God who has departed from the relationship. God urged His people through the prophet Malachi: "Return to Me, and I will return to you" (Mal. 3:7). Likewise in the New Testament James declared, "Draw near to God and He will draw near to you" (James 4:8). Throughout the historic accounts of revival are repeated references to the nearness and palpable presence of God in the midst of people. Just as in the days of Malachi when God's people asked, *"In what way shall we return?"* (Mal. 3:7), so God's people are often unaware of how far they have departed from God until He leads them to return. In times of revival, God's people suddenly become aware of how far they have strayed from God, and they return.

Fourth, true revival always leads to holiness. You cannot continue to practice sin and simultaneously experience spiritual renewal. In Isaiah 1, God rejected His people's worship when they entered the place of worship with sin-filled lives

(Isa. 1:1–20). When the prophet Isaiah experienced a fresh encounter with God, his immediate concern was his lack of holiness (Isa. 6:5). More than our worship or our service for Him, God desires holiness (Lev. 11:44; I Pet. 1:15–16). While some people suggest there can be a revival of worship or prayer without repentance, we do not see this as possible or biblical. Only after God restores us to holiness are we free to pray, worship, and serve Him in the manner He deserves.

Fifth, when revival occurs, people are filled with the Holy Spirit. Preaching becomes powerful when anointed by the Spirit. Duncan Campbell declared that after he experienced personal revival, he would preach sermons he had delivered before, but now they were characterized by divine power. The congregation can sing the same songs, yet now they are invigorated by the Spirit, and the times of corporate worship are characterized by joy and the presence of God's Spirit.

Sixth, revival stimulates an attitude of willing obedience to whatever God requires. Much of carnal Christianity comes not from ignorance of what God expects but from hearts unwilling to do what God has clearly commanded. Revival, because it draws people back to the Lord, inevitably produces an eagerness to do His bidding.

Most important, revival brings God's people back into a love relationship with Him. Christianity is not a religion. It is a relationship. As God demonstrated so graphically through the prophet Hosea, to forsake God is to commit spiritual adultery. Rejecting God is not merely breaking a command or neglecting a precept. It is a blatant repudiation of the One who dearly loves you. When revival comes, people recognize their sin for what it is: a renunciation of God and a violation of the love relationship. That is why, in times of revival, people often declare that God's salvation is too good for them considering the way they had coldly rejected the love of Jesus their Savior.[11]

Even as we submit our definition of revival for your consideration, we recognize that it falls short of fully encompassing all that is involved in spiritual renewal. Yet as we discuss and illustrate these emphases in the following pages, we encourage you to undertake a serious study of this critical subject. Much has been written and many insights have been offered that are worthy of close examination.

Misconceptions Concerning Revival

As we look at the critical subject of revival, we must consider some key issues and address some common misunderstandings if we are to understand what Scripture teaches about revival. We will identify some of these here, but we will take the remainder of the book to address them in greater detail.

Revival Can Be Produced through Human Efforts

This misunderstanding is a subset of the age-old debate within Christendom between Calvinism and Arminianism. John Calvin upheld the absolute sovereignty of God in effecting people's salvation as well as in convicting them of sin. According to Calvin, nothing good could occur in Christians' lives apart from the Spirit's regenerating and sanctifying work. Jacob Arminius, on the other hand, believed people could partake in the process of salvation through specific actions. Such steps as believing and confessing sin appeared to him clear evidence that people participated in their own salvation.

This debate has carried over into our understanding of revival. While clearly God is the One who brings life, He also expects His people to meet His prerequisites for revival. Second Chronicles 7:14 declares that if God's people "humble themselves, and pray and seek My face, and turn from their wicked ways, then I will hear from heaven, and will forgive their sin and heal their land." This verse clearly identifies actions God's people must take for revival to come.

The great revivals in history began with people who had a keen sense of God's sovereignty. Jonathan Edwards noted the most spiritual fruit he witnessed in revival resulted from preaching on "God's absolute sovereignty."[12] Charles Finney is the revivalist best known for introducing "new measures" that he believed could be used to produce results in revival meetings. We will look at this approach in later chapters. However, Finney also strongly believed in prayer and would enlist prayer warriors such as Father Nash to precede him to cities in order to intercede for the city before Finney arrived to preach. Those who experienced revival clearly understood that despite people's participation it was ultimately a divine work.

Revival Is for Unbelievers to Be Converted

Those familiar with contemporary revival meetings recognize the primary emphasis in most of them is evangelism. When you mention you just attended a series of revival meetings, the most typical response is, "How many people were saved?" Not, "How many were revived?" *Revive* comes from the Latin word *re*, meaning "again," and *vivier* meaning "live." For this discussion the key part of this word is *re*. To live again requires that you have lived previously. Revival does not create life. It resuscitates it. Consequently, revival is for those who previously experienced life but whose spiritual life has grown barren and anemic because of sin.

What confuses some people seeking to understand revival is that conversions always accompany periods of revival. People *are* saved during times of spiritual renewal. When God moves powerfully among His people, the natural consequence is that revived Christians impact the lives of unbelievers around them. Conversions are a repercussion of revival, not a core aspect of it. Jesus declared that His people were to be salt and light (Matt. 5:13–16). When salt is functioning as it should, the meat it touches is preserved. When a light shines as it is designed, darkness is dispelled. There is no need to scurry about a room trying to rid it of darkness; one must simply turn on a light. In revival, salt is made salty again, and lights are made to shine brightly once more. Once this occurs, the surrounding environment is immediately impacted.

The problem today is that churches are striving to win their world to Christ without having first been revived themselves. The result is spiritually comatose church members going door-to-door asking unbelievers if they would like to have what they have—spiritual anemia! Such an invitation is patently unappealing. It explains the high dropout rate in the church today. Newborn spiritual babes are being placed into churches filled with spiritually lethargic people. It is a recipe for disillusionment.

Revival Can Occur without Repentance

We have touched on this misconception earlier. The confusion surrounding the need for repentance in revival stems in part from too broad a use of the word *revival*. For some a revival is anything a Christian does that is reenergized. So a "prayer revival" is when Christians become motivated to begin attending the weekly prayer meeting or to commit to personal prayer several times during the week. While this could be a consequence of revival, a renewed interest in and commitment to prayer is not in itself revival. This could merely be the result of a prayer conference your church recently held where a motivational speaker convinced you your life would be better if you were a person of prayer.

Likewise, many are speaking today of a "worship revival." That is, people are enjoying attending worship services to a degree they had not been previously. While invigorated worship certainly results from revival, a renewed interest in worship is not identical to revival. When young people declare they have begun to enjoy worship services, it could mean their church worship leader recently introduced drums and electric guitars to the worship team. Or perhaps a new preacher has come who delivers livelier sermons. There can be many reasons for a renewed enjoyment of worship services, but they are not necessarily evidence of spiritual renewal.

People can experience a revival in anything from classic car styles to retro clothes, music, and movies. Yet true biblical revival deals specifically with one's relationship to God. Only one thing ultimately quenches our relationship with Him, and that is sin. Sins of idolatry, commission, and omission are lethal to spiritual vitality. Sin has only one remedy, and that is repentance. Without repentance there is no revival.

Revival Always Involves a Deep Demonstration of Emotion

One of the distinguishing characteristics of revival as well as one of the greatest points of criticism has centered on its emotional responses. When Jonathan Edwards preached his famous sermon "Sinners in the Hands of an Angry God," those listening in the audience fainted and cried out in terror. Over the history of revivals, people have cried out, wailed, fallen to the ground, fainted, shrieked, moaned, and laughed. Charles Finney noted in one service, "The Spirit of God came upon them with such power that it was like opening a battery upon them."[13] In a meeting attended by many skeptical college students, Jonathan Goforth noted that the Holy Spirit suddenly "swept like an avalanche through the university students."[14] Goforth, who witnessed a great revival in China, observed: "If the Almighty Spirit moves in sovereign power on the hearts and consciences of men the outcomes must be above the normal. . . . [Might] as well expect a hurricane, an earthquake, or a flood to leave nothing abnormal in its course, as to expect a true Revival that is not accompanied by events quite out of the ordinary experience."[15] One could legitimately enquire how a personal encounter with Almighty God could not affect someone's emotions. When Isaiah came face-to-face with God enthroned, he cried out, "Woe is me" (Isa. 6:5). When the beloved disciple encountered the risen Christ on the isle of Patmos, he fell to the ground as a dead man (Rev. 1:17). If we are not experiencing a deep emotional response when we encounter our Creator and Judge, we may need to ask why not.

Nevertheless, to assume revivals are nothing more than mass emotionalism is a misconception. Many revivals have been orderly and free of excessive affectations. During the Asbury revival in 1970, college students testified and worshiped for 185 straight hours, but the services were orderly, and students politely waited their turn to testify. Charles Spurgeon experienced almost continuous revival in his church, and yet services were peaceable and focused on the preached Word. Deeply stirred emotions are a possible result of revival, but they do not constitute revival itself.

There Is Only One Kind of Revival

In essence, this is true. However, genuine revival is conducted in two major ways. One is leader directed and Word centered. The other is laity led and testimony driven. A classic example of the former is the First Great Awakening. This moving of God was led primarily by pastors, including Jonathan Edwards, Gilbert Tennant, and Theodore Frelinghuysen along with the itinerant preacher George Whitefield. The services were focused on preaching and teaching of Scripture. The pastors and preachers controlled the order of the service, and the focal point was their exposition and application of Scripture.

The latter type of revival, laity driven and testimony centered, was exemplified by the Laymen's Prayer Revival of 1957–58 and the Asbury Revival of 1970. In these cases no prominent pastors dominated the movement with their preaching. Rather, laypeople took an active role, praying and testifying. In some ways this form of revival can spread more rapidly because its advance does not depend on a Whitefield or Edwards to do the preaching. In the Asbury Revival the president of the school was out of the country when revival came. When teams of revived Asbury College students traveled across the country testifying to what had happened, more than 130 college campuses soon felt the impact. It has been said that "revival comes through prayer, but testimony spreads the flame."[16]

We would make two general observations about laity-led, testimony-driven revivals. First, they tend to be more prone to abuse. While a man such as Jonathan Edwards witnessed dramatic occurrences during periods of revival, he discouraged excessive forms of emotionalism. If people acted or spoke inappropriately, they were silenced. Further, pastor-led, Word-centered revivals tend to be more rooted in Scripture, which is much more reliable than people's feelings and testimonies. Testimony-driven revivals can be as genuine as Word-driven revivals, but they invite people unschooled in theology or who are easily misled by their emotions to affect the spirit of the entire meeting. Some have argued that the great revival under Evan Roberts in Wales was harmed because he did not place preaching at the center and he was not always discerning in screening who was allowed to testify in the meetings.[17] Some of the testimonies became deeply emotional and at times suggested things that were unbiblical. A second observation is that Word-centered revivals tend to last longer than testimony-driven movements. This may be because they are generally more firmly grounded in Scripture and led by church leaders.

Revivals Are Merely an Attempt to Take a Shortcut from Hard Work and Evangelism

Some critics have charged that all the time spent praying for revival could be better spent by church members doing door-to-door evangelism. While a heartfelt desire for revival never negates our responsibility to make disciples of all nations, to accuse advocates of revival of being lazy is to demonstrate a gross ignorance of what revival entails. Jonathan Edwards believed church history was cyclical, highlighted by great spiritual harvests in which God revived His church and brought large numbers of converts into His kingdom in short periods of time. This did not cancel Edwards's sense of responsibility for nurturing his flock, as he was famous for spending an average of thirteen hours every day in his study preparing to preach and teach those God placed in his care. Edwards recognized that in only a few months God could accomplish more than he could in years of laborious ministry.

Those who view a longing for revival as a desire to avoid hard work do not understand what happens in revival. During such times vast numbers of people, previously unchurched, are born again. In Wales 100,000 people were added to the churches in six months. During the Laymen's Prayer Revival estimates of conversions range as high as one million people in one year. Clearly when God chooses to move in the midst of His people, He can accomplish more in one month than normal church programming can achieve over a decade. When Christians witness what happens in revival, they have an overriding passion to see it happen again and again.

Those who led in revival were anything but lazy. Preachers might preach nightly for seven straight weeks. Worship services would regularly go until late at night with afterglow meetings lasting until the early morning hours. The swarms of people seeking counsel, the attacks from critics, and their own earnest desire to know what God wanted them to do next produced enormous pressure on those responsible for leading revival. Evan Roberts, who was still a young man when revival came to Wales in 1904, was so spent after six months that he retired to a private home in England and never returned to revival ministry.

Issues to Be Examined

Along with these misconceptions are several important issues that must be examined in any serious study of revival. The following are some of the most challenging issues related to revival. We will touch on them here but will address them more fully throughout the remainder of the book.

Does Revival Represent What Normal Christianity Should Be, or Is It Something Extraordinary?

For those who experience revival, the presence of God is almost overwhelming, the preaching is often dynamic, the testimonies of transformed lives are compelling, and the singing is transcendent. Having experienced this, it is difficult to go back to business as usual. The inevitable questions follow: is that what normal church and Christianity are supposed to be like all the time? Is anything less sub-Christian? To this Brian Edwards notes: "Revival is not normal any more than spiritual decline and backsliding are normal. These are opposite ends of the normal life of the church. Revival is supernormal and backsliding is subnormal."[18] Revival can be a spiritual mountaintop experience. However, such experiences are always designed to prepare us for life lived in the valley.

What Role Do People Play in Revival? Why Does God Work Mightily through Some People and Not Others?

To quote Brian Edwards, "God has almost always used particular men to lead His work. That is His method."[19] Any study of the kinds of people God used in revival reveals an extremely wide diversity. Some, such as George Whitefield, were among the most powerful preachers in church history. Others, such as William M'Culloch of Cambuslang, Scotland, possessed no unusual gifts. It has been said of him, "M'Culloch's personal qualifications for his office were not such as to mark him out as a probable leader in a great revival movement. He seems to have been possessed of more than average scholarship, but for the pulpit he had virtually no gifts. His voice was thin and weak and his utterance slow."[20] Yet God worked powerfully through M'Culloch even as He used ministers with far greater pulpit skills.

We will examine more thoroughly the characteristics of numerous leaders of revival throughout this book, but we can conclude that those God used mightily to revive His people were people of fervent prayer who truly believed that with God all things are possible. They also were deeply burdened that the people around them desperately needed a fresh encounter with God. Those God chose to use to impact their generation were willing to pay whatever price was necessary to be effective instruments in God's hands.

Evan Roberts, who saw 100,000 people in Wales come to faith in Christ in six months, was once sharing with a group of people about the mysteries of God. Suddenly a young woman exclaimed, "Mr. Roberts, how fortunate you are to know all these things! I wish I knew them also." In response, Roberts solemnly asked, "Are you willing to pay the price?"[21] That question resounds throughout the ages to all who desire their lives to be used powerfully by God.

What Role Does Prayer Play in Revival?

John Greenfield has noted, "Prayer always precedes Pentecost."[22] Perhaps the only common denominator you find when you study the facets related to revival is prayer. While at times a revival will be highlighted by dynamic preaching or emotional testimonies, you never need to peer back far to discover that in every great outpouring of God's Spirit, people were praying. Prayer always precedes revival. It plays a prominent role during revival, and revival always leaves a praying people in its wake. However, prayer does not guarantee revival. Our fervent praying never holds God hostage to our requests. He remains sovereign and will visit His people afresh on His terms and in His timing. Today record numbers of ministries and prayer groups across North America are committed to praying for revival. Yet as of this writing, large scale, national revival has not occurred in North America as a result of this praying. As we will see, no revival has occurred without prayer, but praying for it does not guarantee it will come.

Why Do Revivals Come to an End?

For those who have participated in revival, it is a blessed and exhilarating experience. When you are in the midst of the outpouring of God's Spirit, it seems as if heaven descends to earth and the angelic hosts join God's people in worship. With church leaders humbled before God, ordinary believers confessing their sins and being reconciled with one another, unbelievers experiencing profound conversions, young adults feeling called into full-time Christian ministry, one would think the church would continue from that point onward to function in the environment of continuous revival. But that does not happen. In fact, Brian Edwards suggests that revival rarely outlasts one generation.[23]

There are many reasons why revivals do not linger. At times it is because a radical element gains a prominent role in the movement, and God withdraws His blessing. In some cases pride fills the hearts of those in leadership, and God no longer entrusts His mighty work into their hands. A broader answer to the question may be that God never intends for revival to be a permanent reality. Revival is *restorative* not *normative*. Revival brings people back into the intimate, consecrated walk with God they had previously forsaken. This comes through brokenness and repentance. A revival might last many weeks where people confess grievous sins night after night. But eventually God's people have been purified and forgiven, and they must then move on to their calling of daily living for Him. Sometimes revival comes to a close because God has accomplished the work He set out to do.

Why Does God Bring Revival to Some Places and Not to Others?

This is another intriguing question. Canada, for instance, has never had a nation-wide revival. Yet it has experienced regional revivals such as in the Maritimes under Henry Alline in the eighteenth century and in Saskatoon in 1972. J. Edwin Orr, the premier revival historian, observed that the Laymen's Prayer Revival, a movement he referred to as "The Event of the Century," actually began in Canada.[24] However, although the 1857–58 awakening began in Canada, it never had the impact it did on the United States. Certainly geographic, demographic, religious, and cultural factors played a role. Anyone who knows Canada understands its religious landscape differs significantly from its southern neighbor. Yet revival is not restricted to culture. Great revivals have swept countries as diverse as Scotland, the Congo, China, and Indonesia. Why does revival come to one church and not another? Why does God use some people like John Wesley, Charles Finney, and Evan Roberts to bring revival and not others? This is an issue shrouded in mystery and ultimately only explained by God's sovereign will.

Is Satan Active in Revivals, and If So, How Can He Still Function in the Midst of a Great Work of God?

It has always been enigmatic that people could be in the presence of a powerful outpouring of God's Spirit and yet become an instrument of Satan. It seems inconceivable that Judas, one of Jesus' twelve disciples, could walk closely with Jesus for three years, watch Him perform astounding miracles, listen to His profound teaching, and receive His loving attention, yet choose to do the unthinkable and betray his Lord. But it is possible. Satan does some of his most devious and destructive work in the midst of the mighty acts of God.

During the revival that occurred in Northampton under Jonathan Edwards in 1735, many lives were gloriously transformed, and large numbers were converted. Then, on Sunday morning, June 1, 1735, Joseph Hawley II, a respected leader in Northampton society, a faithful member of the church, and Jonathan Edwards's uncle, committed suicide by slitting his own throat.[25] Hawley had struggled with depression, but this violent, hopeless act by a man who sat in the same services week after week as people experiencing revival shocked people. Even in the midst of glorious spiritual renewal, Satan was prowling like a roaring lion seeking whom he might devour. When God was accomplishing a great work, the forces of evil were desperately launching a counterattack.

Satan first seeks to destroy God's work, and failing that, he duplicates it. As we will see, one of the enemy's most cunning strategies is to introduce a counterfeit element into the stream of revival. Often this measure, when exposed and denounced by the media and the general public, is sufficient to discredit the legitimate aspects of revival as well. It seems strange that, despite the multitudinous prayers, the forceful worship services, and widespread public surrender to God's will in times of revival, Satan is not held at bay. Rather, evil is present, even in the midst of revival. As preachers preach powerful sermons, some of them are tempted to believe they are great orators. As people publicly confess their sin, some revel in the attention they receive as they hold the microphone. Even as some lives are being genuinely transformed, others may falsify changes in their lives. While some are honestly sharing what God has said to them, Satan is leading others to make wild declarations and to fabricate dreams and visions. God has won the decisive battle against Satan and his hellish forces, but the war has not yet ended. Even as an army will fight more desperately when its back is against a wall, so the spiritual forces of wickedness battle most desperately when they see God's kingdom advancing. Periods of revival are not times to let down your guard to the warfare continually waged in the spiritual realms.

Historically What Role Have Young People Played in Revival?

A fascinating issue related to revival is the involvement of young people. Many of the revival preachers, such as John Wesley, George Whitefield, Charles Finney, and Evan Roberts, were young men when God used them. Numerous great movements of God occurred on college campuses such as Yale, Howard Payne University, Wheaton College, and Asbury College.[26] The revival under Jonathan Edwards in Northampton in 1735 began among young people.[27] Written accounts of great revivals show that those first stirred by the revival fires were often youth and young adults. Surely this factor provides significant guidance to those who long to see revival come in their day. Rather than demeaning young people in the church or consigning them to the "youth building" while the adults have their revival meeting, churches would be wise to invest heavily in the spiritual nurturing of their young people. Churches that lose their young people and fill their pews on Sundays with gray hair will have a much more difficult time experiencing revival.

What Is the Role of Public Confession?

One of the most provocative aspects of revival is the practice of public confession. Sharing grievous sins in public not only arouses great emotions, but it can also lead to many forms of abuse. Confession can at times be more tantalizing than sanctifying. Immature people can enjoy the public attention they receive as they testify rather than being broken over what they are admitting. The need for public versus private confession is a point of debate. Is it not enough to go to God, against whom we have sinned, and confess our sins to Him (Ps. 51:4)? What is the need of telling everyone else in our church, many of whom previously thought highly of us? Is there something therapeutic or redemptive about God's people publicly renouncing their sins? Some have argued that public confession tarnishes the church's reputation in the community. Yet often through times of confession, such as at Asbury College, revival has burst forth in full bloom. J. Edwin Orr observed, "Confession of sins is a neglected doctrine. It only comes into its rightful place in times of revival."[28] Orr also gave this sage advice to those wondering if they should confess their sins publicly: "Let the circle of the sin committed be the circle of the confession made."[29] When confessing sins publicly, believers are wise to limit details to the essential facts and to glory in God's gracious act of pardon rather than in the shameful behavior being renounced.

What about Sins of the Past?

Another controversial subject that recurs in times of revival concerns past sins. What effect do they have on the present? If a middle-aged woman had an abortion as an unmarried teenager, does that sin still need to be confessed publicly, decades later? During times of revival, people may conduct an exhaustive inventory of every sin they ever committed and seek to confess them in order to be set free. Yet where is the line? Does every unconfessed sin from our past weigh heavily on our soul? Is spiritual powerlessness today the result of unconfessed sin from days gone by? What about past sins we have forgotten? Do unremembered, unresolved sins stifle our spiritual life years later? When we experience spiritual defeat, should we immediately begin reviewing our distant past to determine if our present unpleasant circumstances are the result of a forgotten sin? How does the Holy Spirit alert us to those things He knows we must deal with in order to be set free?

How Do We Deal with Corporate Sins?

What is corporate sin? Consider a church that had a bitter split twenty years ago. Amid much acrimony, a splinter group angrily departed and formed its own church. For decades the two congregations have had no interaction with each other and have made no attempts to reconcile. Now a new generation of church leaders has arisen.

They were only children when their parents divided. These second-generation church leaders are sensitive to the fact that God is not blessing their congregations. The questions are: should the present generation repent for sins committed by former members? Do later generations bear the guilt and consequences for their parents' misdeeds?

Can churches or nations sin corporately; and, if so, how do they find cleansing and release from their sin? Why are some churches plagued by continual scandal and heinous sin while others are relatively free from it?

We know churches that were birthed in sin. The founding pastor was having an adulterous relationship while starting the church. Not surprisingly, an inordinate number of the church's leaders also committed adultery and ultimately experienced divorce. Numerous new churches have been formed as a result of angry division in a former congregation. Does God bless such churches? If the way an organization begins plays a determinative role in its future, what does this suggest for the many congregations littered across the North American landscape that were birthed in bitterness and unforgiveness?

We know churches that endured repeated scandals among their ministers and church leaders. The founding pastor of the church was eventually fired for adultery, and five senior pastors later the church had to fire yet another senior pastor for immorality. Some churches, it seems, have had immorality, divisiveness, or lack of faith passed on in their DNA. If a church or a family appears to have inherited an ungodly heritage that continually repeats itself, how does it purge itself of its sin?

These are some of the issues we will probe during subsequent chapters. As we have already seen, revival is a complex subject. It is a divine work contingent on God's sovereignty. As we gain a greater understanding of how God works in revival, we will be better prepared to be His instrument should He choose to revive His people today.

QUESTIONS FOR REFLECTION AND DISCUSSION

1. What are some issues you are concerned about in revival?
2. In light of what you have read so far, how would you define revival? What do you believe are its fundamental characteristics?
3. How do you sense God wants to revive your life and your church?

CHAPTER 3

Current Status of the Church and the World: Why We Need Revival

The church today needs many things, but its most critical shortfall is not larger attendance, money, buildings, or programs. Its greatest need is for revival. Our generation must experience revival, or our churches face increasing irrelevance and ultimately God's judgment. There are those who would adamantly disagree. They would effusively point to the proliferation of megachurches emerging across the country and the world. They would highlight the sophisticated new approaches to evangelism and the numerous programs and technological wizardry available to assist churches in their mission. Yet we are reminded of the early church at Laodicea, which apparently also had all the markings of ecclesiastical success except for one thing: God's pleasure. God noted that this congregation had grown spiritually lukewarm. They were neither hot nor cold but middle of the road, comfortably irrelevant. God's word to them: repent or perish (Rev. 3:14–20).

We love the church and have invested much of our lives encouraging and teaching God's people. We are not alarmists, crying wolf for the sake of sensationalism. However, just as doctors would be irresponsible to tell their patients there was nothing wrong with them to prevent upsetting them, so it would be a gross abdication of duty to declare the church healthy when there are clear signs it is in serious trouble. The following is an overview of the present state of the church as well as society at large. It is not exhaustive, and we readily acknowledge that others would portray conditions differently. Nevertheless, the issues we raise may help bring focus to the plight of today's church. As you consider the church's condition, our prayer is that you, too, will feel compelled to cry out to God for revival.

Condition of the Church

We do not pretend to be leading authorities on the state of the church. Nevertheless, we do spend most of our time speaking with people in churches of various denominations across North America. We also regularly meet with pastors and church leaders around the world. We have witnessed God's activity in diverse places and have also heard the heartache of ministers who expressed frustration and bewilderment in knowing how to lead their congregations. The following are some of the current trends we see that suggest to us the church desperately needs revival.

CURRENT CONDITION OF THE CHURCH

1. False Confidence of Megachurch
2. Biblical Illiteracy
3. Minimal Corporate Praying and Testifying
4. Loss of a Shepherd's Heart
5. Rampant Immorality
6. Numerical Decline and Stagnation

---

1. False Confidence of the Megachurch

If you lived in medieval times, you might take comfort in seeing a series of lofty castles lining the major highways of the land. The sight of the majestic towers and thick walls would provide you with a sense of security should an invading army approach. Imagine, however, that an opposing horde does sweep into your country. Town after town is brutally pillaged, its men put to the sword, and its women and children led into dismal captivity. Imagine that when the enemy marches toward your village, you frantically hurry your family to a nearby castle you have long admired. To your shock and dismay, however, you are informed that the castle is willing to admit you within its walls but it has no food to give you. Further, you are warned that there is an epidemic raging among those inside and you are candidly advised that you might be better off fending for yourself in the countryside. To discover that this mighty fortress is in fact powerless to withstand the rapacious enemy and it is unable to provide basic health for its own inhabitants would be bewildering.

Today's society is witnessing the proliferation of ecclesiastical fortresses dotting the modern landscape. These massive structures, holding enormous congregations, can endue the average Christian with confidence. Surely with such mighty bulwarks, the forces of evil would be defeated if they attempted to invade the territory. However, the reality is that the minions of darkness are ravaging home after home located in the shadows of these citadels. Megachurches are a relatively modern phenomenon. There have always been large churches. The first church in Jerusalem had several thousand members. However, its size was never what was prominent to their ministry. They were led by people who devoted themselves to prayer and studying God's Word (Acts 6:4). The members met together regularly to learn doctrine, to pray, and to enjoy fellowship (Acts 2:42). The early church, though large, attempted to meet the needs of all those in want (Acts 2:44–45). The church, despite a diverse membership, did not tolerate sin (Acts 5:1–11). Scripture does not tell us that citizens in Jerusalem joined the church because it had the most spectacular Christmas musicals in town or because it boasted a fully equipped fitness center for its members. As the early Christians cared for one another and worshipped God with joy, the Lord added many people to their number (Acts 2:47).

Today, however, size and programming are often the defining measurements for ecclesiastical success. People assume that if you attain large numbers God must be pleased with you and is blessing your efforts. Nothing is inherently wrong with having many members. But much of what some megachurch leaders advocate is unbiblical. Size has become the compelling measurement of "success." When a church grows to unusual dimensions, the pastor writes a book explaining how others can do as he did and then offers seminars on church growth that immediately draw hordes of church leaders desperately seeking that one seminar or technique that will vault them into the hallowed sphere of successful ministers.

Numerical growth has become the overriding goal driving the agenda of many church leaders. If preaching on sin offends people and causes them to shop for another church home, then sermons will be crafted to focus on the positive rather than the "negative." Pastors of some of the largest churches in North America today meticulously avoid mentioning unpleasant subjects such as sin or repentance, and the result is that their churches have swelled to enormous proportions. Now a new set of clone churches is springing up all across the country.

Bill Hybels, an influential megachurch leader, popularized the seeker-driven model to church growth. It has been effective in attracting large numbers of unchurched people within its walls. However, a recent study initiated by Hybels's church, Willow Creek, discovered that their methodology, which has been mimicked by thousands of churches around the world, has not grown people into mature Christians. Their methodology achieved numerical growth but not spiritual growth. Notes Hybels, "Some of the stuff we have put millions of dollars into thinking it would really help our people grow and develop spiritually, when the data actually came back it wasn't helping people that much. Other things that we didn't put much money into and didn't put much staff against is stuff our people are crying out for."[1] The reality is that drawing a crowd is not the same as building a church.

Megachurches can develop an voracious appetite for finances and members. It costs a fortune to stage the elaborate, Broadway-caliber musical performances that draw large audiences. Despite boasting huge crowds, megachurch budgets have an insatiable need for more money and thus more donors. To meet their skyrocketing costs, megachurches will often attract and devour disgruntled church members from other congregations. Survey a typical megachurch, and you will discover a wide array of people who once attended or were leaders of other churches. As when a giant department store moves into a small town and the locally owned merchants soon begin filing for bankruptcy, smaller congregations can't compete. Over the last several decades hundreds of small- and medium-sized churches have floundered and closed their doors in the shadows of a megachurch that was devouring every church attender it could entice within its walls. Impressive church empires have been built while God's kingdom has sadly gone wanting. Many studies have demonstrated that much of the megachurch growth is merely a redistribution of the saints and not a winning of the unchurched population. Tragically many of the cities that boast the largest number of megachurches also have some of the highest crime and divorce rates in the country. While the impressive structures and slick advertising of the superchurches today may provide a sense of comfort to Christians in an increasingly secular world, these colossal organizations have not demonstrated that they are God's preferred instrument for bringing national revival.

2. Biblical Illiteracy

While churches may boast they "preach the Bible," it seems to us that not since pre-reformation days have church members been as biblically illiterate. There are several possible reasons for this. For one, much of the preaching being done today is not a verse-by-verse exposition of Scripture, but it rather resembles a self-help seminar: "Ten Tips for Raising Great Kids" or "Five Ways to Stay Fit in a Fast-Food World." Usually there is a token Bible verse referring to the family or to the fact that our bodies are the temple of God. Then the remainder of the sermon is built not on Scripture but on a recent article in *Reader's Digest.* Clearly claiming to be a "Bible-believing church" does not ensure that the Bible is faithfully being preached or taught.

There is also a tendency among many modern pastors to teach rather than preach, to instruct rather than exhort. This trend has been exacerbated by the extensive use of PowerPoint. Now preachers give their people outlines of their sermons so they will maintain their interest throughout the presentation. Listeners are expected to follow the speaker by filling in the blanks in their sermon outlines. The result is that listeners measure the success of the sermon on whether they filled in all the blanks rather than on whether they experienced life change. The Sunday sermon has become a helpful seminar. Now the "old-fashioned" approach of *exhorting* the people of God to practice God's commands seems strangely anachronistic. The shortage of biblical preaching today is exacerbated by the availability of sermons online. Now, with a click of a mouse, pastors can go on the Internet and download sermon manuscripts replete with outlines, PowerPoint presentations, and handouts. Which day of the week receives the most hits? Saturday evening of course. For many modern preachers, there seems to be far more pressing issues to attend to throughout the week than devoting themselves to prayer and the study of God's Word.

Another trend in today's churches is to project the Scripture passage on a large screen at the front of the auditorium. This is done so people who did not bring their Bibles do not have to feel awkward because the scriptural text is conveniently illuminated in bold letters right in front of them. However, what was done to make seekers feel more comfortable in worship services has had a deadening effect on church members. *They* no longer feel the need to bring their Bibles to church. After all, why lug it all the way to church on Sunday when the relevant verses will be posted on the projector screen? The result is that God's people are not handling God's Word as they once did. In times past church members would have a Bible in their hands when the pastor addressed a passage. Readers would notice the context of the verses being preached. Their eyes might be drawn to the surrounding verses, or they might notice a cross-reference leading them to examine a parallel passage. They could mark their Bibles at that place for further study. Now many of those attending services could not tell you the Scripture reference used that morning once it disappears from the screen. For numerous reasons modern church members are largely ignorant of in-depth biblical teaching and are therefore easy prey for shallow fads driven by simplistic clichés.

3. Minimal Corporate Praying and Testifying

A third alarming characteristic of the modern church is the minimal attention given to corporate prayer and the testimony of believers. The early church regularly prayed together in corporate settings. In earlier days the pastoral prayer was a focal point of many church worship services. Charles Spurgeon, one of the first megachurch pastors of the modern era, prepared his pastoral prayer as carefully as he did his famous sermons. Often people who visited London and went to hear the great orator preach would come away as impacted by his prayers as by his peerless preaching.

Time restraints have caused many pastors and worship leaders to jettison anything but the most trite, clichéd prayers that rarely last a minute. People who do not hear genuine, heartfelt praying from the pulpit have no model of what they should be doing in private.

Corporate prayer has become almost nonexistent in most churches today. Even weekly "prayer meetings" are often really a Bible study with two or three faithful church members called upon to pray briefly at the end of the hour. We have asked many pastors why they do so little praying in their prayer meetings. The common response has been: "People won't come if we just pray." So the problem is compounded. Today's prayer meetings are designed to make people who don't enjoy praying feel comfortable. In many churches today the number of people attending a church meeting is the defining measure of success, not what happens to the people when they show up.

Historically revival has spread on the wings of testimony. Hearing from someone who had a profound encounter with God electrified the listeners. However, in churches striving for a polished, professional feel to their services, the risk of allowing untrained laypersons to speak in front of a microphone seems too high. What if they drone on? What if they say something inappropriate? What if they are boring? Often when we are speaking in churches, we'll be given an extensive outline detailing every minute of the service. Even baptisms, which are supposed to be people's defining moment to testify to what Christ has done in their lives, are often conducted mechanically and impersonally. In larger churches new believers are baptized one after another during the offertory or while announcements are being made. No opportunity for a verbal witness is given. Some of the most powerful moments we have experienced in worship have occurred when people testified in their unpolished manner about the transformational work God performed in their lives.

4. Loss of a Shepherd's Heart

An issue closely related to the megachurch phenomenon is the CEO model many pastors have adopted for their leadership style. Biblically, the word *pastor* connotes images of a shepherd. Shepherds walk with and care for their flocks. They live among the sheep, protect them from danger, and bind up their wounds. When a sheep wanders off, the shepherd searches high and low until he recovers the wayward animal (Luke 15:4–7). Shepherds do not become frustrated with sheep when they act sheepish. They know it's their nature to behave that way. That is why sheep require shepherds for their survival.

With the advent of the megachurch, however, pastors began adopting business leadership models rather than biblical patterns. Pastors began presuming to determine the vision for their churches and to view anyone who disagreed with them as their opponent. If the pastor decided the church needed to build an extensive facility, he expected the members to enthusiastically rally behind his vision. Those who expressed misgivings were castigated as "holding the church back" and were forced out of leadership positions or even expelled from the membership. Rather than having a shepherd's concern for every lost sheep, misguided pastors accept the fallacy that you have to lose a lot of people before the membership becomes fully aligned with the new vision. Many new pastors clear out the existing staff wholesale, regardless of their tenure or their openness to working with the new leader. The manner in which some pastors fire their staff would cause Wall Street CEOs to blush.

The image of revival actually threatens and frightens many church leaders because they equate it with a loss of control. At the heart of this issue is the question of who leads the church, the pastor or Christ. If you insist that people keep their emotions under control, that services not run too long, that nothing unexpected occurs, then revival is an unwelcome concept. In truth revival is not convenient, and it cannot be scheduled or choreographed. When people have a profound encounter with the Holy Spirit, keeping them silent is difficult. Services can be filled with emotion. They can last hours, even days. Times of renewal, when the Holy Spirit comes in great power, can be mystifying to those outside the church, leading to criticism and even ridicule (Acts 2:13). For these reasons it is small wonder church leaders are often the most resistant to praying for revival.

5. Rampant Immorality

The modern church is sadly a reflection of the moral depravity of its society. It used to be "news" when a pastor or church leader was exposed for being involved in lewd and immoral behavior. Now rarely a week passes without reports of pastors committing adultery, youth ministers soliciting a prostitute, and worship leaders downloading pornographic images on their church computers. People in the congregations are not being challenged to live holy lives. The divorce rate in the church is comparable to the national average. Drug use and promiscuity among church teens is common.

Even a superficial survey of the church reveals that its members are not distinctly holy and set apart from the world the way Scripture commands. One of the principal reasons for this is church leadership. Many pastors are reluctant to preach against sin for fear of offending people. They are uncomfortable preaching against something they are personally struggling with. The high standards for ministers laid out in Scripture have been explained away or excused as being unrealistic. Many fallen ministers become indignant when told that because of their sin they are no longer qualified to hold pastoral office. Churches have been bludgeoned with charges of being judgmental and unforgiving, and the knee-jerk reaction is to overlook immorality, even in the pastor and worship leaders. As a result, many churches today are led by people who have grievously sinned and who no longer have the moral authority to speak against the sin being practiced by church members.

The church is also rife with sins that do not necessarily make headlines but that are equally stultifying to its spiritual vibrancy. Church splits have become epidemic. Communities witness members of congregations parting so acrimoniously that they will not even speak to one another if they pass on the sidewalk. Within the church, members carry long-term grudges and refuse to forgive one another. Members of the worship team conduct well-known adulterous affairs yet sing on the platform every Sunday.

6. Numerical Decline and Stagnation

A telling sign that revival is required is when the numbers of those attending and joining the church dwindle. While numbers must be carefully interpreted, they can provide a benchmark of the church's health. The Southern Baptist Convention is the largest Protestant denomination in North America. In recent years thousands of its churches report not one baptism during an entire year. Recent statistics reveal the only age category among SBC churches reporting an increase in baptisms was four-year-olds. Surely when the ministry of thousands of churches cannot produce one convert over the course of an entire year, it is time to get on our knees and cry out for revival.

Conclusion

The condition of Christianity today is certainly not all bleak. There are some outstanding churches today. But in the midst of the successes are many congregations that have become spiritually powerless. The majority of churches in America today are plateaued or in decline. Thousands of churches cannot produce one convert in an entire year. Ministerial burnout is occurring at epidemic proportions. The number of unchurched Americans is at record levels. Clearly the church needs to be awakened. Truly we live in a day that desperately calls for revival.

Current Status of Society

Ever since Adam and Eve's fall, the world has been spiritually darkened. Modern society is no exception. Today's media is aggressively challenging and mocking Christian values and beliefs. Government laws and court decisions continually infringe on Christian practices. North American society is becoming increasingly hostile and embittered toward God's work. Here are a few examples:

CONDITION OF SOCIETY

1. Media Hostile to Christianity
2. Pressures to Be Politically Correct
3. Loss of Confidence in Leaders
4. Pressures from World Religions
5. Materialism
6. Rampant Immorality
7. Obsession with Recreation and Pleasure

---

1. Media Hostile to Christianity

Today's media is vehemently opposed to Christian teaching. The vast majority of modern reporters do not hold a Christian view of God, if they believe in any god at all. The openly hostile and disparaging way the media presents the Christian church and its doctrines is a disturbing trend. In an age in which tolerance has been elevated to the noblest of virtues, the media seemingly has tolerance for almost any lewd or perverted behavior or any extreme religious view except what is Christian. Nightly sitcoms regularly portray people committing adultery or seeking to satisfy their sexual desires. These programs run a laugh track in the background and encourage people to chuckle at the characters' indiscretions. While alternative lifestyles are regularly portrayed on television as wholesome and loving, it is almost impossible to find a depiction of a Christian minister or someone with strong Christian convictions on television without having them lampooned. Likewise, scientific theories that purport to undergird evolution are heralded in the media as pure science, despite the fact that these theories often require a greater leap of faith than a straightforward belief in an intelligent design of the universe.

What especially irritates the modern media is that Christianity refuses to adopt the modern moral code of relativism. Christianity does not embrace the mantra that there is no such thing as right and wrong or absolute truth. The media despises the word *sin*. It also routinely blasphemes the Lord's name and ridicules biblical teachings. Yet any effort to curb the excesses and abuses of the media is immediately denounced as censorship. When millions of Christians spend dozens of hours every week watching television and movies, it is impossible to avoid the spiritually deadening effect the media has on their souls.

2. Pressures to Be Politically Correct

Modern society places enormous pressure on people to be politically correct. The values and standards of the liberal media are placed into the sacred pantheon of hallowed societal views to which everyone must adhere or suffer the heinous label of being politically incorrect. Such insistence comes regardless of how these opinions contradict Scripture. For example, an extremely strong homosexual agenda in American society demands to be accepted and affirmed by the modern church. Certainly Christians should love those who practice homosexuality just as God loves them. Nevertheless, the gay community deeply resents the fact that Christians believe the Bible condemns their lifestyle and calls it sin. In this regard, the homosexual community does not seek tolerance, for it already has that. It demands an acknowledgment of legitimacy from the church. Yet where is the tolerance for those who believe that God made people heterosexual? Many churches today have succumbed to this relentless pressure and have changed their constitutions to allow for homosexual members and ministers. In their efforts to become inclusive, such denominations have typically spiraled downward in attendance and spiritual influence.

This matter of political correctness has many other ramifications. Divorce, for example, claims roughly 40 percent of today's marriages. Churches are filled with single-parent families. With so many people in congregations suffering from the devastation of divorce, it is extremely challenging for ministers to uphold biblical teachings on the subject. When was the last time you heard a sermon on Malachi 2:16, "For the LORD God of Israel says that He hates divorce"? The preacher who dares to speak on this verse would either feel pressured to explain it away completely or face a maelstrom of invective from his congregation. While clearly God does not hate divorcees, God does detest what divorce does to people and to the sanctity of marriage that He authored. The church was designed to be a light and a witness to a darkened world. But when the world enters the church and begins to censor its message, the church loses its prophetic voice. The church must be taught what the Bible says and then have the courage to uphold holiness while expressing compassion for all who fall short.

3. Loss of Confidence in Leaders

Today's world has too many politicians and too few statesmen. Society is inundated with government officeholders who routinely break their promises and prove to be untrustworthy. Scandals in government occur routinely. With the revelations during Richard Nixon's and later Bill Clinton's presidency, American society had their worst concerns confirmed that even the nation's highest offices are not immune to adultery, corruption, and deception. Immoral activities that would have immediately ended someone's political career in the past are now exposed but declared to be no one's business. The corporate world has also been rocked with greed and corruption in monumental proportions. Public offices once carrying widespread public respect are now viewed with growing cynicism. In truth the biggest change has been in the revelation to the public of immorality, not the occurrence of it.

The church has been profoundly affected by the distrust and skepticism of leaders today. With the omnipresence of the Internet, facts as well as rumors of scandal surrounding leaders are instantly disseminated around the world. The overall mood of this generation is mistrust. Today's church leaders are being viewed as skeptically as government and corporate leaders, at times even more so.

4. Pressures from World Religions

September 11, 2001, changed the world but especially America. The United States was founded primarily by Christians who sought liberty to worship God in a manner that suited their consciences. Although becoming increasingly secularized, the nation still carries vestiges of its Christian foundations. Yet on that fateful day Americans awoke to the disturbing reality that radical religious groups around the world are adamantly and violently opposed to Christianity. Furthermore, some organizations recruit and train people to destroy the worldwide influence of the church. There are an estimated sixty thousand Christian martyrs worldwide every year.

After September 11, many people in North America began noticing the massive mosques as well as Hindu and Buddhist temples rapidly emerging in suburban American neighborhoods. The land once considered to be Christian was obviously not so any more. In response to September 11, many government spokespeople went out of their way to proclaim their respect for and protection of people's various faiths. The irony is that while government officials assured world religions of their respect for their faith, media outlets continued to pour out a relentless stream of blasphemous and derogatory broadcasts that misrepresented and demeaned Christianity. Clearly the Christian church in America no longer enjoys the hegemony and societal support it once did. In fact, today there are more unchurched Americans than at any time in history. Today's average American has little knowledge of the Bible or core Christian teaching. As the Christian church lies largely dormant across America today, the religions of the world are aggressively spreading across the land.

5. Materialism

North America is obsessed with materialism. The baby boomer generation has enjoyed unprecedented wealth and prosperity. Leisure industries have emerged to satisfy the insatiable appetites people have for recreation and entertainment. The advertising industry spends billions of dollars annually to make North Americans dissatisfied. Television evangelists have joined this parade, promising gullible listeners that God wants them to be wealthy and to indulge themselves. We know an American church leader who met with a Christian pastor in China several years ago who suffered greatly for his faith. The pastor told the American that Chinese Christians were fervently praying for American Christians. The American, somewhat startled that someone who had suffered imprisonment for his faith was praying for those who enjoyed religious liberty, asked why they were praying for America. "Because it seems we are handling our adversity far better than you are handling your prosperity" was the reply. In the wealthy nations of North America and Western Europe, materialism is choking the life out of the church. With our bigger buildings and seeker-driven programs, we court materialism rather than denouncing it.

6. Rampant Immorality

Today's society revels in its freedom to indulge in the grossest forms of immorality. To outcries against child pornography being sold over the Internet, defenders denounce censorship of an art form. Prime-time television regularly portrays violence, sex, profanity, and blasphemy. In the name of freedom of speech, broadcasters fill the airwaves with the vilest forms of sexual degradation. Reality shows exploit people's selfishness and perversions. In an ever-increasing effort to find something that will shock the public, the media sinks lower and lower for its material.

Public morality as a whole has fallen to record lows. There is a strong movement to make same-sex marriages recognized by the state. Millions of abortions have been performed in the United States. Drug use seems impervious to police efforts. In an age when there is no publicly accepted standard of right and wrong, everyone does what is right in his own eyes.

7. Obsession with Recreation and Pleasure

The decline of the Roman Empire, some theorists believe, began when its people became obsessed with sports and entertainment. The entertainment that satisfied the Roman public also became increasingly violent and immoral. In North American society the largest stadiums and auditoriums are not used for public worship but for sporting events. The heroes of the modern age are athletes who are often still in their teens. The celebrity cult in America enables gifted athletes to gain lucrative advertising endorsements and to garner mind-boggling multimillion-dollar salaries. These athletes have become role models for today's youth, even though many of them have never finished school or are living immorally. Steroid and drug use among athletes are not uncommon in their efforts to rise to the top of their games.

Sports is a multibillion-dollar industry. On Saturdays college football stadiums can fill up with 100,000 spectators. On Sunday afternoons millions of North Americans remain glued to their television sets as sporting events are presented throughout the day. All week long television, radio, and newspaper reporters speculate and analyze how teams and athletes will perform that week. Many long-winded preachers have watched with dismay as church members slipped out of the auditorium before the service was over so they would not miss the opening kickoff. On special event days such as Super Bowl Sunday, many churches don't even try to compete; and instead of conducting their regular evening service, they simply broadcast the game on their large screens in the auditorium.

Conclusion

North American society is in grave need of revival. People are turning away from God and the church in record numbers. Immorality is being legitimized and made politically correct by the media. Society's condition will not be rectified by the church's making incremental adjustments to its calendar or programming. Our time desperately cries out for revival.

QUESTIONS FOR REFLECTION AND DISCUSSION

1. What evidence do you see that indicates the church needs revival? What evidence do you see that suggests society needs revival?
2. Do you believe the church is taking its need for revival seriously? Why or why not?
3. What do you think it will take for society to return to God?
4. How are you presently praying for revival? How seriously are you taking the need for revival in your day?

CHAPTER 4

God's People Tend to Depart from Him

Revival in Northampton

In December 1734 the Holy Spirit began working mightily in the Northampton congregation led by a thirty-one-year-old pastor named Jonathan Edwards. The sudden deaths of two young adults prompted a spontaneous turning to God among the young people. By early 1735 the church was filled to capacity. Within six months three hundred people had been converted. As America became swept up in a Great Awakening during the following years, Edwards befriended many of the revival leaders such as George Whitefield. During this exhilarating period, Edwards penned his thoughts and observations, leaving for posterity some of the most insightful writings on spiritual awakening ever written. Nevertheless, the revival fires eventually died out. Then in 1740, revival swept over his congregation once again. Eventually the tide of revival receded once again. On the heels of revival, a faction developed within his church, fueled by disgruntled members. In 1750 this group succeeded in dismissing Edwards as pastor despite the fact that he was a godly man at the center of God's unmistakable activity. Here was a congregation at the epicenter of a great awakening. Yet some people in the church were disoriented to God to the point of ousting their pastor and quenching the Holy Spirit's work.

Those who walk closely with their Lord are perplexed at how others can choose to turn their backs on their heavenly Father. God created us to enjoy a love relationship with Him. He invites us to join Him in His worldwide redemptive work. He is not a distant Creator but a loving, personal God. His expectations of us are neither mysterious nor impossible to understand or to follow. Deuteronomy 30:11–16 says:

"This commandment which I command you today is not too mysterious for you, nor is it far off. It is not in heaven, that you should say, 'Who will ascend into heaven for us and bring it to us, that we may hear it and do it?' Nor is it beyond the sea, that you should say, 'Who will go over the sea for us and bring it to us, that we may hear it and do it?' But the word is very near you, in your mouth and in your heart, that you may do it.

"See, I have set before you today life and good, death and evil, in that I command you today to love the LORD your God, to walk in His ways, and to keep His commandments, His statutes, and His judgments, that you may live and multiply; and the LORD your God will bless you in the land which you go to possess."

God asks us to do three things: (1) love Him; (2) walk in His ways; and (3) keep His commands. More than anything else God desires our love. His ways are contrary to our own self-destructive inclinations and foreign to the world's dangerous temptations. His will is not obscure or mysterious so that we must consult a religious guru to explain God's Word to us. As Christians, God's Holy Spirit is present to guide and empower us in every act of obedience. God has done everything necessary to enable us to obey Him, follow Him, and participate with Him in His redemptive mission.

Cracked Cisterns

Despite God's amazing invitation to walk in intimate, vibrant, victorious fellowship with Him, God's people inevitably forsake Him, enticed away by temporal substitutes. Read about the Israelites' departure and listen to the cry of God's heart as He describes how His people callously forsook Him:

"What injustice have your fathers found in Me, that they have gone far from Me, have followed idols, and have become idolaters? Neither did they say, 'Where is the LORD . . .' I brought you into a bountiful country, to eat its fruit and its goodness. But when you entered, you defiled My land and made My heritage an abomination. The priests did not say, 'Where is the LORD?' And those who handle the law did not know Me; the rulers also transgressed against Me; the prophets prophesied by Baal, and walked after things that do not profit.

"Therefore I will yet bring charges against you," says the LORD . . .
"see if there has been such a thing. Has a nation changed its gods, which
are not gods? But My people have changed their Glory for what does not
profit. Be astonished, O heavens, at this, and be horribly afraid; be very
desolate," says the LORD. "For My people have committed two evils: They
have forsaken Me, the fountain of living waters, and hewn themselves
cisterns—broken cisterns that can hold no water." (Jer. 2:5–13)

God created within each person a capacity for wholeness and joy that only He
can satisfy. Jesus called Himself the living water (John 4:14). He is a wellspring that
flows with life-giving water, refreshing the parched dryness wherever it flows. God
alone is able to endue us with life as He fills us with Himself. His word says, "'The
LORD . . . is your life'" (Deut. 30:20). Jesus said, "'I am . . . the life'" (John 14:6).
In our day Christians continue to reject the living water of Christ to seek surrogate,
worldly gods that cannot satisfy. The twofold tragedy is that not only do we foolishly
reject our loving heavenly Father, but the artificial substitutes we replace Him with
cannot sustain us. They may offer temporary comfort and pleasure, but only God
can provide abundant life.

Old Testament Pattern

The Old Testament clearly details the self-destructive cycle God's people repeatedly
succumbed to. After God delivered the Israelites from their miserable bondage in
Egypt, He miraculously supplied them with daily food and water. He soundly defeated
their enemies. His mighty miracles included unleashing ten devastating plagues on
the Egyptians and parting the Red Sea. Their relationship with Almighty God gave
the Israelites access to inexhaustible provision and power. But when Moses ascended
Mount Sinai to meet with God, the Israelites grew restless. They wanted a god who
would serve them rather than rule them so they ordered Aaron to make them an idol
(Exod. 32). It seems ludicrous. These people had walked through a sea, eaten food
from heaven, and witnessed fire and lightning on the mountain of God, yet they
readily forsook their relationship with God to worship a golden calf they made themselves. God's people would repeatedly betray Him to embrace things that were lifeless
and impotent. This foolish choice cost them the future God intended for them. The
apostle Paul declared, "For the wages of sin is death" (Rom. 6:23). Turning from God
always brings spiritual death. That is the only alternative to the living water of life.

Later, after Joshua brought the children of Israel into the promised land, they continually repeated the deadly cycle of apostasy. They would walk with God temporarily and experience the victorious, abundant life He promised. But then the book of Judges repeatedly states, "Another generation arose after them who did not know the LORD nor the work which He had done for Israel. Then the children of Israel did evil in the sight of the LORD, and served the Baals" (Judg. 2:10–11). Each time the Lord would discipline His people for their rebellion, and they would eventually cry out to Him for mercy. The Lord would have compassion on them and rescue them once more. Tragically His people didn't wait long before they rejected Him again. This disastrous process was repeated for generations (Judg. 7–10; 12–15; 4:1–4; 6:1–11; 8:33–35; 10:6–10; 13:1–5; 21:25). Church history echoes this same tragic pattern of deliverance, idolatry, betrayal, and repentance. Unmistakably people's hearts tend to gravitate away from God.

Shifting Hearts

God "has blessed us with every spiritual blessing" (Eph. 1:3). "His divine power has given to us all things that pertain to life and godliness" (2 Pet. 1:3). God has done amazing things for us, yet we continue to depart from Him. How and why does this happen? How does a church depart from God? God explains: "'But if your heart turns away so that you do not hear, and are drawn away, and worship other gods and serve them, I announce to you today that you shall surely perish'" (Deut. 30:17–18).

Apostasy does not begin with wrong activity. It originates from a change of heart. Alienation from God follows a downward course. It commences as a distraction. Your focus is diverted from God to your circumstances, to people, or to worldly enticements. People seldom realize what is happening until they have drifted far from Him. They begin struggling to obey Him. They make ungodly choices, rationalizing their neglect to follow what God says. They grow comfortable in their worldly living so their hearts are impervious to the Holy Spirit's call to return. Eventually they turn to substitutes for God. Idols do not condemn their sin or convict them of their ungodly behavior. Substitutes do not hold them accountable or ask them to do things they do not want to do. Eventually, like the Israelites of old, they "worship other gods and serve them" (Deut. 30:17). This is how a person, a family, a church, a denomination, or even a nation departs from God.

God knew His people would be habitually tempted to depart from Him so He issued a solemn warning:

"But if your heart turns away . . . I announce to you today that you shall surely perish; you shall not prolong your days. . . . I call heaven and earth as witnesses today against you, that I have set before you life and death, blessing and cursing; therefore choose life, that both you and your descendants may live; that you may love the LORD your God, that you may obey His voice, and that you may cling to Him, for He is your life." (Deut. 30:17–20)

God loves us and wants us to choose life, not destruction. He gives two options, there is no compromise. God desires a love relationship with His people. We are to love Him wholeheartedly and obey Him fully. Then Scripture promises us abundant life. Only God can offer us life because the Lord Himself *is* life.

You may think that warnings of life and death are restricted to the Old Testament. Many Christians tend to think God changed halfway through the Bible and since New Testament times He no longer brings consequences on His people for their sin. Consider what the risen Christ said to the church at Ephesus: "I have this against you, that you have left your first love. Remember therefore from where you have fallen; repent and do the first works, or else I will come to you quickly and remove your lampstand [church, Rev. 1:20] from its place—unless you repent" (Rev. 2:4–5).

Any departure from Christ is serious. In fact, it can be fatal. Around the world today Christians are experiencing grievous consequences for their sin while churches are dying and disbanding. One reason for this is that Christians have refused to repent and return to their first love for Christ. Therefore, as a result, they are no longer walking closely with God so they are in no position to serve Him. He will not allow His people to make a public mockery of His name. There is too much at stake for them and for the unbelievers who observe their lives. Spiritual betrayal is a grave matter.

Disobedience

The process known as "backsliding" is gradual. It is much like a marriage that degenerates from devotion, to inattention, to apathy, to neglect, to enmity, and finally to rejection. Forsaking a loved one does not normally occur instantly or with a solitary act. It is a process that, if left unchecked, leads to enormous pain.

What are the symptoms of a heart that has drifted from God? Two clear indicators will be evident in an individual's life or in a congregation: (1) disobedience and

(2) substitutes for God. As a doctor looks for symptoms to make a diagnosis for someone who is ill, let's probe some of the indicators of a heart that has departed from the Lord. First, notice the clear connection Jesus made between obedience and love:

"If you love Me, keep My commandments." (John 14:15)

"He who has My commandments and keeps them, it is he who loves Me." (John 14:21)

"If anyone loves Me, he will keep My word. . . . He who does not love Me does not keep My words." (John 14:23–24)

Jesus announced that it is spiritually impossible to love Him and not to obey Him. The symptom is disobedience; the malady is lovelessness. Love will obey. We may strongly protest and say, "Lord, it's not that I don't love You; it's just that I'm having trouble obeying You."

God would say, "If you are struggling to follow Me, it is because you do not love Me." If you misunderstand this truth, you will always be frustrated in your attempts to get right with God. You will vainly attempt to reform your behavior, and you will inevitably fail. Do you know how to solve a disobedience problem? Return to your love relationship with God. Then you will resolve the obedience problems in your life. "Walk in the Spirit, and you shall not fulfill the lust of the flesh" (Gal. 5:16).

Has God asked something of you in times past and you obeyed without question, yet now you struggle with the same issue? For example, often new believers freely forgive others while longtime Christians may resist granting forgiveness. Or have you noticed that new converts will often eagerly share their faith with others while those who are "mature" in the faith may seldom tell others about the joy they have in Christ? When Christ gives a command in His Word and you begin to argue with Him, you demonstrate that your heart has shifted. Examine the following Scriptures to see how you or your church is demonstrating your love for Christ:

- Do you love your fellow believers as Christ loves you? "A new commandment I give to you, that you love one another; as I have loved you" (John 13:34).
- Do you forgive others so you may be forgiven? "Whenever you stand praying, if you have anything against anyone, forgive him, that your Father in heaven may also forgive you your trespasses" (Mark 11:25).

- Is your church known as a people who pray? "It is written, 'My house is a house of prayer'" (Luke 19:46).
- Do you give generously to the Lord's work as well as practice justice, mercy, and faith? "Woe to you, . . . hypocrites! For you pay tithe . . . and have neglected the weightier matters of the law: justice and mercy and faith. These you ought to have done, without leaving the others undone" (Matt. 23:23).
- Are you actively seeking to make disciples of the nations, including those around your community? "Go therefore and make disciples of all the nations, baptizing them . . . [and] teaching them to observe all things that I have commanded you" (Matt. 28:19–20).
- Are you bearing witness to Christ in the power of His Spirit? "You shall receive power when the Holy Spirit has come upon you; and you shall be witnesses to Me in Jerusalem, and in all Judea and Samaria, and to the end of the earth" (Acts 1:8).
- Are you experiencing genuine unity with other believers in your church, with other churches, and with Christians in other denominations? "They may be made perfect in one, and that the world may know that You have sent Me, and have loved them as You have loved Me" (John 17:23).

If you notice that you or your church are no longer obeying the Lord's commands, this is a clear sign of departure from God. Many people in a church may sincerely seek God's will and sense He is leading their church in a particular direction. However, some church members may worry about finances or may launch a storm of protest at the direction being proposed for the congregation. If the church decides to appease the naysayers and not move forward with what God told them to do, the heart of the church has begun to shift. Over time a church can so deviate from God's will that even those who were once receptive to Him become hard of heart. In misguided zeal to pursue church unity, many congregations have chosen corporate disobedience instead. God's Word warns: "Beware, brethren, lest there be in any of you an evil heart of unbelief in departing from the living God; but exhort one another daily, while it is called 'Today,' lest any of you be hardened through the deceitfulness of sin" (Heb. 3:12–13).

Another sign of a cold or lukewarm heart is turning to substitutes for God.

The Woman at the Well

On a trip through Samaria, Jesus stopped to rest at Jacob's well near the town of Sychar. As a woman came to draw water, Jesus asked her for a drink. Jesus knew this woman had looked for meaning and happiness in relationships with men. He guided her into a discussion about living water. Notice in the following passage two ways the woman accepted alternatives for a divine relationship:

> Jesus answered and said to her, "If you knew the gift of God, and who it is who says to you, 'Give Me a drink,' you would have asked Him, and He would have given you living water. . . . Whoever drinks of this water will thirst again, but whoever drinks of the water that I shall give him will never thirst. But the water that I shall give him will become in him a fountain of water springing up into everlasting life."
>
> The woman said to Him, "Sir, give me this water, that I may not thirst, nor come here to draw."
>
> Jesus said to her, "Go, call your husband, and come here."
>
> The woman answered and said, "I have no husband."
>
> Jesus said to her, "You have well said, 'I have no husband,' for you have had five husbands, and the one whom you now have is not your husband; in that you spoke truly."
>
> The woman said to Him, "Sir, I perceive that You are a prophet. Our fathers worshiped on this mountain, and you Jews say that in Jerusalem is the place where one ought to worship."
>
> Jesus said to her, "Woman, believe Me, the hour is coming when you will neither on this mountain, nor in Jerusalem, worship the Father. . . . But the hour is coming, and now is, when the true worshipers will worship the Father in spirit and truth; for the Father is seeking such to worship Him." (John 4:10, 13–23)

The Samaritan woman obviously had an enormous void in her life that she had unsuccessfully attempted to fill with a succession of husbands. When one man couldn't meet her deep longings, she looked for another. By the time she met Jesus she was working on partner number six.

Today large numbers of people are turning to sexual relationships or to other forms of human relationship to satisfy needs only God can meet. No human can fulfill the spiritual longing that is present in every person. God reserves the right to that deep, personal place in our hearts. Yet we seek to comfort ourselves in relationships, passions, pleasure, academia, sports, or various other pursuits. None of these satisfies our spiritual thirst for living water. That is a need only Jesus can meet.

The Samaritan woman also discussed religious worship practices with Jesus. Did you notice the focus of her question was not on God? She was concerned about the place of worship and external rituals. Worship for her was merely a collection of traditional religious activities. She knew nothing about a vibrant relationship with God. How different her demeanor was once Jesus opened her eyes to the truth. Here at last was what she had been desperately seeking for years.

Religious activity and tradition can never replace a relationship with God. No wonder multitudes of people reject the religion and stuffy rituals of those who claim to worship God but who have no relationship with Him. Religious activities abound today. But who needs more of that? However, nothing can compare with actually knowing and experiencing the living God. Why would we exchange a vital relationship with the living Lord for a set of religious activities? We can grow so busy being "religious" that we fail to experience life in Him.

Idols of the Heart

The Bible is filled with examples of people who chose alternates for God. Throughout history God's people have continually rejected God to pursue the favored idols of their day. We are as vulnerable to this temptation as any generation before us. Anytime we turn to anyone or anything when we should be turning to God, we reveal the idol in our lives. Scripture describes idols of the heart:

> "These men have set up their idols in their hearts, and put before them that
> which causes them to stumble into iniquity. . . . Therefore say to the house
> of Israel, 'Thus says the Lord God: "Repent, turn away from your idols,
> and turn your faces away from all your abominations."'" (Ezek. 14:3, 6)

The people had set up physical idols in their houses but this displayed the fact that these gods had also found their way into their affections. By turning to idols, they deserted God. Their hearts shifted. Graciously, God was planning to recapture the hearts of His people (Ezek. 14:5). Isn't it tragic to think that, after all God did for Israel, He continually had to win back their love? Could that be true of us? After all God has done for us in Christ, is it possible that we, too, have erected idols in our hearts and have rejected Christ who gave His life for us?

Common Idols

In the story of the woman at the well, we saw two common idols: people and religious activity. Let's look at some other prevalent substitutes for God. The apostle Paul warned: "For this you know, that no fornicator, unclean person, nor covetous man, who is an idolater, has any inheritance in the kingdom of Christ and God" (Eph. 5:5).

According to God's Word, sexual immorality, impurity, and greed are idols of the heart. Each of these could involve a one-time act, or they may be a habitual practice or attitude. When we turn to these to receive what only God can give, they become idols. A person who practices these sins has clearly departed from God. Read about additional idols:

> Thus says the Lord: "Cursed is the man who trusts in man and makes flesh his strength, Whose heart departs from the Lord." (Jer. 17:5)

> "Some trust in chariots, and some in horses, but we will remember the name of the Lord God." (Ps. 20:7)

> "These people draw near to Me with their mouth, and honor Me with their lips, but their heart is far from Me. And in vain they worship Me, teaching as doctrines the commandments of men." (Matt. 15:8–9)

> "No one can serve two masters; for either he will hate the one and love the other, or else he will be loyal to the one and despise the other. You cannot serve God and mammon [money]." (Matt. 6:24)

> "He who loves father or mother more than Me is not worthy of Me. And he who loves son or daughter more than Me is not worthy of Me." (Matt. 10:37)

> "If anyone desires to come after Me, let him deny himself, and take up his cross daily, and follow Me. For whoever desires to save his life will lose it, but whoever loses his life for My sake will save it." (Luke 9:23–24)

> "You search the Scriptures, for in them you think you have eternal life; and these are they which testify of Me. But you are not willing to come to Me that you may have life." (John 5:39–40)

Do not love the world or the things in the world. If anyone loves the world, the love of the Father is not in him. For all that is in the world—the lust of the flesh, the lust of the eyes, and the pride of life—is not of the Father but is of the world. (I John 2:15–16)

Let's look at a summary list of idols we can turn to:

- political or miltary strength (Ps. 20:7)
- sexual immorality (Eph. 5:5)
- impurity (Eph. 5:5)
- greed (Eph. 5:5)
- trusting in people or help from others (Jer. 17:5)
- ritual worship and following human teachings (Matt. 15:8–9)
- greed (Matt. 6:24)
- relationships (Matt. 10:37)
- self (Luke 9:23–24)
- Bible study for the attainment of head knowledge (John 5:39–40)
- materialism (I John 2:15)
- career, job, or work (I John 2:16)

Do some of these surprise you? Not everything on the list is evil or wrong to do. However, if we allow anything to take God's place in our lives, our loyalty is misplaced. The above is not a complete list of substitutes for a love relationship with God. Could devotion to a hobby, television, community service, or even to church work usurp our love relationship with God? Yes. Anything, or any combination of things, that captures your heart—your love—can become an idol.

Substitutes for God

When we move away from God, we replace Him, His purposes, and His ways with something from the world. A major tragedy of the Christian community is that individuals and churches often exchange work, ritual, religious activity, advertising, buildings, and programs for a love relationship with God. Where we once turned to Him, we now look to someone or something else.

We live in a day of rampant materialism. God's people often become as entrapped and enamored with the trinkets and temporary worldly comforts as unbelievers. Notice Scripture's warnings:

"Beware that you do not forget the LORD your God by not keeping His commandments, His judgments, and His statutes which I command you today, lest—when you have eaten and are full, and have built beautiful houses and dwell in them; and when your herds and your flocks multiply, and your silver and your gold are multiplied, and all that you have is multiplied; when your heart is lifted up, and you forget the LORD your God . . . then you say in your heart, 'My power and the might of my hand have gained me this wealth.'" (Deut. 8:11–14, 17)

Is anything presently in your life edging God out of your attention and priorities? Think about success or prosperity. Pride causes us to exaggerate our own importance. Wealth often leads to a desire for more possessions. Jesus said, "'Take heed and beware of covetousness, for one's life does not consist in the abundance of the things he possesses'" (Luke 12:15). Material possessions are not the only substitutes we turn to in place of God. Look over the following three lists for some other possible idols:

Substitutes for God's Presence

- We may place our trust in methods, programs, or people to accomplish spiritual growth and church growth rather than trusting God.
- We may substitute emotional hype, pageantry, entertainment, or ritual for the reality of His intimate presence in worship.
- Rather than enjoying God's presence as we read Scripture and pray, we merely spend a few moments doing a daily devotional reading.

Substitutes for God's Purposes

- We may conduct baptism and the Lord's Supper services as tradition or ritual when God intended them to be times of public testimony, remembrance of Him, personal examination, and renewal of fellowship.
- We may spend much of our time and resources on selfish pleasures and ignore justice for the oppressed or meeting the needs of the poor.
- We may conduct evangelistic visits primarily to invite people to church to meet an attendance goal when God wants them to come to Him.

Substitutes for God's Ways

- We walk by sight when God tells us to live by faith (Heb. 11:1, 6).
- We affirm and focus on self when God says to deny self.

- We pursue positions of influence and prestige when God says humble yourself.
- We cling to what we have when God says to give it away for the kingdom's sake (Matt. 16:25).
- We coerce people to serve when God says pray for Him to thrust forth laborers (Matt. 9:38).

God warns us about forgetting Him: "'If you by any means forget the LORD your God, and follow other gods, and serve them and worship them, I testify against you this day that you shall surely perish'" (Deut. 8:19). You may consider God's promise of destruction for idolatry to be extremely severe. It is. That reveals how seriously God views sin and rebellion. The Bible teaches that God is jealous of our love. He created us and deserves our devotion. As a result God is the relentless enemy of anything that challenges His rightful place in our lives.

QUESTIONS FOR REFLECTION AND DISCUSSION

1. If God evaluated your record of obedience to Him what would He conclude about your love for Him?
2. How does your commitment and eagerness to obey whatever God says reflect your love for Christ?
3. Has anything crept into your life that is becoming a substitute for God?
4. Is your greatest joy and desire to have fellowship with Christ? What do you enjoy more than spending time in fellowship and worship of God?

CHAPTER 5

God's Plumb Line:
The Divine Standard for Holy Living

Revival in Korea

According to Jonathan Goforth, the Korean revival of 1907 commenced when the Central Presbyterian Church held an eight-day week of universal prayer. Many of its members sensed that God was about to renew the church, yet each service concluded in normal fashion. As the final service drew to a close, Elder Keel suddenly rose to his feet. People were startled when this greatly respected church leader confessed, "I am an Achan."[1] He tearfully admitted that a year earlier he had managed the financial affairs of a deceased friend's widow. In the process he pocketed some of the estate's money. He admitted his sin, vowed to make immediate restitution, and acknowledged that his sin was hindering the Spirit's work in their church. Immediately a powerful conviction of sin swept over the congregation. People lined up to confess their sins, and revival burst forth.

The church had been conducting its usual weekly activities for years without the manifested power of the Holy Spirit. When they came abruptly face-to-face with God's holy expectations for His people, they were suddenly aware of how far they had departed from God. The apostle Paul noted this about God's law: "I would not have known sin except through the law. For I would not have known covetousness unless the law had said, 'You shall not covet'" (Rom. 7:7). God's law laid out the requirements for holiness. It established a plumb line by which we can evaluate our behavior.

God's Purpose

Jesus identified the most important commandment: "You shall love the LORD your God with all your heart, with all your soul, with all your mind, and with all your strength. This is the first commandment" (Mark 12:30).

This is God's desire for you—a love relationship with Him. Jesus said, "'This is eternal life, that they may know You, the only true God, and Jesus Christ whom You have sent'" (John 17:3).

The commandment quoted in Mark 12:30 was from the Old Testament and was originally addressed to God's people, the Israelites, not to individuals. God's love is experienced most completely in the midst of His people. God has fashioned His people into a living body—the church. Out of their divine relationship, God will disclose His character and power. In a love relationship with God, God's people will demonstrate a similar quality of love for one another, revealing to the world they are Jesus' disciples. Jesus prayed:

> "I do not pray for these alone, but also for those who will believe in Me
> through their word; that they all may be one, as You, Father, are in Me,
> and I in You; that they also may be one in Us, that the world may believe
> that You sent Me. And the glory which You gave Me I have given them,
> that they may be one just as We are one: I in them, and You in Me; that
> they may be made perfect in one, and that the world may know that You
> have sent Me, and have loved them as You have loved Me."
> (John 17:20–23)

When God's people relate to one another as God intended, the watching world comes to believe the truth of the gospel.

Departing

Because we live in an evil world, sin will tempt you and your church to depart from Him. A church, as a body, can sin against God (1 John 4:16). Many Christians and churches have grown so anesthetized to sin through constant exposure that they have lost their sensitivity to its destructive power. Believers become so accustomed to living without intimacy with God that the church no longer even holds up the ideal. The result is the church looks less like Christ and more and more like a religious organization. Because congregations are not taught the Scriptures thoroughly, they don't see how their lives and actions fall short of God's standards. Rather than feeling conviction for their sin, they identify every difficulty they face as spiritual warfare. How does God get the attention of people who are disoriented to Him?

God's Plumb Line

God used the image of a builder's plumb line to describe His response when the people of Israel wandered from Him:

> "Behold, the Lord stood on a wall made with a plumb line, with a plumb line in His hand. And the LORD said to me, 'Amos, what do you see?' And I said, 'A plumb line.' Then the Lord said: 'Behold, I am setting a plumb line in the midst of My people Israel; I will not pass by them anymore.'" (Amos 7:7–8)

God built His people like a straight wall—true to plumb. When we depart from Him, we are like a warped wall, unsightly and unsteady. We may not even recognize how close we are to complete collapse. To help His people, God holds a plumb line beside our lives so we can see how far we have departed from Him.

The Leaning Tower of Pisa

The famous bell tower in Pisa, Italy, is known worldwide for its irregular slant. Its construction began in 1173 and was not completed for two hundred years. The tower is 179 feet tall and made from solid marble. The ground beneath the tower is not solid enough to support its weight and the structure began to sink on one side even before the construction was completed. Today the tower leans more than seventeen feet off center. The walls are straight, but the building is crooked. The problem is with the foundation; if it was firm and perfectly horizontal, the walls would be perpendicular. If a gigantic crane pulled the walls to plumb again, the problem would return as soon as the tower was let loose. Without a solid, level foundation the tower would inevitably sink and be off center again.

In a similar way your spiritual life has its foundation in a love relationship with God. The way you live your life, practice your faith, and obey God's commands can be represented by the tower. If your life (or your church) is out of line with God's plan, that is merely visible evidence of a foundational problem. The issue is your love relationship. Jesus said, "If anyone loves Me, he will keep My word" (John 14:23).

The Bible reveals His nature, His purposes, and His ways. Scripture serves as God's plumb line for how His people should live. When we recognize we have departed from God's instructions, we know we have a problem. The issue is we have left our love relationship with Him. You cannot love God fully and habitually disobey Him. It is spiritually impossible. If you are disobeying God, it is because you do not love Him as you should. "He who does not love Me does not keep My words" (John 14:24).

God's Plumb Line for Ephesus

In His message to the first-century churches, the risen Christ invited them to hear and respond to Him. Addressing the church at Ephesus, the Lord commended their hard work, perseverance, and intolerance of evil. Yet they had a fatal flaw. Jesus set a plumb line alongside their church so they would clearly know what was wrong.

> "I have this against you, that you have left your first love. Remember
> therefore from where you have fallen; repent and do the first works, or else
> I will come to you quickly and remove your lampstand from its place—
> unless you repent. . . . He who has an ear, let him hear what the Spirit says
> to the churches. To him who overcomes I will give to eat from the tree of
> life, which is in the midst of the Paradise of God." (Rev. 2:4–7)

The reason we need revival is because we have forsaken our love relationship with God. God invites us to repent and return to Him. His word to the church at Ephesus indicates that failure to repent is fatal. When He said He would remove their lampstand, He was referring to the church (Rev. 1:20). To the extent that we fail to return to our first love, we will miss out on the abundant life God intends, and a lost world will continue its march into a hopeless eternity.

As you continue to read, let the Lord set the plumb line of Scriptures alongside your life, your family, your church, your denomination, and your nation. Ask Him to show you any place you have deviated from Him. When you see the signs of departure, remember that restoration begins in your heart. Let God bring you to a place of brokenness over your estranged relationship. "For godly sorrow produces repentance leading to salvation, not to be regretted" (2 Cor. 7:10). Out of the brokenness of your damaged relationship, God can restore you to a close walk with Him that exceeds anything you could have imagined possible.

A Testimony of God's Grace: The Shantung Revival

In 1920 Christian missionaries in North China were grieved over the spiritually lethargic condition of their churches. Members showed scant interest for spiritual concerns. The missionaries began to wonder if many of the people in the churches had accepted Christianity intellectually but had never been spiritually born again.

They began to devote one day a month to praying together for revival. In March 1927, the Chinese southern revolutionary army burned Nanking, and missionaries were ordered to Chefoo for possible evacuation. While the missionaries were gathered together waiting to see if they could continue their work or not, they began to study the Scriptures and to ask the Lord why they had been removed from their work. God spoke to them through His Word.

A group of missionaries asked Marie Monsen, an Evangelical Lutheran missionary from Norway, to join their prayer meetings. God used her to challenge them to get right with Him. The group spent days before the Lord. They confessed every known sin. They were reconciled with one another. God was drawing His people back to Himself. Marie asked people three penetrating questions:

1. Have you been born of the Spirit?
2. What evidence do you have of the new birth?
3. Have you been filled with the Holy Spirit?

The hunger for spiritual vitality caused people to do much soul-searching. C. L. Culpepper, one of the missionaries present, observed, "We felt an electric excitement, a feeling that God was preparing us for something we had never known before."[2] Christians, especially church leaders, were revived and filled with the Holy Spirit. Once God's people drew close to Him, He used them powerfully to impact China for Christ.

God set His plumb line against the lives of the Chinese church leaders, and they saw that they fell short of His expectations. An evangelist for twenty-five years, Mr. Chow realized he was trusting in his good works for salvation but not in Christ. He gave his life to Christ, and thenceforth he refused to be paid for his preaching. Lucy Wright, a missionary nurse for nine years, realized she had only joined the church but had not been born again. She trusted Christ for the first time. By 1932 thousands of people were coming to Christ. In one school all six hundred girls and nine hundred out of one thousand boys trusted Christ during ten days of meetings.

The revival produced exponential results. New converts went everywhere telling people what Jesus had done for them. Those who turned to Christ took down their "house gods" and burned them. The hearts of God's people were full of praise and thanksgiving. Joyful singing filled the services. New hymns were written, and Scriptures were put to music. Believers developed an insatiable hunger for God's Word. Bible classes met nightly. Enrollment in Bible schools and seminaries increased dramatically. Spiritually stagnant churches were reinvigorated. Church attendance multiplied and members enthusiastically participated in worship, prayer, and discipleship. Prayer meetings lasted two or three hours as people got right with God and prayed for unbelievers. Broken families and relationships were healed.[3] Once God's people realized how far they had drifted from Him, they enthusiastically returned, and soon vast regions of China were feeling the impact.

God's Revealed Word

God has provided clear guidelines in Scripture concerning His expectations of His people. The following are some of the truths people most often misunderstand or neglect. When revival comes, these particular truths suddenly become clear, calling for a radical response from believers and nonbelievers alike. Ask the Holy Spirit to evaluate your life in light of the following.

God's Word Is Authoritative

Those who experience revival are people with a deep reverence for God's Word and a readiness to obey what it says. The Bible declares: "All Scripture is given by inspiration of God, and is profitable for doctrine, for reproof, for correction, for instruction in righteousness" (2 Tim. 3:16). While Christian churches routinely preach and teach from the Bible, Stephen Olford suggested that in times of revival, "God's word comes alive."[4] Then the Bible is not only preached; it is proclaimed *with conviction.* Martin Lloyd Jones observed that revival never begins in churches or denominations where fundamental doctrines of the faith are compromised.[5] Brian Edwards said it more plainly, "Revival never begins with the liberal wing of the church."[6] Spiritual renewal comes when God's Word is fearlessly and faithfully preached and taught. Octavious Winslow observed: "Nothing perhaps more strongly indicates the tone of a believer's spirituality, than the light in which the scriptures are regarded by him."[7] God expects His Scriptures to be preached, taught, and obeyed reverently and wholeheartedly. In the atmosphere of scriptural fidelity, revival is most likely to occur. Conversely, nothing is more deadening to spirituality than careless treatment of the Bible and its instruction.

Salvation Is in Christ Alone

First Timothy 2:5 declares: "For there is one God and one Mediator between God and men, the Man Christ Jesus." Revival occurs where Christ is exalted among His people. In times of pluralism, Christ as the sole means of salvation is compromised or questioned, and the church declines. Martin Lloyd Jones said: "Revival, above everything else, is the glorification of the Lord Jesus Christ, the Son of God. It is the restoration of him to the center of the life of the Church."[8] Jonathan Goforth observed: "The call to revival must be a call to exalt Jesus Christ in our hearts."[9]

All Have Sinned

Scripture clearly states, "All have sinned and fall short of the glory of God" (Rom. 3:23). Revival comes only after people develop a profound awareness that they have sinned against a holy God. Significantly, Romans 6:23, which declares that the wages of sin is death, was not written to unbelievers but to Christians in Rome. Sin kills spiritual vitality, destroys marriages, severs relationships, and decimates church unity. Sin deadens the passion for God's Word and for prayer and invalidates Christian witness. A deep sensitivity to sin and its devastating consequences among God's people is always a prerequisite for revival.

Jonathan Edwards's famous sermon, "Sinners in the Hands of an Angry God" graphically depicted sin's deadly nature. On July 8, 1741, Edwards preached in Enfield, Connecticut, from Deuteronomy 32:35, "Vengeance is Mine, and recompense; their foot shall slip in due time; for the day of their calamity is at hand, and the things to come hasten upon them." As Edwards preached and explained the reality of what it means to sin against an absolutely holy God, a terrifying sense of conviction for their sins came upon the people, and many of them cried out in dread. Once people recognized the gravity and pervasiveness of their wickedness, they returned to God immediately. Amid the Holy Spirit's powerful work during the Welsh Revival in 1860, an observer said, "It is the broken prayers of the most abandoned characters, confessing their sins and crying for mercy in their simple and childlike language, that affect the people most. I will defy the hardest and most callous sinner to remain five minutes within hearing of these prayers without being melted to tears."[10] When the Spirit of God moves among His people to revive them, they view their sin with the same holy repugnance God does.

Those Who Reject God's Salvation Perish

John 3:16 is a beloved verse memorized by many children and new believers; it presents the gospel message in stark detail. God sent His Son because He knew the consequences if there was no provision for people's salvation. When the church ignores or refuses to believe in the dreadful fate of those who choose to reject the gospel, Christians no longer have the passion to plead with sinners to repent of their evil ways. When revival comes, the horrific reality of hell is acknowledged and preached uncompromisingly. The church is always in danger of losing the concern for people going into a Christless eternity separated from the Father.

Genuine Salvation Leads to Spiritual Fruit

Galatians 5:22–23 lays out the visible evidence that someone has been born again. "But the fruit of the Spirit is love, joy, peace, longsuffering, kindness, goodness, faithfulness, gentleness, self-control." Those in whom the Holy Spirit dwells will increasingly demonstrate spiritual fruit in their lives as the Holy Spirit continues His sanctifying work within them. When God's people are not characterized by the fruits of His Spirit, the need for revival is unmistakable.

A natural result of abiding in Christ is joy (John 15:11). Christians who have no joy must understand that their hearts have wandered from God. Many accounts of revival testify that worship services were previously joyless. However, when God's people are revived, they experience a new and deeper quality of joy. The singing and praying become characterized by irrepressible gladness. Worship songs are composed to express the newfound joy God has brought. A witness of the Welsh Revival observed of those who had been revived "they have enjoyed more happiness in one hour of communion with God, than they had during many years of wasteful life."[11]

Believers Obey Christ as Lord

Jesus asked those who professed to be His disciples, "But why do you call me 'Lord, Lord,' and not do the things which I say?" (Luke 6:46). Jesus identified true disciples as men and women who obeyed what He commanded (John 15:14). During periods of revival, many tearfully confess that they know what God commanded them to do but they resisted. People who ignored God's leading to go on international missions repent and apply to be missionaries. Those who have refused to forgive finally extend forgiveness to those who wronged them. People who were puffed up with pride embrace the Spirit's work as He humbles them. Many who have long resisted the Holy Spirit's conviction concerning a sinful habit thoroughly renounce it at last.

Those who stole, confess and repay. During the Saskatoon Revival, the *Star Phoenix* reported on November 12, 1971 in its article "Renewed Morality Found in Wake of Revival" that there was "a surge of people making up for past dishonesty." Local businesses were being inundated with people returning to confess their crimes. The federal tax department received checks in the mail with letters of apology regarding previously misrepresented income tax claims. Church treasurers confessed to "borrowing" church funds. Times of revival reveal how deeply the sins of greed, lust, and pride have become normative in the church.[12] Once people are made right with God, they will go to enormous lengths to do what they know God has been asking them to do.

Believers are Characterized by Holiness

Scripture exhorts: "But as He who called you is holy, you also be holy in all your conduct, because it is written, 'Be holy, for I am holy'" (1 Pet. 1:15–16). The church is to be *in* the world but not *of* the world (John 17:15). Over time the line between "in" and "of" inevitably grows fuzzy, and as it does, the spiritual vitality of God's people wanes. The lack of holiness immediately smites God's people whenever they are awakened to their spiritual condition. The saintly Robert Murray McCheyne regularly prayed, "God, make me as holy as it is possible for a sinner saved by grace on this earth to be."[13] As a result of this unswerving desire, God mightily used McCheyne's life to consecrate the people around him.

Holiness in Brownwood

On January 22, 1995, John Avant began a sermon series on the Ten Commandments at his church at Coggin Avenue Baptist Church in Brownwood, Texas. At the close of the early service, Chris Robeson, a student at Howard Payne University in Brownwood, came forward to share how God encountered him. Others immediately came under conviction of their own sin. Twenty-two people were converted or called into Christian ministry before the service ended. God began to work powerfully among the people in subsequent services. Henry Blackaby arrived soon afterward to preach at the church and at a series of services at Howard Payne. During that time revival continued to spread across the university campus. Students came under great conviction that they had not been living holy lives. People lined up at the microphones to confess tearfully their sins as they committed themselves anew to sanctified living. When holy God demonstrates His lordship over people, the results are often dramatic.[14]

God's People Forgive

Jesus commanded His followers to forgive those who offended them (Matt. 5:44). Likewise Jesus taught that God would forgive them in the same way they extended grace to those who injured them (Matt. 6:12; 18:35). God expects His people to forgive because He has given us the ministry of reconciliation (2 Cor. 5:18–21). There is no acceptable excuse for a Christian to withhold forgiveness from anyone.

Forgiveness in Saskatoon

Forgiveness has been used by God as a divine spark plug for revival. In October 1972, Ebenezer Baptist Church in Saskaton, Canada, launched a week of services aimed at spiritual renewal. Initially the response was modest, but two of the church leaders were brothers, Sam and Arnold Derksen, who had been angry at each other for thirteen years. For the previous two years they had not spoken to each other. Many in the congregation were unaware of the depth of their animosity. However, their pastor, Rev. Bill McLeod, knew that such unforgiveness was stifling the Spirit's work in the congregation. One evening before the service began, McLeod brought the two brothers together and sought to have them reconciled. At first each was hardened toward the other and refused to acknowledge responsibility. However, the Holy Spirit eventually brought great conviction to them both until their pride was broken and they confessed their fault and asked each other's forgiveness. People sitting in the auditorium upstairs could hear their weeping as they were reconciled. As they confessed their sin in that evening's service, the Holy Spirit brought many others under conviction of their own sin. In the following service, the brothers sang a duet. Revival pulsated through that church that lasted seven weeks and spread across Canada, ultimately impacting the United States and many places around the world.[15]

God's People Pray

God does not expect His people merely to pray during their daily devotionals. Believers are to pray without ceasing (1 Thess. 5:17). When the place of prayer is forsaken, it is evidence that God's people need revival. Those who know they can do nothing apart from abiding in Christ will cry out to God continually (John 15:5). People who become self-confident and proud will find they are too busy to pray. One of the first signs revival may be coming is a renewed interest among God's people in prayer. Once revival has come, prayer meetings will overflow with eager participants.

Materialism Is Renounced

Scripture warns that the love of money is a root of all sorts of evil (I Tim. 6:10). Biblical history is replete with tragic examples of how God's people, once they became prosperous, forgot God and became consumed with materialism. Material wealth tempts God's people to trust in their own devices rather than in Christ. Prosperous churches can spend large sums to advertise their church on television, radio, and on billboards rather than relying on Christ to build His church as He promised (Matt. 16:18). In commenting on the revival in his church, Robert Murray McCheyne noted: "How glorious it is to have revival without the fanfare of trumpets! How blessed to have revival without advertising and organization! How blessed to be in the midst of meetings where the Holy Spirit takes full control and the Lord Jesus, Himself, is the center of attention. Not a penny was spent in any way on advertising these meetings!"[16] Perhaps one reason revival has not come through the efforts of a megachurch today is because they have such ample resources. It is too easy to trust in catchy brochures, clever advertisements, and musical extravaganzas rather than wait upon the Holy Spirit to do His work in His time.

Spiritually renewed believers let go of their attachment to wealth. Many confess that possessions have controlled their hearts, rendering them unwilling to heed God's voice. In times of revival, Christians frequently admit to improper use of funds or to acting without financial integrity. The twin sins of dishonesty and greed affect numerous people in thousands of congregations, and only the Holy Spirit's activity exposes the damage caused by the love of money.

Conclusion

God has given us a plumb line so we can measure whether or not we have departed from His standards. Apart from the convicting work of the Holy Spirit, we can convince ourselves we have not wandered from God even though there is compelling evidence to the contrary. We are much like those in the prophet Malachi's day. When he chastised God's people for straying from God, they were incredulous. "In what way shall we return?" (Mal. 3:7), they replied. Though they were far from God, they remained oblivious to how far away their sin had led them.

Along with God's plumb line Christians also need the active, convicting work of the Holy Spirit to open our spiritual eyes to the gravity of our spiritual condition. According to Romans 8:16, "The Spirit Himself bears witness with our spirit that we are children of God." The Holy Spirit convicts of sin, righteousness, and judgment (John 16:8). He will take God's standard and hold it against our lives to reveal where we stand. *Any* departure from God is serious. When the Spirit reveals that you have strayed from God in *any* way, immediately and earnestly return to Him before you have gone any farther.

QUESTIONS FOR REFLECTION AND DISCUSSION

1. Think about your life immediately after you became a Christian. Has your joy and love for God waned, or has it increased since that time? Is there any way in which your heart has departed from God?

2. Have you lost your reverence for and commitment to obey God's Word?

3. Do you believe there is salvation in no one else but Jesus Christ? How does that belief affect the way you are living?

4. How does the reality of hell compel you to pray for and witness to those who do not know Christ?

5. Are you obeying Christ with all your heart? In what ways has your commitment to obey God diminished?

6. Consider whether the following spiritual fruit is evident in your life: love, joy, peace, long-suffering, kindness, goodness, faithfulness, gentleness, self-control. Have you been making excuses for the absence of any of these characteristics?

7. How have you been compromising God's righteous standards?

8. Have you forgiven every person who has offended you? If not, what is preventing you?

9. Is your prayer life pleasing to God? Has your prayer life been distracted by things you value more than communing with God?

10. Has materialism invaded your life? Do you truly love God more than any possession or amount of wealth? If so, what is the evidence?

CHAPTER 6

The Biblical Record of Revival

R evival is a biblical phenomenon mentioned throughout the Old and New Testaments.[1] Scripture records numerous instances when individuals repented of their sin and were restored in their relationship with God. The Bible also testifies to the many times when God's people repented corporately and committed themselves afresh to the Lord. While Scripture records a wide diversity of revival experiences, there are also some common threads woven throughout each one. The following are examples of revivals found in the Scriptures.

Revival under Samuel

The nation of Israel was birthed out of revival. When God set about His work of delivering the Hebrews from bondage and transforming them into a holy nation, He began by calling Moses. When Moses first encountered God at the burning bush, God's instructions were: "Take your sandals off your feet, for the place where you stand is holy ground" (Exod. 3:5). Moses first had to experience personal cleansing and renewal before he was prepared to lead God's people. When Moses led the Israelites to Mount Sinai after they had been freed from captivity, God told Moses: "Go to the people and consecrate them today and tomorrow, and let them wash their clothes. And let them be ready for the third day. For on the third day the Lord will come down upon Mount Sinai in the sight of all the people" (Exod. 19:10–11). As God began to establish the laws and practices of this new nation, He first cleansed them to prepare them to be His people.

In Samuel's day, however, the nation of Israel fully emerged, and this too came out of a time of renewal. As a young man Samuel learned a valuable lesson in his personal relationship with God: "For those who honor Me I will honor, and those who despise Me shall be lightly esteemed" (I Sam. 2:30). Samuel honored God all his life, and as a result God's hand was always on him. Sadly, the same could not be said for the Israelites.

During the ministry of the priest Eli, the Israelites grew disoriented to the Lord. Because the people abandoned Him, God allowed them to face their problems without His assistance or protection. They went into battle against their mortal enemies, the Philistines, and lost four thousand men in a devastating defeat. The leaders returned to camp and lamented: "Why has the LORD defeated us today before the Philistines? Let us bring the ark of the covenant of the LORD from Shiloh to us, that when it comes among us it may save us from the hand of our enemies" (I Sam. 4:3).

The Israelites made three serious mistakes. First, they assumed that because they were God's people they could live any way they wanted and yet enjoy God's blessing and protection. Their second mistake was believing they could initiate God's activity through their actions. They did not seek direction from the Lord but made their own plans and assumed God would bless them. Third, they turned to a substitute for God. They placed their trust in the ark of the covenant rather than in the God of the ark. The ark represented God's presence. However, they made a subtle but significant shift in their thinking. They began to treat the symbol of God's presence as a good luck charm rather than as a representation of their relationship with Him. They took "it" with them so "it" would save them.

Idolatry is essentially turning one's trust from the person of God to someone or something else. God allowed His people to experience the futility of trusting in a substitute. The ark, despite its sacred history, did not save them. Once again the Israelites were beaten, and they lost thirty thousand soldiers in a stunning defeat. The enemy captured the ark and killed Eli's two sons. Upon hearing the disastrous news, the priest Eli collapsed, broke his neck, and died (I Sam. 4:18).

Seven months later the Philistines returned the ark to Israel, and it was lodged at Kiriath Jearim for safekeeping. Subsequently Israel was without the manifest presence of God. Twenty years later the people finally *lamented after the Lord.* They came to realize the futility of life apart from God's direct involvement and leadership in their lives. Samuel led them to destroy their foreign gods and return to the Lord.

> Samuel spoke to all the house of Israel, saying, "If you return to the LORD
> with all your hearts, then put away the foreign gods and the Ashtoreths from
> among you, and prepare your hearts for the LORD, and serve Him only; and
> He will deliver you from the hand of the Philistines." So the children of
> Israel put away the Baals and the Ashtoreths, and served the LORD only.

And Samuel said, "Gather all Israel to Mizpah, and I will pray to the LORD for you." So they gathered together at Mizpah, drew water, and poured it out before the LORD. And they fasted that day, and said there, "We have sinned against the LORD." And Samuel judged the children of Israel at Mizpah.

Now when the Philistines heard that the children of Israel had gathered together at Mizpah, the lords of the Philistines went up against Israel. And when the children of Israel heard of it, they were afraid of the Philistines. So the children of Israel said to Samuel, "Do not cease to cry out to the LORD our God for us, that He may save us from the hand of the Philistines."

And Samuel took a suckling lamb and offered it as a whole burnt offering to the LORD. Then Samuel cried out to the LORD for Israel, and the LORD answered him. (I Sam. 7:3–9)

The Israelites met together to fast, confess their sin, and offer sacrifices to the Lord. Samuel, as their spiritual leader, prayed for the people, and God answered him.

Now as Samuel was offering up the burnt offering, the Philistines drew near to battle against Israel. But the LORD thundered with a loud thunder upon the Philistines that day, and so confused them that they were overcome before Israel. And the men of Israel went out of Mizpah and pursued the Philistines, and drove them back as far as below Beth Car. Then Samuel took a stone and set it up between Mizpah and Shen, and called its name Ebenezer, saying, "Thus far the LORD has helped us."

So the Philistines were subdued, and they did not come anymore into the territory of Israel. And the hand of the LORD was against the Philistines all the days of Samuel. (I Sam. 7:10–13)

Summary

The preceding account clearly demonstrates the process of biblical revival. During Eli's day the leaders failed to walk closely with God, and inevitably God's people forsook Him as well. The people turned their hearts away from God and depended upon man-made planning and resources just as the rest of the world did. Therefore God judged His people by allowing their enemies to strike them down. When the people recognized they were powerless without God, they cried out to Him for deliverance. By repenting of their sin, the people returned to God, and He responded by returning to them. With God working in their midst once more, no enemy or crisis could overcome God's people.

Revival under King Asa

Asa, King of Judah, had a family heritage of faith. He was the great-great-grandson of King David. Asa's father, King Abijah, trusted the Lord and guided the people to follow God's requirements. Asa was brought up to believe in the Lord and faithfully serve Him. When Asa became king, he "did what was good and right in the eyes of the LORD his God, for he removed the altars of the foreign gods and the high places, and broke down the sacred pillars and cut down the wooden images. He commanded Judah to seek the LORD God of their fathers, and to observe the law and the commandment" (2 Chron. 14:2–4).

Malcom McDow and Alvin Reid point out the difference between reform and revival. "Reform focuses on practices; revival focuses on people."[2] We might say reform changes behavior but only revival alters hearts. King Asa instigated reform by removing the abominable idols and sacred pillars that had captured the hearts of God's people. For more than ten years the land of Judah enjoyed peace and prosperity. Most people, especially those who observed the wicked nation of Israel to the north, would have commended Judah's religious practices. But God knew His people's hearts were still not wholly for Him.

God allowed a fierce enemy to rise up to invade Judah. King Asa, recognizing the hopelessness of their situation apart from divine intervention, prayed, "LORD, it is nothing for You to help, whether with many or with those who have no power; help us, O LORD our God, for we rest on You" (2 Chron. 14:11). God gave Asa a miraculous victory. The people then stood at a crossroad. Having experienced victory and prosperity, they could go the way of their fathers and turn their backs on God, or they could firmly place their faith in Him. At that time the prophet Azariah delivered a classic revival message to God's people:

> Now the Spirit of God came upon Azariah the son of Oded. And he
> went out to meet Asa, and said to him: "Hear me, Asa, and all Judah and
> Benjamin. The LORD is with you while you are with Him. If you seek
> Him, He will be found by you; but if you forsake Him, He will forsake
> you. For a long time Israel has been without the true God, without a

teaching priest, and without law; but when in their trouble they turned to the LORD God of Israel, and sought Him, He was found by them. And in those times there was no peace to the one who went out, nor to the one who came in, but great turmoil was on all the inhabitants of the lands. So nation was destroyed by nation, and city by city, for God troubled them with every adversity. But you, be strong and do not let your hands be weak, for your work shall be rewarded!" (2 Chron. 15:1–7)

Clearly if God's people seek Him, they will find Him. This truth is underscored throughout the Bible (Deut. 4:29; I Chron. 28:9; Jer. 29:13–14; Matt. 7:7–12; Acts 15:17; 17:27). Revival occurs when God's people return to Him and God draws near to His people. However, as the prophet Azariah explained, when God's people turn away from Him, God allows them to experience calamity apart from His protection.

King Asa needed this reminder from the Lord. God had not left Israel; they had abandoned Him. God would be with His people when they returned to Him. God was calling them back into a right relationship with Him. If they would seek the Lord, He would be found. But, if they forsook God, they would find themselves alone and apart from Him.

And when Asa heard these words and the prophecy of Oded the prophet, he took courage, and removed the abominable idols from all the land . . . ; and he restored the altar of the LORD that was before the vestibule of the LORD. Then he gathered all Judah and Benjamin, and those who dwelt with them from Ephraim, Manasseh, and Simeon, for they came over to him in great numbers from Israel when they saw that the LORD his God was with him.

So they gathered together at Jerusalem in the third month, in the fifteenth year of the reign of Asa. And they offered to the LORD at that time seven hundred bulls and seven thousand sheep from the spoil they had brought. Then they entered into a covenant to seek the LORD God of their fathers with all their heart and with all their soul; and whoever would not seek the LORD God of Israel was to be put to death, whether small or great, whether man or woman. Then they took an oath before the LORD with a loud voice, with shouting and trumpets and rams' horns. And all Judah rejoiced at the oath, for they had sworn with all their heart and sought Him with all their soul; and He was found by them, and the LORD gave them rest all around. (2 Chron. 15:8–15)

Asa prepared for the return to the Lord by removing the detestable idols and repairing the Lord's altar. Then he summoned the people for a solemn assembly. This was serious business. The nation's future hinged on the people's fervent response, and the passage says they "entered into a covenant to seek the LORD" (2 Chron. 15:12). There are nine biblical references to King Asa and his people diligently pursuing God; and as the passage above reveals, God responded to their search and blessed them.

Summary

The Bible clearly demonstrates a pattern of revival: God's people would reject Him and invoke His discipline. Then the Lord would call on them to return to Him. The great joy of revival came after the people repented of their evil ways and enthusiastically returned to a love relationship with God.

Revival under King Hezekiah

Ahaz was the epitome of wicked leadership. He closed down the Lord's temple and blatantly worshipped pagan gods. He even sacrificed his own sons to idols. Because of his wickedness, "the LORD his God delivered him into the hand of the king of Syria. They defeated him, and carried away a great multitude of them as captives, and brought them to Damascus. Then he was also delivered into the hand of the king of Israel, who defeated him with a great slaughter" (2 Chron. 28:5).

Spiritually, the nation reached a low ebb under Ahaz's leadership. Then Hezekiah, his son, became king of Judah following his father's wicked sixteen-year reign. Notably many of those who led their nation in revival began their rule as young men. Samuel began serving God when he was a boy. King Asa was a young man when he assumed the throne. Hezekiah was twenty-five. Josiah was eight. God has often sparked revivals through young people. Although still a young man, Hezekiah chose not to follow in his evil father's footsteps.

> Hezekiah became king when he was twenty-five years old, and he reigned twenty-nine years in Jerusalem. . . . And he did what was right in the sight of the LORD, according to all that his father David had done.
>
> In the first year of his reign, in the first month, he opened the doors of the house of the LORD and repaired them. Then he brought in the priests and the Levites, and gathered them in the East Square, and said

to them: "Hear me, Levites! Now sanctify yourselves, sanctify the house of the LORD God of your fathers, and carry out the rubbish from the holy place. For our fathers have trespassed and done evil in the eyes of the LORD our God; they have forsaken Him, have turned their faces away from the dwelling place of the LORD, and turned their backs on Him. . . . Therefore the wrath of the LORD fell upon Judah and Jerusalem, and He has given them up to trouble, to desolation, and to jeering, as you see with your eyes. For indeed, because of this our fathers have fallen by the sword; and our sons, our daughters, and our wives are in captivity.

"Now it is in my heart to make a covenant with the LORD God of Israel, that His fierce wrath may turn away from us."
(2 Chron. 29:1–6, 8–10)

A wise spiritual leader recognizes the symptoms of spiritual sickness in the midst of God's people. Hezekiah knew the previous generation had forsaken the Lord. He recognized that destruction, death, and the captivity of Jerusalem were signs of God's judgment on His people for their sin. Hezekiah knew it was time to cry out to the Lord for spiritual renewal. In preparation Hezekiah had the temple repaired, cleansed, and rededicated to the Lord.

There was so much accumulated filth in the temple it could not facilitate worship. The Levites spent sixteen days consecrating the temple and removing the debris. Then Hezekiah gathered the city officials and went to the temple to offer sacrifices to the Lord. The temple musicians were called into service to assist with the worship. "The service of the house of the LORD was set in order. Then Hezekiah and all the people rejoiced that God had prepared the people, since the events took place so suddenly" (2 Chron. 29:35–36).

Hezekiah sent word to all Israel and Judah, calling them to assemble for the Passover celebration. Though the time had already passed for that year's celebration, there was a sense of urgency to gather immediately.

Then the runners went throughout all Israel and Judah with the letters from the king and his leaders, and spoke according to the command of the king: "Children of Israel, return to the LORD God of Abraham, Isaac, and Israel; then He will return to the remnant of you who have escaped from the hand of the kings of Assyria. And do not be like your fathers and your brethren, who trespassed against the LORD God of their fathers, so that He gave them up to desolation, as you see. Now do not be stiff-necked, as your fathers were, but yield yourselves to the LORD; and enter His sanctuary, which He has sanctified forever, and serve the LORD your God, that the fierceness of His wrath may turn away from you. For if you return to the LORD, your brethren and your children will be treated with compassion by those who lead them captive, so that they may come back to this land; for the LORD your God is gracious and merciful, and will not turn His face from you if you return to Him." (2 Chron. 30:6–9)

Just as King Asa had done, so Hezekiah sought to make a covenant with God (2 Chron. 29:10). Hezekiah recognized God's severe judgment as a consequence of Judah's breaking its sacred promises to Him. The young king implored the people to return to the Lord. This was a call to worship, but not everyone wanted to honor the Lord. Detractors scorned and ridiculed the messengers. Others, however, humbled themselves and gathered to worship. And "the hand of God was on Judah to give them singleness of heart to obey the command of the king and the leaders, at the word of the LORD" (2 Chron. 30:12). Hezekiah prayed for the people, "And the LORD listened to Hezekiah and healed the people" (2 Chron. 30:20). When God's people repented of their sin and worshipped Him, the covenant relationship of love was reestablished. The people experienced great joy in their worship. In fact, they decided to celebrate the feast seven more days. Everything changed once their relationship with God was restored.

"Then the whole assembly agreed to keep the feast another seven days, and they kept it another seven days with gladness. . . . A great number of priests sanctified themselves. The whole assembly of Judah rejoiced. . . . So there was great joy in Jerusalem, for since the time of Solomon the son of David, king of Israel, there had been nothing like this in Jerusalem. Then the priests, the Levites, arose and blessed the people, and their voice was heard; and their prayer came up to His holy dwelling place, to heaven." (2 Chron. 30:23–27)

As a demonstration of repentance, the people set out from the assembly to rid the surrounding area of every remnant of idolatry: "Now when all this was finished, all Israel who were present went out to the cities of Judah and broke the sacred pillars in pieces, cut down the wooden images, and threw down the high places and the altars—from all Judah, Benjamin, Ephraim, and Manasseh—until they had utterly destroyed them all" (2 Chron. 31:1). Once God's people are revived, the nation and the surrounding nations soon feel the impact.

During the next five months, the people generously brought tithes "of everything" (2 Chron. 31:5) to the Lord. "And when Hezekiah and the leaders came and saw the heaps, they blessed the LORD and His people Israel" (2 Chron. 31:8). Another consequence of revival is generous giving. A reluctance to give to the Lord is a symptom of a strained relationship with God. When believers turn their trust back to the Lord, giving flows naturally out of a thankful heart.

Summary

King Hezekiah inherited a nation that had abandoned faith in God and had forsaken the place of worship. Before godliness could flourish in the land, the religious leaders had to be renewed, and the place of worship had to be cleansed. This took time. But, when the leaders were prepared, most of the people eagerly followed their lead. The result of returning to God was great joy among His people. Here is a summary of Hezekiah's work: "He did what was good and right and true before the LORD his God. And in every work that he began in the service of the house of God, in the law and in the commandment, to seek his God, he did it with all his heart. So he prospered" (2 Chron. 31:20–21).

Revival under Josiah

Josiah's heritage certainly did not predispose him to lead a revival. His grandfather, King Manasseh, was the most wicked king in Judah's history. Sadly, his reign of fifty-five years lasted the longest. Manasseh's son Amon was so evil that his servants murdered him (2 Chron. 33:24). Amon's killers were then executed, and eight-year-old Josiah was placed on the throne.

When Josiah began his reign, the temple was once again in shambles. The Book of the Law had been lost. King Josiah did not even know the Lord's requirements for His people. At age sixteen, Josiah began to seek the Lord (2 Chron. 34:3). At twenty he began to purge the land of its idolatry. When he was twenty-six, Josiah commissioned the repairing of the temple. While cleaning the temple, Hilkiah, the priest, found the Book of the Law. When Josiah heard the law read, he evaluated his nation's behavior in light of what God had said. When this young king realized his people had departed from God and that they now faced impending judgment, Josiah cried out to God, tearing his robes in brokenness and repentance (2 Chron. 34:19).

Josiah must have felt betrayed by his father and grandfather who reigned before him. Now that Josiah saw clearly the symptoms of a people who had departed from the Lord, he needed direction. Josiah sought a word from the Lord through the prophetess Huldah. "Go, inquire of the LORD for me, and for those who are left in Israel and Judah, concerning the words of the book that is found; for great is the wrath of the LORD that is poured out on us, because our fathers have not kept the word of the LORD, to do according to all that is written in this book" (2 Chron. 34:21).

Huldah brought back a message from God:

"Thus says the LORD: 'Behold, I will bring calamity on this place and on its inhabitants, all the curses that are written in the book which they have read before the king of Judah, because they have forsaken Me and burned incense to other gods, that they might provoke Me to anger with all the works of their hands. Therefore My wrath will be poured out on this place, and not be quenched.'" (2 Chron. 34:24–25)

Tragically it was too late for Josiah to save his nation from judgment. Despite his strenuous efforts to reform his nation, the people's hearts were too hardened in their sin. While some did return to the Lord, later events proved that the revival under Josiah was not deep or long lasting. Because the people's transformation was not permanent, God ultimately judged His people. God is extremely patient, but He does not withhold His judgment forever. About forty years later God told the prophet Jeremiah: "Do not pray for this people, for their good. When they fast, I will not hear their cry; and when they offer burnt offering and grain offering, I will not accept them. But I will consume them by the sword, by the famine, and by the pestilence" (Jer. 14:11–12).

Jeremiah was a contemporary of King Josiah. By the end of Jeremiah's prophetic ministry, God told him it was too late even to intercede for the people. God's call to His people is repent or perish. When we hear that call, we must respond quickly. The time will come when judgment is unavoidable. Fortunately for Josiah, God saw His receptive heart and delayed sending judgment until after his reign.

"Because your heart was tender, and you humbled yourself before God when you heard His words against this place and against its inhabitants, and you humbled yourself before Me, and you tore your clothes and wept before Me, I also have heard you," says the LORD. "Surely I will gather you to your fathers, and you shall be gathered to your grave in peace; and your eyes shall not see all the calamity which I will bring on this place and its inhabitants." (2 Chron. 34:27–28)

God recognized that Josiah was brokenhearted over his people's sins. Josiah's humility saved an entire generation from judgment. Significantly, God spared Josiah's generation after he responded but before the people repented. A leader's repentance secured God's response. Josiah then guided the people to return to the Lord.

> Then the king sent and gathered all the elders of Judah and Jerusalem. The king went up to the house of the LORD, with all the men of Judah and the inhabitants of Jerusalem—the priests and the Levites, and all the people, great and small. And he read in their hearing all the words of the Book of the Covenant which had been found in the house of the LORD. Then the king stood in his place and made a covenant before the LORD, to follow the LORD, and to keep His commandments and His testimonies and His statutes with all his heart and all his soul, to perform the words of the covenant that were written in this book. And he made all who were present in Jerusalem and Benjamin take a stand. So the inhabitants of Jerusalem did according to the covenant of God, the God of their fathers. Thus Josiah removed all the abominations from all the country that belonged to the children of Israel, and made all who were present in Israel diligently serve the LORD their God. All his days they did not depart from following the LORD God of their fathers. (2 Chron. 34:29–33)

Summary

Like Kings Asa and Hezekiah, Josiah made a covenant to follow God and keep His law "with all his heart and all his soul" (2 Chron. 34:31). The people gave evidence of their return to the Lord by removing their false gods. Once they repented, Josiah guided them in their return. This was a stirring time of celebration and praise for all God did in delivering them from Egyptian bondage. After repentance joy returns to worship. The Scripture records that "There had been no Passover kept in Israel like that since the days of Samuel the prophet" (2 Chron. 35:18).

Revival under Ezra and Nehemiah

God told the prophet Jeremiah to cease praying for the people because God's judgment was now certain. In 586 BC the Babylonian armies under King Nebuchadnezzer razed Jerusalem's walls, burned the temple, and carried Judah's leaders away into seventy years of exile. After that time, as God began to bring the people back to Jerusalem, a significant revival took place under the joint leadership of Ezra the priest and Nehemiah the governor. This widespread renewal began on the day of the Feast of Trumpets.

> Now all the people gathered together as one man in the open square that was in front of the Water Gate; and they told Ezra the scribe to bring the Book of the Law of Moses, which the LORD had commanded Israel. So Ezra the priest brought the Law before the assembly of men and women and all who could hear with understanding on the first day of the seventh month. Then he read from it in the open square that was in front of the Water Gate from morning until midday, before the men and women and those who could understand; and the ears of all the people were attentive to the Book of the Law.
>
> So Ezra the scribe stood on a platform of wood which they had made for the purpose. . . . And Ezra opened the book in the sight of all the people, for he was standing above all the people; and when he opened it, all the people stood up. And Ezra blessed the LORD, the great God. Then all the people answered, "Amen, Amen!" while lifting up their hands. And they bowed their heads and worshiped the LORD with their faces to the ground. (Neh. 8:1–6)

Imagine standing outdoors in a crowd for six hours listening attentively to the reading of Scripture! Yet everyone came to listen, and the people knew they must take God seriously. There is a profound difference between *listening* and *hearing.* Apparently the people not only listened to what was said; they heard the message loud and clear. The nation had suffered decades of bondage because preceding generations ignored God's Word. As the Scriptures were read aloud, the people heard how God created them to be a special nation. They recalled the miracles God performed on their behalf. They lived through the dire consequences resulting from God's people rejecting Him. As the words of Scripture enlightened God's people, they began to weep and humble themselves before the Lord. They stood convicted by the truth of God's Word. There were no excuses, no attempts to justify their sin. They now understood that their lives and the well-being of their families depended on their response to what they heard that day. This revival experience began with the reading of God's Word and a meaningful time of worship. "The Levites, helped the people to understand the Law; and the people stood in their place. So they read distinctly from the book, in the Law of God; and they gave the sense, and helped them to understand the reading" (Neh. 8:7–8).

As the people mourned their sinful history, the spiritual leaders responded with an intriguing directive:

> Nehemiah, who was the governor, Ezra the priest and scribe, and the
> Levites who taught the people said to all the people, "This day is holy to
> the LORD your God; do not mourn nor weep." For all the people wept,
> when they heard the words of the Law. Then he said to them, "Go your
> way, eat the fat, drink the sweet, and send portions to those for whom
> nothing is prepared; for this day is holy to our LORD. Do not sorrow, for
> the joy of the LORD is your strength." (Neh. 8:9–10)

Much as the apostle Paul set aside his wretched past and pressed forward to the hope of his calling (Phil. 3:12–14), so the leaders urged the people not to dwell on their failures. Rather, the day had come to rejoice in God's salvation and His deliverance from their captivity. The focus was not on the past but on how they chose to follow the Lord in the present. Genuine worship, experiencing the joy of God's presence, would strengthen the people for the eventual working out of their repentance. The Israelites experienced great joy in worship, but that could not bring about revival, nor could any amount of prayer, feasting, fasting, or Scripture study. God required repentance, a turning away from wrong and returning to Him.

On the day following the Feast of Trumpets, the leaders gathered to gain instruction on continuing their return to the Lord: "Now on the second day the heads of the fathers' houses of all the people, with the priests and Levites, were gathered to Ezra the scribe, in order to understand the words of the Law. And they found written in the Law, which the LORD had commanded by Moses, that the children of Israel should dwell in booths during the feast of the seventh month" (Neh. 8:13–14).

The Jewish calendar was important for God's people. The next event for them to observe was the Day of Atonement on the tenth day of the seventh month (Lev. 23:27). The Feast of Tabernacles lasted a week (Lev. 23:34–43). The leaders saw that the people were too discouraged and weak to deal thoroughly with their sin as the Day of Atonement required. So they bypassed the Day of Atonement and celebrated the Feast of Tabernacles.

For eight days they celebrated the mighty deeds of God's provision for the people during their wandering in the wilderness. "And there was very great gladness"

(Neh. 8:17). As the leaders declared earlier, the joy of the Lord strengthened the people (Neh. 8:10). Now the people were ready to deal with their sin through repentance. Two days later the people assembled for a special purpose: "Now on the twenty-fourth day of this month the children of Israel were assembled with fasting, in sackcloth, and with dust on their heads. Then those of Israelite lineage separated themselves from all foreigners; and they stood and confessed their sins and the iniquities of their fathers. And they stood up in their place and read from the Book of the Law of the LORD their God for one-fourth of the day; and for another fourth they confessed and worshiped the LORD their God" (Neh. 9:1–3)

Clearly the repentance God required was extensive and thorough. God was not looking for lip service. He did not ask people merely to say they were sorry or to check a box on a card indicating they would like to rededicate themselves. Repentance, to be acceptable to Almighty God, must be radical, total, and unforgettable. The people demonstrated in several ways that they were serious about renouncing their sin. Following a time of confession, Nehemiah rehearsed the mighty acts God performed for His people; he recounted the nation's spiritual markers. He detailed God's judgment on the land because of the nation's sins. He confirmed that God was justified in how He acted in judgment. Then Nehemiah guided the people to reaffirm their covenant relationship with God. Revival began with genuine worship and ended with worship.

Summary

The revival experience in Nehemiah's day teaches us several things. First, godly leaders can guide God's people to return to Him. Ezra did this by reading Scripture. There is no more powerful instrument to bring conviction of sin than God's Word. Further, the religious leaders helped the people understand what Scripture said. They made sure no one who was listening missed the implications for their lives. The repentance called for was *thorough* and *public*. The nation as a whole had sinned, and now together they repented.

The people also corporately renewed their covenant with God (Neh. 9:38–10:39). God relates to His people through a covenant relationship. A covenant is a promise between two people that guides how they will relate to each other. God remains true to His Word; God's people forsake the covenant and must renew their vows. Last, as in all the revivals examined in this chapter, joy was prominent. Just as sin brings death (Rom. 6:23), so repentance brings life. While repentance can often be heart wrenching and tear filled, if it is done properly, it will ultimately result in profound joy. Evidence that spiritual life is once again flourishing is the joy on people's faces and in their worship of God.

Revival is fragile, and it generally does not last more than one generation. Spiritual vitality can be modeled, but in each generation believers must cultivate their own intimate walk with God. The offspring from Nehemiah's generation drifted away from a close walk with God and replaced it with legalism and ritual. The sect of the Pharisees developed a complex and extensive religious system that demanded the letter of the law but neglected its spirit. By the time the long-awaited Messiah came to earth, these religious leaders were so disoriented to God they murdered His Son. As we study how God related to people in biblical times, we see how He will interact with us. Walking closely with God in covenant is a choice every generation must make.

For Further Study

Below are other instances recorded in Scripture where God's people returned to Him or renewed their relationship with Him.

- Jacob led his family to repent (Gen. 34–35).
- Moses renewed the covenant between God and the people (Exod. 34:10–17).
- Elijah challenged the false prophets on Mount Carmel (1 Kings 18:16–46).
- Jehoshaphat pointed people to God in a time of crisis (2 Chron. 20).
- Jehoiada and Joash initiated reform (2 Chron. 23–24).
- Joel called a sacred assembly (Joel 1–2).
- Ezra dealt with the sin of intermarriage (Ezra 9–10).

QUESTIONS FOR REFLECTION AND DISCUSSION

1. What intrigued you most as you read the biblical accounts of revival?
2. What role did spiritual leaders play in these revivals? How might church leaders today be instrumental in revival?
3. What role did worship play in revival?
4. What role did Scripture play in revival?
5. Why do you think it was important for Nehemiah to rehearse the mighty acts of God during the "revival meeting"? How meaningful would it be

for your congregation to remember all the ways God has worked in your church in years past?

6. What were some examples that people genuinely had repented? What were the fruits of revival?

CHAPTER 7

Biblical Foundations for Revival

A Testimony of Returning to the Lord at His Table

Claude once received an urgent plea to help a congregation in distress. Their pastor was dismissed for sexual immorality, and several of the remaining leaders were indulging in carnality. Lay leaders were struggling for control of the church while they sought a new pastor. Meanwhile many members were leaving the church to escape the pain caused by wounding words and offensive behavior. Attendance dwindled, and the church languished under the suffocating cloud of sin. The church was dying.

Although Claude only had a few days free in which to help them, he agreed to lead them back to the Lord. Claude knew the people needed to deal radically with their sin. Experience had taught him that congregations often resent being confronted directly with their wickedness.

Claude decided to lead the people in a time of preparation for celebrating the Lord's Supper. Together Claude and the congregation embarked on a time of spiritual examination. On the first evening Claude taught the people about God's pattern for revival and spiritual awakening. He showed them the direct connection between a church getting right with God and God's using them to reach their community for Christ. He read from I Corinthians 11 concerning the importance of preparing to participate reverently in the Lord's Supper. The people were sobered by the thought that some of the church members in Corinth were weakened, others were sick, and some had died because they treated Christ and His table carelessly. The people only had three days that week to prepare for the Lord's Supper, but they were eager for Claude to help them.

Claude led them to look back at the cross and the love Jesus demonstrated for them by His suffering and death. People shared their personal stories of His compassion for them and their devotion to Him. Then they asked themselves a series of questions:

1. Am I in the faith? (2 Cor. 13:5)
2. Are there unconfessed sins in my life hindering my fellowship with God?
3. Do I have idols in my heart I must relinquish?
4. Are there items in my home that do not honor my faith in Christ?
5. Have I offended others in any way? Have I sought forgiveness and reconciliation with those I have wounded?
6. Am I bitter or unforgiving toward someone who has offended me?
7. Do I harbor pride in my spirit manifested by cynicism, haughtiness, boastfulness, or snobbery?

During those three days of preparation, the people began confessing and repenting. They took specific actions to deal with their sin. They consecrated themselves and their homes, cleansing both of anything quenching holiness in their lives. They sought reconciliation with one another. They prayed together to gain victory over sin. They stayed late into the night, and God worked deeply in their lives. Several experienced deliverance from bondage to their past. Many made significant commitments to the Lord. A new spirit became evident.

The night before the Lord's Supper, a woman said to Claude, "I've got something in my life I'm not ready to deal with yet. I'll not be here tomorrow." People were beginning to fear meeting the Lord in worship unprepared. Another woman approached him, weeping. She had become aware of many broken relationships in her life, and she felt she couldn't possibly get them all right before the next day. Claude encouraged her to come anyway because she needed the strength and spiritual nourishment she would receive at the Lord's Supper to achieve the reconciliation required of her.

The people celebrated the Lord's Supper the final day of Claude's time with them with a fresh sense of wholeness and purity. People experienced afresh the forgiveness provided by the cross. They had reached a new dimension of love for God.

After the service a young woman approached Claude with a question. It became clear she was not a Christian. She finally said, "I think this is what I've been looking for all my life." Claude told her how to enter a saving relationship with Jesus Christ. Claude explained she would have to die to self and embrace new life through Christ.

Claude later learned the young lady owned the New Age bookstore in town. She attended the meetings with her parents. After she sat and listened to believers confessing and repenting of their sins for hours, night after night, her response was, "This is what I've been looking for all my life!" She finally found a remedy for the guilt of her sin. She could be forgiven. She was set free.

Months later the church called a new pastor. Two months afterward, the day before Thanksgiving, the church was filled, and six people made professions of faith. By the spring of the next year, they launched a building program because they were outgrowing their space. Not only were they reaching their city, but they also developed a ministry to world athletes and tourists that was touching the world. As this body of believers obediently followed Christ's command to observe the Lord's Supper reverently, God brought revival to their midst. The same church that once languished in sin now flourished with new life.

Human beings are capricious and easily distracted. Worldly concerns constantly draw us away from fellowship with God. In Old Testament times God made provision for the renewal of His people. He set aside times of refreshing that were called holy convocations or sacred assemblies ("solemn assemblies" in KJV).

Solemn assemblies were days for God's people to gather for a sacred task. They were prescribed as times to:

- demonstrate obedience to God, His commands and decrees
- remember God's provisions for His people
- acknowledge God's ownership of all their resources
- offer sacrifices
- recognize God in His holiness
- confess and repent of personal and corporate sin
- renew fellowship and the covenant with God

Scheduled Times for Revival

Leviticus 23 and Numbers 28–29 identify seven prescribed days each year to be celebrated as sacred assemblies. These days were:

1. First day of the Feast of the Passover (fifteenth day of the first month)
2. Seventh day of the Feast of the Passover (twenty-first day of the first month)
3. Feast of Firstfruits (Pentecost—fifty days after Passover)

4. Feast of Trumpets (first day of the seventh month)

5. Day of Atonement (tenth day of the seventh month)

6. First day of the Feast of Tabernacles (fifteenth day of the seventh month)

7. Eighth day of the Feast of Tabernacles (twenty-second day of the seventh month)

Revivals often took place on these scheduled days because these times allowed God's people to set aside their individual concerns and corporately remember what God had done for them. By joining together, God's people enjoyed a special dynamic that facilitated spiritual renewal.

In addition to these seven annual events designed to help people maintain close fellowship with God, the Sabbath Day was also to function as a sacred assembly. The Sabbath was originally designed by God so His people could never go more than one week without resting from work and focusing on Him.

When these prescribed days accomplished their intended purpose, God's people stayed in a right relationship with Him. But when these special days became mere holidays, or when they regressed into ritual or religious tradition, they failed to draw people back into fellowship with God. In fact, God condemned the observance of these days when they were not used to enhance His people's relationship with Him (Isa. 1:10–15). The Israelites assumed God would be pleased with the crowds of people gathered for services and the mounds of offerings they collected. But here is God's response to religious ritual:

> "To what purpose is the multitude of your sacrifices to Me?" says the
> LORD. "I have enough of burnt offerings of rams and the fat of fed
> cattle. I do not delight in the blood of bulls, or of lambs or goats.
> When you come to appear before Me, who has required this from your
> hand to trample My courts? Bring no more futile sacrifices, incense is an
> abomination to Me. The New Moons, the sabbaths, and the calling of
> assemblies—I cannot endure iniquity and the sacred meeting. Your New
> Moons and your appointed feasts My soul hates; they are a trouble to Me,
> I am weary of bearing them. When you spread out your hands, I will hide
> My eyes from you; even though you make many prayers, I will not hear.
> Your hands are full of blood." (Isa. 1:11–15)

Now as in Old Testament days, we must understand that seasonal parties and the mindless carrying out of religious traditions actually elicits God's rebuke rather than His pleasure.

In the face of God's remedial judgments, the prophet Joel saw that the people must quickly repent. He issued a call to an emergency assembly for the people to hasten back to the Lord. In response God forgave His people, and He said, "'I will restore to you the years that the swarming locust has eaten'" (Joel 2:25). God revives His people when they repent, but it would be unnecessary if God's people would regularly renew their commitment to Him through scheduled times of worship and communion with the Lord.

New Testament Assemblies

The Old Testament term *sacred assembly* does not appear in the New Testament. Because most of the Jerusalem Christians were of Jewish ancestry, they continued to practice the Hebrew customs and laws even after they were born again. Up until the time of the Roman emperor Constantine, Jewish believers continued to celebrate the Jewish feasts but with a focus on the fulfillment they found in Christ. Two important New Testament events occurred in connection with prescribed Jewish sacred assemblies. Both were occasions of great importance to the early church.

Pentecost

After Jesus ascended to heaven, the Jerusalem Christians spent ten days praying and awaiting the coming of the Holy Spirit, just as Jesus instructed them to do. The Holy Spirit descended on the disciples in the upper room on the Day of Pentecost, which was one of three major Jewish holidays. The Day of Pentecost was also known as the Feast of Weeks. *Pentecost* comes from the Greek word meaning "fifty." This holiday came fifty days after Passover and was to coincide with the reaping of the grain harvest. It celebrated God's goodness in providing for His people. While the early Christians met to thank the Lord for His gracious provision for them, the Holy Spirit brought God's presence directly to their lives. Now they were empowered to do anything God commanded them to do. Peter's life provides a striking illustration of the difference the Holy Spirit made: a few weeks earlier he lacked the courage to confess Christ to a servant girl; now he preached boldly and three thousand converts came to Christ (Acts 2).

Peter's Deliverance

When King Herod began to persecute the church, he had James executed. This so pleased the Jews that he arrested Peter with the intention of killing him too. Since it was the Feast of Unleavened Bread (Passover week), Herod put Peter in prison to try him the day after the Passover celebrations ended. It was deemed improper to execute people during that time! The last day of Passover was a scheduled day of sacred assembly. That evening the Christians met in a house to pray for Peter. God dramatically intervened and delivered Peter from prison. Shortly thereafter the Lord struck King Herod down, and he died, but Peter lived to provide strong leadership for the early church (Acts 12).

Applications for Today

These biblical examples point us to several issues today's churches should address.

Regular Times of Renewal in the Church

Christians must recognize that they, too, are prone to neglect their love relationship with God. It is important for churches to provide regular opportunities for the congregation to gather as a body and focus their attention on the Lord. Special times set aside for prolonged prayer, baptismal services, and services devoted to the Lord's Supper are ways to do this. Many congregations regularly set aside times for meeting to worship, pray, and share testimonies.

Personal Times with the Lord

The best way to maintain an intimate personal walk with God is to meet with Him regularly. The psalmist declared: "With my whole heart I have sought You; oh, let me not wander from Your commandments! Your word I have hidden in my heart that I might not sin against You" (Ps. 119:10–11). Daily seeking God in His Word keeps us close to Him. When we forsake our meetings with God, our heart is already beginning to shift away from Him. God declared: "I spoke to you, rising up early and speaking, but you did not hear, and I called you, but you did not answer" (Jer. 7:13).

The Lord's Day

The Christian observance of the Sabbath provides a regular time for returning to God in fellowship. The Lord's day ought to be kept holy and used as a time to do good (Matt. 12:12). Without falling into legalism like the Pharisees, we need to consecrate the day to the Lord. We are to focus especially on God, His Word, and fellowship with His people. We are to avoid self-indulgent pleasure seeking and when possible, regular work on the Lord's day. God knows we need rest from our work, just as He set the example in creation (Gen. 2:1–3). The Lord's day suspends our usual busy schedule and provides a time to reflect, to confess our sin, and to seek God's forgiveness and cleansing. The Sabbath is meant to be a positive day of celebration and renewal. It should be a time for ministry to the needy as it was for Jesus. It should be dedicated wholly to the Lord.

Sacrifice and Offering

Because of the affluence and comfort many people enjoy today, we have forgotten the Lord (see the warning in Deut. 6:10–12). The tithe and the presentation of sacrifices and offerings were instituted by God to remind His people of His sovereignty. Because of greed and disobedience, many Christians are robbing God by withholding what He asks them to give. For this reason many are unknowingly living as idolaters under the curse and wrath of God (Mal. 3:6–12; Eph. 5:5–6). Through regular times of offering, we can guard ourselves against the encroachment of greed and materialism.

Gathering the People

In sacred assemblies all the people gathered to meet with God. Churches are often satisfied to conduct meetings that only a small percentage of the church members attend. For God to do a church-wide work of cleansing and renewal, everyone must be urged to participate in the sacred gathering. God is looking for corporate repentance. Some sins need to be renounced by the whole body. Churches need to ask the Lord to show them ways to summon people for collective prayer, worship, and repentance. The need for spiritual awakening like the one in Joel 1–2 would be lessened if congregations would take opportunities to stand before God in reverence and humility.

Lessons from Biblical Revivals

We see the call for repentance in the New Testament. The Old Testament, however, is the foundation of our understanding of how God relates to His people. Several factors were common to corporate revival experiences recorded in the Old Testament.

Revivals Began with Leaders

Often it was the king or a prophet who led the people back to God. Other leaders were drawn in as revival spread. Revival generally called for multiple leaders to help people know what to do. The king would call on the prophet. Nehemiah, the governor, summoned leaders of all the families together to seek their counsel. Together spiritual leaders could gain from one another wisdom and sensitivity to the Lord.

Revival Often Came after God's People Experienced Severe Discipline or after They Were Warned of Coming Judgment

In most cases the discipline had already come, and the people were crying out to God for help in the middle of their distress. Sometimes recognition of serious sin caused the people to fear God's judgment so they returned to the Lord before it came. In Nineveh, Jonah preached a one-sentence message announcing God's coming judgment, and the king and all the people felt compelled to repent in sackcloth and ashes (Jon. 3:4–10).

Revivals Occurred at Times Scheduled for Revival or for Covenant Renewal

While no one can dictate to God when He will come in power, God has often chosen to use times of public gathering to visit His people and renew them. Some examples include the Feast of Trumpets, Feast of Tabernacles, and Passover. Revival is not always spontaneous. According to Scripture, when God's people sincerely seek Him, He will be found (Jer. 29:13).

All of God's People Were Expected to Attend the Scheduled Meetings

Revival was serious business for God's people. No excuses were acceptable. The life of the nation depended on their response. The leaders knew that the sin of one person could bring God's judgment on the nation. Leaders called all the people to return to the Lord. On one occasion they threatened to remove a person from the genealogies of Israel if he did not report at the appointed time. On another occasion God's coming judgment was so close the leaders threatened to kill anyone who did not join in returning to the Lord. We, of course, would not recommend that approach. But it does point out that the leaders of Israel knew well that God dealt with them corporately as well as individually. This might also speak to the habit of many churches to segregate their gatherings by age group. At times churches will hold separate revival meetings for the youth and children or senior adults. There are sacred times in the church when the entire church body needs to stand before the Lord together to repent and commit themselves afresh to be God's holy people.

Leaders Gave Clear Guidance to the People about Revival

As part of these worship experiences, the leaders helped the people:

- remember what God did for them in the past
- express worship and praise with rejoicing
- offer offerings and sacrifices
- renew and affirm their covenant with God as His holy people

Revivals Began with Worship

After the people repented of their sin, the joy they experienced as they worshipped and praised God was profound. Joy is the fruit of revival. This is the experience of revival for which we often pray. We yearn for the excitement and joy in the Lord revival produces. However, the only pathway to joy leads directly through periods of repentance and brokenness before the Lord. The refining process must always come first; then comes joy.

Scriptures Were a Vital Part of the Revival Experience

In times of revival, spiritual leaders preached and taught God's Word fearlessly and without compromise. Through God's Word the people came to know God's requirements. They also understood the consequences if they did not return to the Lord. It's important to remember that, while the Scriptures must have a central place, they ultimately point us back to the God of the Scriptures.

Leaders and the People Confessed and Repented of their Sins and the Sins of their Fathers before Them

Confessing the sins of their fathers was an important step in the revival process because God was dealing with the nation as a whole. Although their ancestors were no longer living, the consequences of their sins were still felt generations later. When a group of people sins, that sin can have repercussions for years to come. Likewise, even if we did not belong to the church when the sin took place, we must still bear some of the weight if we do not help the congregation repent and return whole-heartedly to God. The most important factor is to acknowledge the seriousness of the sin. After confession we must determine not to walk the sinful path of our predecessors.

People Demonstrated Repentance

They removed idols, cleansed places of worship, and changed their ways. They took action to display the fruits of repentance. True repentance always results in changed living.

People Obeyed God Wholeheartedly with Joy

They did not have to be forced to change their ways. God communicated to the people the gravity of their condition. Once they recognized their waywardness, the people eagerly joined the process of returning to the Lord. Overcoming sin is humanly impossible, but with God all things are possible. God motivated their hearts to repent. The psalmist declared: "I waited patiently for the LORD; and He inclined to me, and heard my cry. He also brought me up out of a horrible pit, out of the miry clay, and set my feet on a rock, and established my steps. He has put a new song in my mouth—praise to our God; many will see it and fear, and will trust in the LORD" (Ps. 40:1–3).

God Responded by Cleansing, Forgiving, Restoring, and Blessing His Repentant People

God does the sovereign work of revival that no human can do. Only God can forgive, cleanse, and restore. People are generally unaware of how much power their sin has over them. But when they repent and God releases them from sin's bondage, the freedom and joy people experience is beyond what they could have imagined.

T. W. Hunt, prayer leader and author of *The Mind of Christ*, has made these observations about biblical revivals:

- Most were preceded by great wickedness.
- Most were led by multiple leaders.
- They spread from the high officials downward.
- Previously established divine criteria were restored.
- They were characterized by a great love for God's Word.
- Worship, especially as expressed in the great Jewish festivals, had a primary place. It was worship from the heart.
- The temple and the people were purified.

Hunt adds, "The scriptural evidence indicates that if established leaders will not assume their God-given responsibility in revival, then God will produce new leaders in a major social upheaval."[1]

Conclusion

Scripture provides clear guidance on how God revives His people. His standards and ways have not changed. It behooves us to make certain we are responding to Him as He works in our midst. It is imperative that we view sin the way God sees it. And it is critical that we familiarize ourselves with the ways God revives His people, for those are the same ways He will seek to revive us and our church as well.

QUESTIONS FOR REFLECTION AND DISCUSSION

1. Why does God plan for regular times for His people to return to Him?
2. What are some opportune times in the Christian calendar for renewing fellowship with God?
3. What are some ways the Lord's day is no longer honored and kept holy? What are some changes we can make to set the Lord's day apart as holy and make its observance meaningful?
4. Why would involving numerous leaders in times of revival be valuable?
5. Why is it important that churches try to gather all God's people for times of revival?

CHAPTER 8

God's Pattern for Revival: Created for a Love Relationship

od is, by nature, multidimensional while at the same time His nature remains constant (Mal. 3:6). He is mysterious, yet He has promised that those who seek Him will find Him (Jer. 29:12–13). Therefore, while it is impossible to predict exactly what He will do, in light of His absolute sovereignty, patterns and principles seen in the Scriptures and throughout history can help us understand the ways God relates to people. Throughout this book we have isolated particular aspects of revival. In this chapter we will present an overview of the seven stages that occur in revival.

A Cycle of Sin and Revival in the Book of Judges

One of the best places to view clearly the pattern of revival is in the book of Judges. As you read through this biblical account, you will observe the repetitive cycle God's people experienced in their walk with Him. The following is a summary of the pattern seen in Judges.

People Followed God

"The people served the LORD all the days of Joshua, and all the days of the elders who outlived Joshua, who had seen all the great works of the LORD which He had done for Israel" (Judg. 2:7). God did not deliver the Israelites from bondage so they could go to the promised land. Rather, God rescued them so they would be free to enjoy a special relationship with Him (Exod. 19:4). Joshua's generation experienced God's incredible power exercised on their behalf. Joshua was a strong spiritual leader who never wavered in his trust in God. The people he led also chose to trust and follow Joshua's God, and as a result they experienced victory wherever they went.

People Forsook the Lord

"Then the children of Israel did evil in the sight of the LORD, and served the Baals" (Judg. 2:11). We cannot live on yesterday's walk with God, whether that be our parents' faith or our own previous relationship with Him. Every day we must choose afresh to walk with God intimately and obediently. Even though the people heard their parents speak of God's glorious provision and protection, they did not follow their parents' God but turned their attention elsewhere. Choosing to love anything or anyone more than God is to forsake Him.

God Defeated the People through their Enemies

"The anger of the LORD was hot against Israel. So He delivered them into the hands of plunderers who despoiled them; and He sold them into the hands of their enemies all around, so that they could no longer stand before their enemies" (Judg. 2:14). God loves us. He knows our relationship with Him brings life, and our rejection of Him causes death. He will therefore bring whatever is necessary to bear on our lives so we return to Him when we have strayed. He will not allow us to remain comfortable in our sin and rebellion. He will remove His hedge of protection from us and allow us to experience the pain and fear that comes with alienation from our Creator.

People Cried Out for Help

"They were greatly distressed. . . . [and] the LORD was moved to pity by their groaning" (Judg. 2:15, 18). While prosperity will not generally motivate God's people to cry out to Him, tribulation more often brings us to our knees. Revival begins when people recognize their sin and their hearts return to God. Only when we realize our desperate need for God are we in a position to enjoy fully God's presence in our lives.

God Had Compassion and Delivered Them

"The LORD raised up judges who delivered them out of the hand of those who plundered them. . . . For the LORD was moved to pity" (Judg. 2:16, 18). God is an expert at setting people free. When we cry out to Him, His heart is invariably moved with compassion. Regardless of how many times we reject Him and break our promises to Him, His infinite love compels Him to reach out to us and save us.

The above pattern of apostasy, despair, deliverance, and return was repeated throughout the book of Judges. The next chapter in Judges shows the cycle repeating again:

> So the children of Israel did evil in the sight of the LORD. They forgot the LORD their God . . . Therefore the anger of the LORD was hot against Israel, and He sold them into the hand of Cushan-rishathaim king of Mesopotamia; and the children of Israel served Cushan-rishathaim eight years. When the children of Israel cried out to the LORD, the LORD raised up a deliverer for the children of Israel, who delivered them: Othniel . . . The Spirit of the LORD came upon him, and he judged Israel. He went out to war, and the LORD delivered Cushan-rishathaim king of Mesopotamia into his hand; and his hand prevailed over Cushan-rishathaim. So the land had rest for forty years. (Judg. 3:7–11)

Continuing Apostasy

Unfortunately, the pattern of turning away from God and needing to return to Him was not limited to the book of Judges or to the Old Testament. Notice how God called His people back to Him during the days of the early church recorded in the book of Revelation:

- To the church at Ephesus: "I have this against you, that you have left your first love. . . . repent and do the first works, or else I will come to you quickly and remove your lampstand from its place—unless you repent" (Rev. 2:4–5).
- To the church at Pergamos: "I have a few things against you, because you have there those who hold the doctrine of Balaam, who taught Balak to put a stumbling block before the children of Israel, to eat things sacrificed to idols, and to commit sexual immorality. Thus you also have those who hold the doctrine of the Nicolaitans, which thing I hate. Repent, or else I will come to you quickly and will fight against them with the sword of My mouth" (Rev. 2:14–16).
- To the church at Sardis: "I know your works, that you have a name that you are alive, but you are dead. . . . Remember therefore how you have received and heard; hold fast and repent. Therefore if you will not watch,

I will come upon you as a thief, and you will not know what hour I will come upon you" (Rev. 3:I, 3).

- To the church at Laodicea: "I know your works, that you are neither cold nor hot. I could wish you were cold or hot. So then, because you are lukewarm, and neither cold nor hot, I will vomit you out of My mouth. . . . As many as I love, I rebuke and chasten. Therefore be zealous and repent" (Rev. 3:I5–I6, I9).

This same cycle of departure and return to the Lord can also be traced throughout church history. We have designed a diagram that shows the phases of revival. This cycle can be repeated in an individual's life as well as churches, denominations, and nations.

Phases of Revival

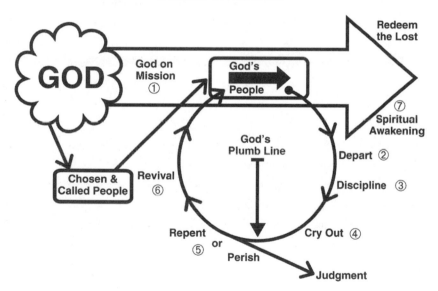

Seven phases of revival can be seen in this diagram:

PHASE I: *God is on mission to redeem a lost world.* He calls people into a love relationship with Him, and He accomplishes His work through them. God is constantly working to bring people around the world into a saving relationship with Himself. As soon as we enter into a personal relationship with God, He will begin to involve us in His redemptive activity. Out of our walk with God, we have the desire and the empowering to serve God.

PHASE 2: *God's people tend to depart from Him, turning to substitutes for His presence, His purposes, and His ways.* The most destructive condition plaguing God's people is the chronic tendency to depart from God. Despite all the heavenly resources and blessings our Lord makes available to us, we inexplicably choose to wander from His watch care.

PHASE 3: *God disciplines His people because of His love.* As His people invariably rebel against Him, God could remain serenely indifferent to the inevitable plight of His creatures. He could mock at our frail attempts to live independent of Him, knowing the eternal consequences we face. But God in His infinite love cannot remain indifferent; His love compels Him to work actively in our lives to make the result of sin patently unappealing in order to lead us back to Himself.

PHASE 4: *God's people cry out to Him for help.* God's discipline becomes increasingly intense until His people cry out to Him. He is patient and long-suffering. Like the father of the prodigal son (Luke 15:11–32), God waits eagerly for His children to return to Him. God will gently seek to restore His people, but if they will not respond, He will increase the intensity of His disciples until they can no longer ignore Him or what He is saying.

PHASE 5: *God calls His people to repent and return to Him or perish.* God has clearly identified the parameters and attitudes of repentance. He doesn't give options. Returning to Him is nonnegotiable. Partial or halfhearted repentance is a contradiction in terms and completely unacceptable. Refusing to repent invites dire consequences. Godly repentance leads to forgiveness and restored life.

PHASE 6: *God revives His repentant people by restoring them to a right relationship with Him.* Repentance brings forgiveness, freedom, and purity. The ultimate result of repentance is renewed fellowship with God. Out of this revitalized relationship flows joy and abundant life (Ps. 51:12).

PHASE 7: *God exalts His Son Jesus among His people and draws unbelievers to saving faith in Him.* When God's people are rightly related to Him, He displays His glory through their lives to a watching world. When people experience God's mighty power working through the church, others will notice and desire a similar experience themselves. Spiritual awakening becomes a natural by-product of a revived people.

God's Purpose for Revival

Although by now it should be self-evident, let's pause and recall why God takes revival so seriously. Revival has many critics within the church who see the focus on renewal as distracting and unnecessary. There are two primary reasons revival is critical. The first is because God takes delight in our love, and He receives glory from our worship and obedience to Him. The second reason is because God chooses to accomplish His redemptive purposes on earth through consecrated people. When God's people depart from their love relationship with Him, they are no longer of use to Him. For both these reasons God will not allow His people simply to walk away from Him. He will pursue them and do whatever is necessary to bring them back into a loving, obedient relationship with Himself.

God Pursues a Love Relationship

The greatest mystery of human history is why God loves His rebellious creation. Why does God continue to reach out to an indifferent, arrogant, foolish people? Why would He pay the ultimate price to obtain redemption for people who were oblivious to what He was doing? Why would the God of heaven care whether His people chose to have fellowship with Him or not (Jer. 7:13)? But God does care. Historically, often when people were enlightened to the great love God has for them, their hearts were melted in shame and remorse for the calloused way they previously responded to His compassion. David Brainerd, the early missionary to the American Indians, testified that his preaching on God's love reduced his listeners to tears rather than his preaching on God's judgment. Grasping, even partially, the incredible love God has for us ought to drive us to our knees in awe and profound gratitude, and it likewise should cause us to grieve every time we fail to properly respond to that love.

God Calls People to Work with Him

The second major reason revival is so important is because it makes God's people serviceable to Him. Throughout human history God has been seeking to bring people into a close relationship with Him so they would be sanctified, useful instruments in His hand.

When God approached Abraham, it was not merely to have fellowship with Him. God also intended to use Abraham's life to bless many others. Genesis 12 tells us God invited Abraham to become involved with Him in His eternal purposes:

> Now the LORD had said to Abram: "Get out of your country, from your family and from your father's house, to a land that I will show you. I will make you a great nation; I will bless you and make your name great; and you shall be a blessing. I will bless those who bless you, and I will curse

him who curses you; and in you all the families of the earth shall be blessed." (Gen. 12:1–3)

The LORD appeared to Abram and said to him, "I am Almighty God; walk before Me and be blameless. . . . And I will establish My covenant between Me and you and your descendants after you in their generations, for an everlasting covenant, to be God to you and your descendants after you." (Gen. 17:1, 7)

"Abraham shall surely become a great and mighty nation, and all the nations of the earth shall be blessed in him. For I have known him, in order that he may command his children and his household after him, that they keep the way of the LORD, to do righteousness and justice." (Gen. 18:18–19)

The focus of these Scriptures is not on Abraham but on God and His activity through Abraham's life. In calling Abraham, God was setting in motion His plan to redeem an entire world. God told Abraham to follow Him, to be blameless, and to teach his children to follow God. God kept his promises to Abraham and built his descendants into a nation and ultimately brought salvation to all humankind through one of Abraham's descendents.

Throughout history God has called people to Himself so He had a holy people through whom to work. When God delivered the Israelites, it was not so they could become wealthy and comfortable in the promised land. Notice the call God gave His people:

Moses went up to God, and the LORD called to him from the mountain, saying, "Thus you shall say to . . . the children of Israel: 'You have seen what I did to the Egyptians, and how I bore you on eagles' wings and brought you to Myself. Now therefore, if you will indeed obey My voice and keep My covenant, then you shall be a special treasure to Me above all people. . . . And you shall be to Me a kingdom of priests and a holy nation.'" (Exod. 19:3–6)

We usually say God brought Israel to the promised land, but God said, "I . . . brought you to Myself" (v. 4). God did not primarily lead them to a *place* but to a *relationship.* That is what set them apart. Out of their relationship with God, the Israelites would be God's special treasure, a kingdom of priests, and a holy nation. God chose Israel for a unique purpose.

"You are a holy people to the LORD your God; the LORD your God has chosen you to be a people for Himself, a special treasure above all the peoples on the face of the earth. The LORD did not set His love on you nor choose you because you were more in number than any other people, for you were the least of all peoples; but because the LORD loves you, and because He would keep the oath which He swore to your fathers, the LORD has brought you out with a mighty hand, and redeemed you from the house of bondage. . . . Therefore know that the LORD your God, He is God, the faithful God who keeps covenant and mercy for a thousand generations with those who love Him and keep His commandments." (Deut. 7:6–9)

God treasures those who are His. You are also to be a holy people set aside for His purposes. Out of your close walk with God, many others can be blessed.

Although God called His people to be a royal priesthood, by the time Jesus came to earth, God's people were no longer walking closely with Him. Many people still attended worship services and performed religious rituals, but they did not walk in fellowship with Him. The religious leaders were so disoriented to God they did not recognize His Son when He stood before them (Luke 19:41–44). In fact, they killed Him.

In Christ, God established a new covenant with a new Israel—the church. This new relationship was based on faith, not on keeping the law. God said through Peter, "You are a chosen generation, a royal priesthood, a holy nation, His own special people, that you may proclaim the praises of Him who called you out of darkness into His marvelous light" (1 Pet. 2:9).

Christians, like the Old Testament nation of Israel, are called out by God for His pleasure and His purposes. God's intent for them is to shine the light of Christ in a spiritually darkened world. His desire for the church is to continue what He began with the people of Israel. God wants to redeem a lost world.

A Chosen Generation

As God's people we are chosen to be trophies of God's amazing grace. We are set apart not because we deserve it but because we belong to Him. We are not our own. What a privilege to belong to the family of Almighty God (Rom. 8:16–17). As our Father, God deserves and expects our obedience for His purposes to redeem our generation.

A Royal Priesthood

God did not establish a kingdom *with* a priesthood, a group of people represented by a few priests who know how to relate to Him. Rather, He said, "You are . . . a royal priesthood." *Every* believer is a priest with access to God. "Royal" implies that each person has a direct relationship with the King of kings and belongs in the royal family. The role of the priest was traditionally to bring a word from God to people. The priest also represented the people before God. Christians have the assignment and privilege to act as God's ambassadors. Each priest is to serve in a priesthood; no one is called to serve alone.

A Holy Nation

The word *holy* means "set apart for God's exclusive use." Christians are to be separated from the values and ways of the world. We should have a radically different outlook on life than the world does. We are to reflect God, His nature, and His ways. We are commanded to be holy as God is holy and to "abstain from fleshly lusts . . . having your conduct honorable among the Gentiles, that . . . they may, by your good works which they observe, glorify God in the day of visitation" (I Pet. 2:11–12).

God is at work through His people to accomplish His redemptive work in the world. His goal is to draw an unbelieving world to faith in Christ so those who accept Christ's salvation surrender to His lordship, and they exalt Him as they serve Him. Paul described this relationship with God:

> All things are of God, who has reconciled us to Himself through Jesus Christ, and has given us the ministry of reconciliation, that is, that God was in Christ reconciling the world to Himself . . . and has committed to us the word of reconciliation. Now then, we are ambassadors for Christ, as though God were pleading through us: we implore you on Christ's behalf, be reconciled to God. (2 Cor. 5:18–20)

Reconciled means "restored to a right relationship." God is the One drawing the world to Himself through Christ and He is doing it through the church, His body. According to Paul, we are Christ's ambassadors and God's fellow workers (2 Cor. 6:1). Our motivation for this work is the love of Christ; His love compels us to deliver His message of redemption.

The task is His. The mission of drawing others to faith in Christ is one we cannot accomplish on our own (John 15:5). God accomplishes the work through us. As God uses us, our lives will become His instruments to build the kingdom of God

(John 15:8, 16). With God working through His church, Christians will accomplish greater things than Jesus did in His earthly ministry. He said, "'He who believes in Me, the works that I do he will do also; and greater works than these he will do, because I go to My Father'" (John 14:12).

The problem is self-evident. The church is not impacting its world the way God intended. Just as the Israelites forgot their calling and became enmeshed in worldly values and pursuits, so Christians today are not reaching society for Christ as God wants. Churches continue holding services, building larger buildings, and launching new programing, but the world becomes increasingly dark and hostile to God. This is a day that desperately cries out for revival.

Conclusion

God is on mission to redeem a lost world. He could use any method at His disposal, but He chooses to work through a holy people consecrated to Him and for His purposes. When God's people sin and turn away from their covenant relationship with Christ, they are no longer in a place to serve God and to bring Him glory. God will discipline His people and draw them back to Himself. Once God's people repent and return to Him, God forgives and cleanses them and will use them once again to accomplish His purposes. God takes our relationship with Him extremely seriously because out of that relationship our life has meaning and purpose as we relate to Him and serve Him.

QUESTIONS FOR REFLECTION AND DISCUSSION

1. Where do you sense your nation is in this cycle of sin and revival? Why?
2. Judges 2:14 says, "The anger of the LORD was hot against Israel. So He delivered them into the hands of plunderers who despoiled them; and He sold them into the hands of their enemies all around, so that they could no longer stand before their enemies." Who are some of the "plunderers" or raiders God may be using in our day to discipline His people?
3. In which of the seven phases of God's pattern for revival and spiritual awakening is your church? Why?
4. When have you been part of a time of repentance in your church? What was it like?
5. In what phase of revival are you personally? What do you think is the next step God wants you to take? When and how do you intend to respond?

CHAPTER 9

God Disciplines His People

I Saw the Lord

In her book *I Saw the Lord*, Ann Graham Lotz tells of her interview with Jane Clayson of *The Early Show* on CBS immediately after the horrific events of 9/11. On national television Clayson commented: "I've heard people say—those who are religious, those who are not—'If God is good, how could God let this happen?' To that, you say . . ." Lotz: "God is so angry when He sees something like this. And I would say also that for several years now, Americans, in a sense, have shaken their fists at God and said, 'God, we want You out of the schools, we want You out of our government, we want You out of our business, we want You out of our marketplace.' And God, who is a gentlemen, has quietly backed out of our national and political life, removing His hand of blessing and protection."[1]

In today's world God is often ignored, openly disobeyed, and even mocked. People brazenly defy God's commands. Yet when tragedies occur, the question is always, "How could a loving God allow such suffering?" Our generation is witnessing a growing number of stunning catastrophes inflicting enormous damage well beyond the resources of even the most powerful nations to handle. In an age of such pervasive danger and massive destruction, people desperately need to know what God is saying and why He is allowing this level of suffering.

The aspect of revival people seem to struggle with most is the truth that God disciplines and ultimately will judge people. In our politically correct age, parents are castigated for disciplining their children. Postmodern culture does not equate love with pain or discomfort. To suggest God disciplines people today is to immediately invite a maelstrom of scorn from people both in and outside the church.

The following is a biblical overview of God's use of correction when His people sin. God would have to deny His nature and refute His values *not* to deal with our sin.

God's Nature

Modern Christians have lost the fear of God. People no longer believe God rebukes His people. Many think the God of judgment and wrath is found only in the ancient pages of the Old Testament. They believe the God of the New Testament is characterized by love and grace. Such thinking reveals a skewed and limited knowledge of what Scripture reveals about God.

God said, "'For I am the LORD, I do not change'" (Mal. 3:6). "Jesus Christ is the same yesterday, today, and forever" (Heb. 13:8). The God we discover in the New Testament is the same God revealed in the pages of the Old Testament. The Lord is One. He doesn't change.

God is beyond our understanding. Yet He has revealed His character to us in Scripture. The fundamental essence of His nature is perfect love. He does nothing apart from pure, unfailing love. He forever proved His loving-kindness through Jesus' death on a cross. He is kind, compassionate, patient, and slow to anger. Likewise God is absolutely holy, pure, and just. God perfectly balances infinite love with absolute righteousness. His judgments are as equally righteous as they are merciful and gracious. He seldom gives us the punishment we deserve. He freely forgives us when we repent and return to Him.

Notice what Scripture indicates about God's nature in response to humanity's sin:

"I know that You are a gracious and merciful God, slow to anger and abundant in lovingkindness, One who relents from doing harm." (Jon. 4:2)

Beloved, let us love one another, for love is of God; and everyone who loves is born of God and knows God. He who does not love does not know God, for God is love. (I John 4:7–8)

"Nevertheless in Your great mercy You did not utterly consume them nor forsake them; for You are God, gracious and merciful." (Neh. 9:31)

"I am the LORD, exercising lovingkindness, judgment, and righteousness in the earth. For in these I delight," says the LORD. (Jer. 9:24)

Against You, You only, have I sinned, and done this evil in Your sight—that You may be found just when You speak, and blameless when You judge. (Ps. 51:4)

In accordance with your hardness and your impenitent heart you are treasuring up for yourself wrath in the day of wrath and revelation of the righteous judgment of God. (Rom. 2:5)

He, being full of compassion, forgave their iniquity, and did not destroy them. Yes, many a time He turned His anger away, and did not stir up all His wrath. (Ps. 78:38)

To the Lord our God belong mercy and forgiveness, though we have rebelled against Him. (Dan. 9:9)

The word of the Lord is right, and all His work is done in truth. He loves righteousness and justice; the earth is full of the goodness of the Lord. (Ps. 33:4–5)

The Lord shall endure forever; He has prepared His throne for judgment. He shall judge the world in righteousness, and He shall administer judgment for the peoples in uprightness. (Ps. 9:7–8)

The Lord of hosts shall be exalted in judgment, and God who is holy shall be hallowed in righteousness. (Isa. 5:16)

The Lord will wait, that He may be gracious to you; and therefore He will be exalted, that He may have mercy on you. For the Lord is a God of justice; blessed are all those who wait for Him. (Isa. 30:18)

The Bible, from Genesis to Revelation, clearly teaches that God disciplines His people, yet many Christians today struggle with the concept of God's wrath. They miss the truth that we ought to fear God. He would not be perfectly loving if He did not likewise detest those things that rob us of life. God knows every ounce of suffering anyone has ever endured because of sin. Consequently, He will not tolerate sin in our lives. The apostle Paul could certainly be confident in his relationship with God. Paul started numerous churches and led many people to faith in Christ. He endured beatings and suffered imprisonment for his faith. Yet when Paul, the once boastful zealot, anticipated the day he would stand before his Lord seated upon His throne, this apostle humbly declared, "For we must all appear before the judgment seat of

Christ, that each one may receive the things done in the body, according to what he has done, whether good or bad. Knowing therefore the terror of the Lord . . ." (2 Cor. 5:10–11). Terror? Why would Paul be afraid to stand before Christ? Surely Paul had one of the greatest heavenly rewards awaiting him of any of the saints. To know Christ had been Paul's life goal (Phil. 3:10), so Paul realized that despite his credentials, his sacrifices, and his successes he was only a creature who would one day stand before his Creator and Judge. Paul did not fear for his eternal salvation. He was not worried about a harsh reprimand. He trembled at the thought of standing before Someone wholly beyond his imagination and understanding. Someone who ruled the universe and whose word brought life into being. Paul *knew* Christ, and that is why, although he loved Him with all his heart, he also quaked at the thought of seeing Him face-to-face.

Like Paul, we must have a holy reverence for God. When we enter His presence on judgment day, we will experience a profound sense of His holiness. We will also see clearly the sin in our lives. The following Scriptures indicate what pleases or displeases God:

> "'Do I have any pleasure at all that the wicked should die?' says the Lord God, 'and not that he should turn from his ways and live? . . . For I have no pleasure in the death of one who dies,' says the Lord God. 'Therefore turn and live!'" (Ezek. 18:23, 32)

> The Lord is not slack concerning His promise, as some count slackness, but is longsuffering toward us, not willing that any should perish but that all should come to repentance. (2 Pet. 3:9)

God does not delight in anyone's destruction. He knows the horrific reality of what it means to "perish" (John 3:16). He wants all people to choose life and turn to Him for salvation.

God's Discipline, Judgment, and Final Judgment

God deals with sin and sinners in three important ways. The first is His *discipline*. Discipline is for God's children. Notice what God said through the prophet Amos: "You only have I known of all the families of the earth; therefore I will punish you for your iniquities" (Amos 3:2). Once people become Christians, they are transformed into new creatures and are made children of God (2 Cor. 5:17; Rom. 8:16–17).

They cannot lose their salvation. However they can drift away from God and become immersed in sin. When this happens, God brings circumstances to bear on His wayward children to make their sinful lives intolerable and to awaken in them a sense of dependency on God. Discipline is God's means of turning His rebellious children away from their sin and back to fellowship with Him.

God primarily uses *judgment* for the purpose of punishment rather than reform. God applies this when His patience with rebellion has come to an end and He chooses to vindicate His holy name. God also uses judgment to provide a warning to others of the grave consequences of unrepented sin. This form of judgment can also be described as "remedial" or "temporal" judgment. It is focused on our present life on earth. It brings severe retribution to those who blatantly mock and disregard God's standards, and it causes others to take warning of what happens when people flaunt their sin before a holy God.

God may inflict judgment on believers as well as unbelievers. For example, the wickedness of the cities of Sodom and Gomorrah was so detestable to God that He brought judgment on the cities and destroyed them (Gen. 19:1–29). The unbelievers of these cities had become so utterly depraved that God severely judged them. Judgment can be withheld if people repent, such as occurred with the city of Nineveh in Jonah's day. However, if people do not turn from their sin, God's judgment is severe.

God also applies judgment to believers when they turn away from Him and refuse to repent or when God wants to make an example to deter others from committing the same offense. Such was the case with Achan (Josh. 7) as well as Ananias and Sapphira (Acts 5:1–11).

Ananias and his wife Sapphira were members of the church in Jerusalem who sold a possession. They brought only a portion of the proceeds to contribute to the church. This couple led their fellow church members to believe they were giving everything to the Lord. They may have been expecting praise and public recognition. However, Peter said:

> "Ananias, why has Satan filled your heart to lie to the Holy Spirit and keep back part of the price of the land for yourself? While it remained, was it not your own? And after it was sold, was it not in your own control? Why have you conceived this thing in your heart? You have not lied to men but to God."
>
> Then Ananias, hearing these words, fell down and breathed his last. So great fear came upon all those who heard these things. . . .

About three hours later . . . his wife came in, not knowing what had happened. And Peter answered her, "Tell me whether you sold the land for so much?"

She said, "Yes, for so much."

Then Peter said to her, "How is it that you have agreed together to test the Spirit of the Lord? Look, the feet of those who have buried your husband are at the door, and they will carry you out." Then immediately she fell down at his feet and breathed her last. . . . So great fear came upon all the church and upon all who heard these things. (Acts 5:3–5, 11)

The Jerusalem church was young and learning what it meant to walk with the Holy Spirit. A wicked influence of deceit could corrupt the entire congregation and its mission to take the gospel throughout the world. God's people had to learn that they could not treat the Holy Spirit lightly (Matt. 12:31). Because their sin could have such a broad and lasting influence, God immediately executed judgment on the sinful couple. The result of God's judgment was "great fear came upon all the church and upon all who heard these things" (Acts 5:11). What was the result on unbelievers after God dealt severely with two church members? Scripture indicates: "And believers were increasingly added to the Lord, multitudes of both men and women" (Acts 5:14). When God's people gained a healthy reverence for the Holy Spirit, they experienced His power working mightily through them, and many people came to faith in Christ as a result.

God's judgment upon Christians is temporal in that it is confined to their lives on earth and does not follow them into eternity. When God judges those who are Christians, they do not lose their salvation, but they can forfeit their possessions, reputation, health, and even their lives.

Final judgment is reserved for unbelievers at the close of history. The word *final* indicates there are no appeals and no further opportunities to amend one's ways. While every person must give an account to Christ for his or her actions on earth (2 Cor. 5:10), those who refuse to accept Christ's offer of salvation will be sentenced to irrevocable, eternal punishment (Matt. 25:31–46; Rev. 20:11–15). Those people whose names are written in the book of life will be admitted into heavenly bliss while those who rejected God will be forever separated from Him (Rev. 20:12). Such final judgment is limited to unbelievers, and it comes at the close of time. In the remainder of this chapter, we will be looking at God's discipline and His judgment upon His people as He seeks to draw them to return to Him.

Truths Concerning God's Discipline

God's discipline is for Christians. It provides unmistakable evidence that God loves them. God is not an indifferent parent who is oblivious to the squalor and filth in which His children are living. God does not look the other way while those He loves race toward harm and destruction. God is an active, participative, caring Father.

God vehemently opposes anything that robs us of enjoying a close relationship with Him. When we, as His children, opt for destructive activities and attitudes, God actively disciplines us. Christ declared: "As many as I love, I rebuke and chasten. Therefore be zealous and repent" (Rev. 3:19). God's discipline is applied to discourage His people's rebellion and to encourage their return to Him. The writer of Hebrews explains God's discipline:

> "My son, do not despise the chastening of the LORD, nor be discouraged when you are rebuked by Him; for whom the LORD loves He chastens, and scourges every son whom He receives."
>
> If you endure chastening, God deals with you as with sons; for what son is there whom a father does not chasten? But if you are without chastening . . . then you are illegitimate and not sons. Furthermore, we have had human fathers who corrected us, and we paid them respect. Shall we not much more readily be in subjection to the Father of spirits and live? For they indeed for a few days chastened us as seemed best to them, but He for our profit, that we may be partakers of His holiness. Now no chastening seems to be joyful for the present, but painful; nevertheless, afterward it yields the peaceable fruit of righteousness to those who have been trained by it. (Heb. 12:5–11)

God knows that fullness of life is found only in a relationship with Him. When we drift from God, we squander our inheritance. Our loving Father cannot remain indifferent as we race headlong to our ruin. He allows us to feel the pain and to suffer the consequences of the lost love relationship so we quickly return to Him.

Parents discipline their children when they do wrong. Parents understand that the discipline may be painful for the moment, but it will save their children from greater harm in the future. Only irresponsible and lazy parents neglect to correct their children. Failing to act when children misbehave may avoid a brief period of unpleasantness, but it will consign the child to future misery. Parents who love their children teach them to live correctly so they experience a healthy and safe life.

Our sin brings great pain. It cost Christ the cross, and it will destroy us. That is why God does everything necessary to turn us away from it. Being disciplined by Him provides evidence we belong to God's family (Heb. 12:7). Those who habitually sin without receiving discipline prove they are not members of God's household (Heb. 12:8). Even though His discipline may be painful, we should embrace it, learn from it, and be set free by it. Knowing God cares enough about us to discipline us ought to greatly encourage us and provide a sense of security for our Christian life.

A second reason God disciplines us is because He loves every person on the earth and wants each one to know and love Him (John 3:16). When God's people depart from God, they are no longer in a position to lead others to Him. God has no plan B if Christians fail to obey Him. Thus, God disciplines errant believers so they return to Him. Then He works mightily through them to redeem a lost world.

Truths Concerning God's Judgments

As we have seen, God passes judgment on Christians as well as unbelievers. These are God's severe responses to those who refuse to turn from their sin or whose actions could encourage others to sin. As we examine God's methods of judgment, several scriptural truths are important to understand.

- Judgment begins with God's people. "The time has come for judgment to begin at the house of God; and if it begins with us first, what will be the end of those who do not obey the gospel of God?" (I Pet. 4:17). While Christians are exempt from final judgment, they are the first to receive judgment in this life.
- *Every* deed will be judged. "God will bring every work into judgment, including every secret thing, whether good or evil" (Eccles. 12:14).
- Jesus came to bring judgment. "Jesus said, 'For judgment I have come into this world, that those who do not see may see, and that those who see may be made blind'" (John 9:39).
- God's judgments are always right, true, and fair. "'Even so, Lord God Almighty, true and righteous are Your judgments'" (Rev. 16:7).

God's discipline is generally progressive. Although sometimes, such as in the case of Ananias and Sapphira, it is immediate, generally judgment comes after a series of increasingly severe instances of discipline. Each time we do not respond to God, His response becomes more intense.

"If you do not obey Me, and do not observe all these commandments, . . .
I also will do this to you: . . . After all this, if you do not obey Me, then
I will punish you seven times more for your sins. I will break the pride of
your power. . . . If you walk contrary to Me, and are not willing to obey
Me, I will bring on you seven times more plagues, according to your sins.
. . . If by these things you are not reformed by Me, but walk contrary to
Me, then I also will walk contrary to you, and I will punish you yet
seven times for your sins. . . . And after all this, if you do not obey Me,
but walk contrary to Me, then I also will walk contrary to you in fury;
and I, even I, will chastise you seven times for your sins. . . . I will
destroy. . . . I will lay your cities waste . . . I will bring the land to
desolation . . . I will scatter you among the nations." (Lev. 26:14, 16,
18–19, 21, 23–24, 27–28, 30–33)

God is long-suffering and merciful. Yet, if we keep refusing to repent, He will
deal with us accordingly.

Examples of God's Discipline and Judgments

The Scriptures are filled with examples of God's discipline on His wayward people
as well as His judgments. As we have said, His discipline is usually progressive until
it culminates in His judgment. God generally brings only as much discipline to bear
upon us as is necessary to turn us from our sin. However, if we harden our hearts to
the Holy Spirit's convicting activity, God will escalate the severity of His discipline
until it is extremely difficult to continue in our sin.

God can use similar means for His discipline and His judgment. The difference
lies in the severity. For example, a storm that causes financial hardship could be a
form of discipline. A storm that causes death and widespread suffering would be
a form of judgment. Scripture makes it clear that God makes use of natural disasters
to reprimand His people (Deut. 27; 28:15–67; 2 Chron. 6). These include:

- **Natural disasters:** earthquake, volcano, hurricane, tornado, flood, fire,
  drought, hail, famine, insect plague, attack of wild animals
- **Disease:** plague, wasting disease, fever, and leprosy
- **Human conflict or trouble:** war, attack or defeat by an enemy, being
  taken into captivity or bondage, being ruled by enemies, victim of crime,
  victim of immorality, bloodshed, increase in wickedness, broken human
  relationships, economic collapse

While God does use natural disasters as a means of His discipline and judgment, not every crisis is necessarily God's judgment. The earth is not our final home. Scripture indicates it is decaying and under the curse of sin (Rom. 8:18–22). Cancer is not necessarily the result of God's judgment but is due to the fact we inhabit imperfect, earthly bodies. Storms occur because of the way nature functions. Nevertheless, when disasters or conflicts occur, God's people must seek to understand if God is communicating displeasure over sin. Sometimes when God judges groups such as nations, seemingly innocent people are hurt. God's judgments are not always limited to the wicked. Sin's tragedy is that it harms innocent as well as guilty people. But none of us is truly innocent. All have sinned (Rom. 3:23). When Adam and Eve rejected God's command, countless people through the ages suffered as a consequence. When God judged Judah during Ezekiel's day, He said,

> "I will cut off both righteous and wicked from you, therefore My sword
> shall go out of its sheath against all flesh from south to north, that all
> flesh may know that I, the LORD, have drawn My sword out of its sheath;
> it shall not return anymore." Sigh therefore, son of man, with a breaking
> heart, and sigh with bitterness before their eyes. (Ezek. 21:4–6)

While God is consistent in His response to sin, He also deals with us uniquely and individually. The Bible relates a number of means and ways God disciplined individuals and nations. The Holy Spirit convicts people of their sin. If people respond with a heart ready to repent, He does not proceed to discipline them. When people refuse to turn from their sin, God will apply discipline in an increasing degree. The following are some of the methods the Bible says God may use in disciplining His people:

1. *God may refuse to hear their prayers.* "Your iniquities have separated you from your God; and your sins have hidden His face from you, so that He will not hear" (Isa. 59:2). God does not promise always to answer our prayers. Silence is one of His ways to gain people's attention. Scripture warns husbands to treat their wives in an understanding manner lest their prayers be hindered (1 Pet. 3:7). When we sense God is not hearing our prayers, we must quickly find out why.

2. *God may hide His presence from us.* "How long, O LORD? Will You forget me forever? How long will You hide Your face from me?" (Ps. 13:1). Of all of David's anguished pleas with God after he sinned, his most heart-wrenching cry was: "Do not cast me away from Your presence, and do not take Your Holy Spirit from me" (Ps. 51:11). There can be no greater punishment than separation from God.

This is the essence of hell. While God is omnipresent (Ps. 139:7–16), He can hide His presence from us so that we no longer feel He is near.

Often in times of revival, people said God seemed to come near to His people. Tragically, a long time passes before some churches or individuals realize they are far from God. A heartbreaking account of God abandoning His people is found in the book of Ezekiel. God gave the prophet a vision, allowing him to observe the gradual withdrawal of God's presence from His people. First God left the holy of holies, which was the traditional place of His presence. Then He moved to the threshold of the temple (Ezek.10:4). Later God's Spirit moved to the east gate of the temple (Ezek. 11:1). Finally the Lord departed to the Mount of Olives outside the city (Ezek. 11:23). Rabbinic tradition claimed that God's presence remained on the Mount of Olives for three and a half years waiting to see if His people would repent, but they did not. It seems incredible that God's presence could leave the temple and even the city and His people not even notice. Yet not until enemies surrounded the city and threatened their doom did the people cry out for God and discover He was no longer there. Perhaps that is the imagery intended in the book of Revelation when the risen Christ declared He stood at the door of His church and knocked, waiting to see if people would realize He was standing *outside* and would open the door to let Him in (Rev. 3:20).

3. *God may withhold His word so His people do not hear a fresh word from Him.* "'Behold, the days are coming,' says the Lord GOD, 'That I will send a famine on the land, not a famine of bread, nor a thirst for water, but of hearing the words of the LORD. They shall wander from sea to sea, and from north to east; they shall run to and fro, seeking the word of the LORD, but shall not find it'" (Amos 8:11–12). God's Word brings life (Deut. 8:3; John 1:1–4). An absence of a word from God is evidence of God's displeasure with His people. Throughout history, revivals erupted when a preacher came along who *did* have a word from the Lord. People realized they had not been hearing from God, and when they did, great conviction of sin resulted. That accounts for the startling effect of revival preachers such as George Whitefield and D. L. Moody. Suddenly people knew they had heard from God, and they felt compelled to repent.

4. *God may remove the wall of protection from us and those we love.* "'Let Me tell you what I will do to My vineyard [Israel]: I will take away its hedge, and it shall be burned; and break down its wall, and it shall be trampled down. I will lay it waste'" (Isa. 5:5–6). God does not cause every bad thing that happens to people who sin. However, all God must do is remove His protective care from His people, and natural disasters and evil people will do their worst. God's people take His watch care over

them for granted until He withdraws it. Events such as September 11, 2001 have caused heated debate among Christians concerning whether God caused the terrorist attacks as a form of judgment on America. What *is* apparent is that God *allowed* the attacks to occur. In such terrible moments God's people must seek to understand why the Lord at least temporarily removed His hand of protection from their nation.

5. *God may allow us to face the full consequences of our own sinful behavior.* The Bible describes how the Lord allows people to reap what they have sown:

> "God also gave them up to uncleanness, in the lusts of their hearts, to dishonor their bodies among themselves. . . . God gave them up to vile passions. . . . God gave them over to a debased mind, to do those things which are not fitting; being filled with all unrighteousness, sexual immorality, wickedness, covetousness, maliciousness; full of envy, murder, strife, deceit, evil-mindedness; they are whispers, backbiters, haters of God, violent, proud, boasters, inventors of evil things, disobedient to parents, undiscerning, untrustworthy, unloving, unforgiving, unmerciful."
> (Rom. 1:24, 26, 28–31)

Sin is its own worst punishment. It guarantees innumerable painful results. When someone commits adultery, that sin carries inevitable disastrous consequences: alienation from children, family, friends, church members; feelings of guilt, anger, and remorse; loss of position and respect; and financial hardships. That is one of the reasons God warns us not to sin. Every sin ushers in its own aftermath of strife and suffering (Rom. 6:23).

God's People and the Civil War

While God's people have not always made the connection between their sin and their circumstances, they did during the American Civil War. This was the most horrific crisis the United States had faced. That conflict caused the tragic loss of hundreds of thousands of young men. It tore families apart and severely divided the nation. Both government and church leaders recognized that the young nation was undergoing a catastrophic trial with irreparable consequences. Ultimately President Lincoln issued several proclamations urging the people to recognize God's discipline on their nation and to devote a day to prayer, fasting, and repentance. Read below these excerpts from three of Lincoln's proclamations issued between 1861 and 1864. Consider whether there is not an equally urgent need for today's leaders to issue a similar appeal.

Proclamation of a National Fast Day, August 12, 1861

Whereas a joint committee of both houses of Congress has waited on the President of the United States and requested him to recommend a day of public prayer, humiliation, and fasting, to be observed by the people of the United States with religious solemnities, and the offering of fervent supplications to Almighty God. . . .

It is fit and becoming in all people, at all times, to acknowledge and revere the supreme government of God; to bow in humble submission to his chastisements; to confess and deplore their sins and transgressions, in the full conviction that the fear of the Lord is the beginning of wisdom; and to pray with all fervency and contrition for the pardon of their past offenses. . . .

Whereas when our own beloved country, once, by the blessing of God, united, prosperous, and happy, is now afflicted with faction and civil war, it is peculiarly fit for us to recognize the hand of God in this terrible visitation, and in sorrowful remembrance of our own faults and crimes as a nation and as individuals, to humble ourselves before him and to pray for his mercy. . . .

Therefore, I, Abraham Lincoln, President of the United States, do appoint the last Thursday in September next as a day of humiliation, prayer, and fasting for all the people of the nation.

Proclamation of a National Fast Day, March 30, 1863

Whereas, the Senate of the United States, devoutly recognizing the supreme authority and just government of Almighty God in all the affairs of men and of nations, has by a resolution requested the President to designate and set apart a day for national prayer and humiliation:

And whereas, it is the duty of nations as well as of men to own their dependence upon the overruling power of God; to confess their sins and transgressions in humble sorrow, yet with assured hope that genuine repentance will lead to mercy and pardon; and to recognize the sublime truth, announced in the Holy Scriptures and proven by all history, that those nations only are blessed whose God is the Lord;

And insomuch as we know that by his divine law nations, like individuals, are subjected to punishments and chastisements in this world, may we not justly fear that the awful calamity of civil war which now desolates the land may be but a punishment inflicted upon us for our presumptuous sins. . . . We have been the recipients of the choicest bounties of Heaven. We have been preserved, these many years, in peace and prosperity. We have grown in numbers, wealth, and power as no other nation has ever grown; but we have forgotten God. . . . We have vainly imagined, in the deceitfulness of our hearts, that all these blessings were produced by some superior wisdom and virtue of our own. Intoxicated with unbroken success, we have become too self-sufficient to feel the necessity of redeeming and preserving grace, too proud to pray to the God that made us.

It behooves us, then, to humble ourselves before the offended Power, to confess our national sins, and to pray for clemency and forgiveness. . . .

I do hereby request all people to abstain on that day from their ordinary secular pursuits, and to unite at their several places of public worship and their respective homes in keeping the day holy to the Lord. . . . All this being done in sincerity and truth, let us then rest humbly in the hope authorized by the divine teachings, that the united cry of the nation will be heard on high, and answered with blessings no less than the pardon of our national sins, and the restoration of our now divided and suffering country to its former happy condition of unity and peace.

Proclamation for a Day of Prayer, July 7, 1864

Whereas the Senate and House of Representatives, at their last session, adopted a concurrent resolution, which was approved on the second day of July instant, and which was in the words following, namely:

That the President of the United States be requested to appoint a day for humiliation and prayer by the people of the United States; that he request his constitutional advisers at the head of the executive departments to unite with him as chief magistrate of the nation, at the city of Washington, and the members of Congress, and all magistrates, all civil, military, and naval officers, all soldiers, sailors, and marines, with all loyal and law-abiding people, to convene at their usual places of worship, or wherever they may be, to confess and to repent of their manifold sins; to implore the compassion and forgiveness of the Almighty

. . . to implore him, as the supreme ruler of the world, not to destroy us as a people, nor to suffer us to be destroyed by the hostility or the connivance of other nations, or by obstinate adhesion to our own counsels which may be in conflict with his eternal purposes. . . .

Now, therefore, I, Abraham Lincoln . . . do hereby appoint the first Thursday of August next to be observed by the people of the United States as a day of national humiliation and prayer.

I do hereby further invite and request the heads of the executive departments of this government, together with all legislators, all judges and magistrates, and all other persons exercising authority in the land, whether civil, military, or naval, and all soldiers, seamen, and marines in the national service, and all the other loyal and law abiding people of the United States, to assemble in their preferred places of public worship on that day, and there and then to render to the Almighty and merciful Ruler of the universe such homages and such confessions, and to offer to him such supplications, as the Congress of the United States have, in their aforesaid resolution, so solemnly, so earnestly, and so reverently recommended.

This, too, is a day when the church must make the connection between its sin and its present circumstances.

6. *Ultimately God may choose to destroy or bring down those who refuse to repent.* "'Your enemies will build an embankment around you, surround you and close you in on every side, and level you, and your children within you, to the ground; and they will not leave in you one stone upon another, because you did not know the time of your visitation'" (Luke 19:43–44). God has never hesitated to use ungodly instruments to punish His people. God used the wicked Assyrians to punish the northern kingdom of Israel. He used King Nebuchadnezzer to raze Jerusalem. God later allowed the Roman legions to destroy Jerusalem and decimate the temple. God's people would be foolish to assume He will always protect them from their enemies regardless of how they live. As the writer of Hebrews gravely warned, "It is a fearful thing to fall into the hands of the living God" (Heb. 10:31).

If we refuse to repent when God calls us back to Him, He will eventually deal decisively with our stubbornness. He will not wait indefinitely as we continue to blatantly defy Him. If we persist in our resistance, He will bring judgment upon us. The New Testament offers several examples of this happening:

Destruction of Jerusalem

Jesus had prophesied the destruction of Jerusalem that eventually took place in AD 70. This was a judgment on the Jewish people for rejecting God's Messiah (Luke 19:41–44).

Corinthian Christians

Paul rebuked the Corinthian church for not taking the Lord's Supper seriously. They were sinning against the body and blood of Jesus and then hypocritically partaking of the Lord's Supper as if their hearts were pure and true toward God. Paul warned:

> He who eats and drinks in an unworthy manner eats and drinks judgment to himself, not discerning the Lord's body. For this reason many are weak and sick among you, and many sleep. For if we would judge ourselves, we would not be judged. But when we are judged, we are chastened by the Lord, that we may not be condemned with the world. (I Cor. 11:29–32)

Some actually died because they refused to conduct themselves properly during that sacred observance.

Ephesian Church

The risen Christ warned of impending judgment on the church at Ephesus, "Repent and do the first works, or else I will come to you quickly and remove your lampstand [church] from its place—unless you repent" (Rev. 2:5).

Some people have developed a false theology they believe releases them from any personal accountability for sin once they are saved. They argue that God does not punish those who are redeemed and are covered by the blood of Jesus. They suggest that when God looks at them, He only sees Jesus. Two of the examples above involved Christians and churches. Jesus has indeed paid the penalty for all sin—past, present, and future. Our eternal destiny is firmly established when we are born again. However, our relationship with Him and our usefulness to His kingdom purposes can be greatly hindered by our sin.

Spiritual Warfare

When God revives His people, Satan will vehemently oppose that work (I Pet. 5:8). Christians must be prepared for assaults from the spiritual forces of darkness (Eph. 6:10–17). Nevertheless, it is foolish to attribute every difficulty Christians experience to Satan's attacks. When the pastor catches a cold and cannot preach on Sunday, he may have simply caught a virus. Life has setbacks—cars break down, the economy fluctuates. Not every negative event is a bullet from Satan. Scripture is clear that God does allow or use bad circumstances to discipline His people. It would be futile if, every time God disciplined you, you assumed it was spiritual warfare with Satan orchestrating events. If, rather than seeking what God is saying to you through your trying circumstances, you cry out to God for protection from the wiles of Satan, you are missing the point of God's discipline.

Satan and his minions seek to hinder you from serving and glorifying the Lord. The forces of darkness want to discourage you and cause you to lose heart in serving God. God's discipline, on the other hand, is designed to remove anything from your life that is not Christlike. If, for instance, God wants to build the spiritual fruit of patience into your life (Gal. 5:22), He may allow trying circumstances to beset you so you have the opportunity to learn patience. This is not spiritual warfare. It is God allowing ordinary, frustrating life experiences into your life so they serve as His instrument to make you more like Jesus. If you resist this work and cry out to God for deliverance from your situation, you may miss God's sanctifying activity in your life. When hardships come, always ask: Is this an ordinary life experience that comes to every person who lives in a decaying body and a sin-filled world? Is God using these events in my life as a means of pruning me so I become more like Christ? Or is my condition an expression of spiritual warfare since I am a Christian who serves God in an evil and spiritually darkened world?

God Measures His Discipline to Our Hearts

A seventeenth-century puritan pastor named Henry Scougal observed, "God hath several ways of dealing with the souls of men, and it sufficeth if the work be accomplished, whatever the methods have been."[2] God perfectly measures His discipline to our heart's condition. Some people's hearts have so stiffened that major discipline is needed to humble them. For others the slightest expression of disapproval from God is sufficient to drive them to their knees.

A nineteenth-century English pastor named Octavius Winslow noted that God "is a tender, loving Father; so tender and so loving, that not one stroke, nor one cross, nor one trial more does He lay upon us, than is absolutely needful for our good; not a single ingredient does He put in our bitter cup, that is not essential to the perfection of the remedy."[3] Winslow cites the example of Peter when he denied his association with Jesus on the night of the crucifixion. Such a shameful act deserved Jesus' most bitter rebuke. But Jesus in His grace knew what was required for His zealous, over-confident disciple. Jesus merely glanced at Peter (Luke 22:61). That one gentle look crushed Peter's tender heart. He immediately realized the awful thing he had done. That gaze from Jesus broke Peter's heart, and he went out into the night and wept bitterly (Luke 22:62). Oh that each of us would have hearts so receptive toward God that all He need do is glance in our direction for us to grieve over any offense we committed against our beloved Savior. Jonathan Goforth claimed, "The sin of unyieldedness, alone, can keep us from revival."[4]

Conclusion

If we are to respond properly to the sanctifying work of the Holy Spirit in our lives, we must understand the way God works to discipline us as His children. When we choose to sin, we can expect a divine response. If we will quickly repent and return to the Lord, we will once again enjoy fellowship with our Savior. If we harden our hearts to our Lord, God will discipline us. His rebuke will be perfectly placed and measured to bring us back to Him. Should we brace ourselves against His heavenly initiative, God will increase the intensity of His convicting work until we cannot ignore it. Should we become so entrenched in our sin that we resist God's work at all costs, then He will ultimately bring judgment upon us. This judgment will crush us and provide a stark warning to those around us of the foolishness of rebellion against God.

Today God has removed His hedge of protection from many marriages, families, churches, and nations. The trials people face are becoming increasingly severe. God's people must immediately and humbly return to God and restore the close walk with God they once enjoyed.

QUESTIONS FOR REFLECTION AND DISCUSSION

1. How is discipline a display of God's love?
2. What do you think about the way God punished Ananias and Sapphira?
3. Why is God's discipline progressive, increasing in intensity? How have you experienced this in your own life or in your church?
4. How is the story of Job an illustration of the fact that bad things are not always judgment or discipline? (Job 1–2).

5. How could a Christian distinguish between godly discipline and spiritual warfare? Why is it important to know the difference?

6. In what ways, if any, do you sense your church is being or has been disciplined by God?

CHAPTER 10

God's People Cry Out in Repentance

Revival in Tennessee

J. Edwin Orr noted that "confession of sins is a neglected doctrine. It only comes into its rightful place in times of revival."[1] Mark Partin was called as the pastor of Indiana Avenue Baptist Church in LaFollette, Tennessee in 1993.[2] The church had been founded in 1940, but after fifty-three years it had dwindled to eighty-five members, most of them elderly. For the first several years, Partin's ministry followed the normal routine. However, after studying materials such as *Experiencing God* by Henry Blackaby and Claude King and *Seeking Him* by Nancy Leigh DeMoss and Tim Grissom, the congregation sensed that God wanted to do a special work in their midst. On October 20, 2006, the church began a series of revival meetings that would last forty days.

Pastor Partin invited friend and fellow pastor Mark Douglas to come from Florida to preach in the services. At the close of the first meeting, one young lady came forward to pray during the altar call, then the service came to an end. In the second service, held that evening, the tide of revival came in. This is how pastor Partin described it: "We faithfully returned for Sunday evening service. After singing only two songs, God began blowing His sweet breath throughout the congregation. His presence became so strong and real. Streams of people began flowing from their seats directly to the altar. They begged for the opportunity to confess sin. No one had even been asked to confess sin. The Word of God had not even been preached. But God was extending the offer for His people to come before Him; to purify themselves; to be cleansed; to be set free. People were responding."

Douglas remained for two weeks preaching each evening before he finally had to return to his own church. The pastor then took over the preaching. "Night after night people continued to confess their sins. Following the delivery of God's Word and message, complete silence would fall upon the congregation like a veil. Amazingly, in spite of so many people being present, not a sound could be heard . . . no rustling of papers; no movement of bodies shifting; not even the sighs of people breathing . . . nothing! And then breaking through the silence you would hear footsteps. Footsteps that clicked with force and determination to reach the altar; footsteps driven by purpose; footsteps guided by the hand of God."

All manner of sin was confessed during the services. Women admitted to conceiving children out of wedlock and to having abortions. A man wept that he had been called by God into ministry at age nineteen, but he told God no. People confessed adultery, addictions, greed, bitterness, and unforgiveness. The services lasted three to four hours each evening. People felt convicted over sins they committed decades earlier. Individuals would suddenly find themselves at the altar without any recollection of deciding to go forward. Each morning when the church was opened at eight o'clock, people would be waiting to enter the auditorium to pray.

Two things in particular characterized this divine movement. First, there was an overwhelming sense of God's presence. The people attending the services knew they were encountering God. They entered the auditorium each evening anticipating that God would meet them. Second, there was a profound sense of conviction for sin. The congregation increasingly felt the reality of God's presence. They became acutely aware of their sin because an encounter with God always brings conviction for sin.

God Brings His People Back to Himself

Richard Owen Roberts has stated that the message of revival is the message of repentance.[3] When we depart from our relationship with the Lord, He lovingly disciplines us. We need to make the connection between our sin and what is happening to us. If we are experiencing God's discipline, we must respond immediately. The longer we delay, the harder our hearts will become. When we cry out to Him for relief, He invites us to repent and return to Him: "'Return to Me, and I will return to you,' says the LORD of hosts" (Mal. 3:7). Henry Scougal points out: "It is utterly impossible that God should deny His love to a soul wholly devoted to Him, and which desires nothing so much as to serve and please Him, He cannot disdain His own image."[4]

King Solomon understood that God's people would inevitably sin and depart from Him. As he dedicated the temple in Jerusalem, Solomon asked God if He would forgive His people when they cried out to Him. Read Solomon's prayer:

> "If Your people Israel are defeated before an enemy because they have
> sinned against You . . . When the heavens are shut up and there is no rain

because they have sinned against You . . . When there is famine in the land, pestilence or blight or mildew, locusts or grasshoppers; when their enemies besiege them in the land of their cities; whatever plague or whatever sickness there is . . . When they sin against You (for there is no one who does not sin), and You become angry with them and deliver them to the enemy, and they take them captive . . . yet when they come to themselves . . . and repent, and make supplication to You in the land of their captivity, saying, 'We have sinned, we have done wrong, and have committed wickedness'; and when they return to You with all their heart and with all their soul . . . and pray . . . then hear from heaven Your dwelling place their prayer and their supplications, and maintain their cause, and forgive Your people who have sinned against You." (2 Chron. 6:24, 26, 28, 36–39)

Sin is always ultimately against God. Solomon knew God could use drought, famine, plague, blight, mildew, insect plagues, military defeat, and captivity to discipline His people. His question was this: Lord, if You punish Your people because of their sin and they turn their hearts back to You, will you forgive them?

God's Promise for Revival

Here is God's answer: "When I shut up heaven and there is no rain, or command the locusts to devour the land, or send pestilence among My people, if My people who are called by My name will humble themselves, and pray and seek My face, and turn from their wicked ways, then I will hear from heaven, and will forgive their sin and heal their land" (2 Chron. 7:13–14).

God answered yes! If I punish My people and they return to Me, I will forgive and restore them. In His reply to Solomon, God identified four requirements for revival: humility, prayer, seeking God, and repentance leading to a change in behavior. When people fulfill these requirements, God *will* respond by forgiving their sin and healing their land.

Symptoms of Spiritual Illness

Suppose your son has a fever and complains of an earache. You take him to the doctor who finds his temperature to be 102 degrees. His white blood count is high. His right ear is red. These symptoms are not the primary problem. An ear infection is the issue. The doctor could prescribe medication to reduce the fever and dull the pain, but that would not solve the problem. Your son needs an antibiotic to kill the infection.

In a similar way we can clearly observe symptoms of a spiritual illness. We have already identified three characteristics of spiritual sickness:

1. God's discipline indicates a sin problem.
2. Turning to or accepting substitutes for God, His presence, purposes, or ways indicates a spiritual problem.
3. Disobedience to the clear will of God in His Word indicates a problem.

Likewise, when our lives show evidence of sins such as anger, deceit, or infidelity, these are actually symptoms of a deeper issue. They indicate a heart that has left its love relationship with the Father. Nancy Leigh DeMoss notes: "When we cease to sense the seriousness of our sin, we also cease to be moved by the wonder of Christ's sacrifice on the cross for sin."[5] Whenever we recognize the symptoms of spiritual illness in our lives, family, church, denomination, or nation, we must cry out to God for deliverance. We cannot cure ourselves or others of sin. We can beseech the Lord to intervene. The good news is that God is fully prepared to help us. In fact, by the time we call out to Him, He already has everything planned for revival. When God led Israel into captivity because of its sin, He sent a message through Jeremiah. God took the initiative to call His people back to Himself:

> Thus says the LORD of hosts, the God of Israel, to all who were carried away captive, whom I have caused to be carried away from Jerusalem to Babylon: . . . I know the thoughts that I think toward you, says the LORD, thoughts of peace and not of evil, to give you a future and a hope. Then you will call upon Me and go and pray to Me, and I will listen to you. And you will seek Me and find Me, when you search for Me with all your heart. I will be found by you, says the LORD, and I will bring you back from your captivity; I will gather you from all the nations and from all the places where I have driven you, says the LORD, and I will bring you to the place from which I cause you to be carried away captive.
> (Jer. 29:4, 11–14)

Even when He brought disaster on His people, God had everything in place to draw them back to Himself. He was prepared to bless them; He was only waiting for their prayerful cry. When they began to seek Him, He would immediately respond.

God's Requirements for Repentance

God calls His people to repent or perish (Rev. 2:5). Sin is lethal, and we must treat it as such. Jeremiah 6 describes the nation's spiritual condition during Jeremiah's time. The people were extremely sinful, but the leaders were unconcerned about the evil pervading their society. No one grasped the danger in the wicked practices of the day, not even the priests or prophets.

> "From the least of them even to the greatest of them, everyone is given to covetousness; and from the prophet even to the priest, everyone deals falsely. They have also healed the hurt of My people slightly, saying, 'Peace, peace!' When there is no peace. Were they ashamed when they had committed abomination? No! They were not at all ashamed; nor did they know how to blush. . . ." Thus says the LORD: "Stand in the ways and see, and ask for the old paths, where the good way is, and walk in it; then you will find rest for your souls." (Jer. 6:13–16)

In Jeremiah's day, as in ours, genuine repentance was scarce. Repentance is not merely being sorry you got caught, nor is it feeling sorrow about your sin. The motivation to repent is not primarily to avoid God's wrath. The word *repent* indicates a turning away from sin and a wholehearted return to our love relationship with God. Henry Scougal noted: "Repentance is a delightful exercise when it floweth from the principle of love."[6] Remorse is inadequate. Behavior modification is ineffectual. Returning to religious activity is futile. Confession is part of repentance in that we acknowledge our wrongdoing, but repentance involves a broken heart and a decisive return to God. Repentance without absolute humility is not repentance at all; it is at best rededication. "For godly sorrow produces repentance leading to salvation, not to be regretted; but the sorrow of the world produces death" (2 Cor. 7:10).

God wants us to love Him with our entire being. When we return to our love relationship with Him, our lifestyle will reflect the transformation.

> He [John the Baptist] went into all the region around the Jordan, preaching a baptism of repentance for the remission of sins. . . . Then he said to the multitudes that came out to be baptized by him, "Brood of vipers! Who warned you to flee from the wrath to come? Therefore bear fruits worthy of repentance." (Luke 3:3, 7–8)

Paul explained how new life in Christ reflects repentance: "'I have been crucified with Christ; it is no longer I who live, but Christ lives in me; and the life which I now live in the flesh I live by faith in the Son of God, who loved me and gave Himself for me'" (Gal. 2:20). The evidence of repentance is that once again Christ freely lives His life in and through you.

Repentance for God's people, as individuals or as a church, involves a threefold process of change.

An Adjustment of Attitude

An alteration of mind is required wherein we agree with God about the truth of our sin. This is confession. We affirm that what we have done is wrong. If we argue with God about whether we have sinned, we are not in a position to repent! If we make excuses for our behavior, we are unprepared for repentance. We must reach the place David did when he said, "I acknowledge my transgressions . . . Against You, You only, have I sinned, and done this evil in Your sight" (Ps. 51:3–4).

A Change of Heart

Instead of enjoying our sinful ways, we must grieve over our sin as the Father does. If our transgression does not grieve us, we make a mockery of Christ's supreme sacrifice on the cross. David said, "The sacrifices of God are a broken spirit, a broken and contrite heart—these, O God, You will not despise" (Ps. 51:17). Alienation from God begins with a shift of our heart—when we lose sight of our first love. Only after we have returned to loving the Lord can we willingly obey Him. A change of heart is a prerequisite for lasting obedience.

Transformed Desires and Actions

Too many Christians try to walk as close to the world as possible without sinning. We flirt with temptation when we should flee from it. Repentance requires intentional living. We must rid ourselves of any idol of the heart and tear down strongholds keeping us from holiness. We must remove ourselves from tempting situations. These actions require a change of the will.

If you desire to change your will, God will enable you to do so, "for it is God who works in you both to will and to do for His good pleasure" (Phil. 2:13). Once you have allowed God to adjust your heart, you must go on and allow Him to alter your actions as well.

Corporate Repentance

Whenever people sin, repentance is required. This not only includes individuals but also:

- families who sin.
- committees who sin.
- cities that sin.
- churches that sin.
- businesses that sin.
- nations that sin.
- denominations that sin.
- Christian organizations that sin.

All sin is serious. God condemned Judah's spiritual leaders because they treated His people's sins so lightly (Jer. 6:14). We cannot merely move on from or cover over our sin. Sometimes churches try to hide the transgressions of their members because they are concerned about the church's reputation in the community. But sin is an affront to holy God, and God's opinion is what matters most. Notice what God said to His people:

> But I had concern for My holy name, which the house of Israel had profaned among the nations wherever they went.
>
> "Therefore say to the house of Israel, 'Thus says the Lord GOD: "I do not do this for your sake, O house of Israel, but for My holy name's sake, which you have profaned among the nations wherever you went. And I will sanctify My great name, which you have profaned among the nations, which you have profaned in their midst; and the nations will know that I am the Lord," says the Lord GOD, "when I am hallowed in you before their eyes."'" (Ezek. 36:21–23)

The way God's people act reflects on His hallowed name. God is jealous for the glory of His name before a watching world, and He will not allow His people to dishonor Him with impunity. Just because people in the church want to leave their sins in the past or they want to start over, that does not satisfy God's requirements.

Churches must repent of their corporate sins much as individuals do. Without repentance fellowship with God will remain broken. Read from the book of

Revelation the following messages the risen Christ delivered to five churches: (Ephesus: Rev. 2:1, 4–5; Pergamos: Rev. 2:12, 14–16; Thyatira: Rev. 2:18, 20–23; Sardis: Rev. 3:1–3; Laodicea: Rev. 3:14–20).

These five churches were called to repent. Sin committed by a group is still sin. Churches may adopt unbiblical policies and activities. Members may form splinter groups and act in an ungodly manner. Committees can meet to slander and oppose the pastor. Financial leaders of the church can use unethical means to accomplish church goals. Educational leaders can manipulate people to serve. Staff can be unfairly fired. When a church sins, every member must assume a portion of the guilt. At times, however, church members assume that because they did not directly commit the transgression they are not responsible. The refusal to repent can be fatal to churches. How does a church or a religious group repent?

Second Chronicles 7:14, God's Word for His people, outlined His provision for corporate repentance. Before revival comes, God's people must first humble themselves. Pride is the first and greatest barrier to revival. Because of pride, churches are reluctant to admit any wrong. The thought of repenting publicly is repugnant to them. How does God respond when His people try to hide their sin? He tells us, "He who covers his sins will not prosper, But whoever confesses and forsakes them will have mercy" (Prov. 28:13). Congregations, Christian organizations, and families, like individual Christians, must learn to renounce their pride and humble themselves before God. There is no other option.

After humility comes prayer, communicating with God and seeking His face. Hiding from God is impossible. Trying to avoid Him or run from Him is futile. Running *to* Him is the only remedy for our wretched condition. God said to Judah: "'Come now, and let us reason together. . . . Though your sins are like scarlet, they shall be as white as snow; though they are red like crimson, they shall be as wool'" (Isa. 1:18).

When we have humbly sought God's presence, we are in a position to repent. Then we must turn from our wickedness. Repentance, as we have already studied, requires a transformed mind, heart, will, and actions. It results in a changed lifestyle. As with an individual, a repentant church must turn away from its sin. This may require the tearing down of idols, changing the way things are done, getting rid of traditions, selling property, disbanding particular committees, or making restitution for wrongs committed. Saying, "We'll try to do better next time," is insufficient. Repentance requires actions in the present, not just promises for the future.

A Prayerless Church

In April 1994 a small rural church in Tennessee met for a special emphasis on prayer. Following the study, members were given time to share what God had been saying to them. The bivocational pastor stood and confessed, "I have not been a man of prayer, and I have not led you to be a people of prayer. I need to ask you to forgive me."

The conference leader asked the pastor to pray aloud, confessing his sin to the Lord and seeking His forgiveness. Then the church members expressed their forgiveness to their pastor. Together the congregation acknowledged they had not been a people of prayer. As a body they confessed their sin of neglecting to pray. Now eager to get right with the Lord, they joined their hearts and voices in prayers of repentance.

They stood before the Lord to acknowledge collectively their sin, and their pastor led in a prayer of confession. He beseeched God to enable them to become a prayerful congregation. Then the people spread out across the worship center to pray in small groups. They lingered until they sensed God dismissing them.

God did a special work of grace in that church. Following their corporate repentance in 1994, the people began to take prayer seriously. They cultivated their personal prayer lives. They scheduled time for prayer in Bible study gatherings and worship times. They regularly called special prayer meetings. During this time their pastor resigned, and the congregation made prayer a major element in seeking a new pastor.

In the spring of 1995, they called a new pastor on whom God had already placed a burden for personal prayer and for leading a church to be a house of prayer. God's powerful presence became increasingly evident throughout the church ministries. Inactive church members returned. Members dealt decisively with sin. People in the community were drawn to the church, and numerous nonbelievers chose to put their faith in Christ. What had begun with one man's confession of sin grew to transform an entire congregation and the surrounding community. That's what repentance does.

Corporate repentance need not be a complicated or long, drawn-out process. It should not be viewed in a negative light. In fact, repentance is one of the most positive experiences a church can have. Jesus preached, "Repent, for the kingdom of heaven is at hand" (Matt. 4:17). When a body of believers repents, God's powerful presence and resources are poised to pour out over the people, infusing them with joy and renewed life.

The Joy of Repentance

A few years ago a congregation was faced with a sensitive but not uncommon situation. An unmarried couple in the church, new believers, had been living together; and it became obvious they were expecting a child. Extenuating circumstances had prevented them from marrying as soon as they became believers. The woman was separated from a husband who had been abusive and unfaithful but who refused to grant a divorce. The man was from another country and could not obtain employment until his immigration papers arrived.

Nonetheless the pastor and deacons helped the couple recognize that their situation was dishonoring to God and to the church. The couple tearfully repented, and the deacons helped them pay for separate housing immediately. That very week every obstacle to their marriage was suddenly removed. On Sunday this man and woman stood before their church family and humbly confessed their sin. They desired to be married immediately. The congregation's response was overwhelming. Members flew into action cooking, baking, and decorating; and that afternoon the church people gathered back together to celebrate a wedding. This dear couple and their children remain a cherished and vibrant part of that church fellowship to this day.

Rather than ignoring the obvious sin of two believers, church leaders firmly and lovingly addressed the situation and provided assistance to help them do what would honor God. The church family responded with forgiveness and joy that this family was seeking to do what was right. Clearly repentance opens the door for forgiveness, fellowship, and joy, not just for the penitent ones but for the entire Christian community. Repentance is God's provision to bring us back into the abundant life He longs for us to enjoy (Acts 3:19).

A Refiner's Fire

During the Shantung Revival the Holy Spirit brought a profound sense of conviction upon Christians in the churches, including spiritual leaders. Though they were respected in the churches, God saw the sin in their hearts. The nearer God drew to His people, the more agonizing was their conviction for their sin. C. L. Culpepper, a respected missionary leader, testified to his experience under the Holy Spirit's conviction: "The Holy Spirit and God's word continued to probe until I believed I would die under the searching, accusing finger of God. . . . I told my Chinese coworkers that in their compliments of me as an effective worker I had stolen God's glory. My heart was so broken I didn't believe I could live any longer."[7]

When God brings revival, He comes in power to purge His people of their sin and restore them to holiness.

> "The Lord, whom you seek, will suddenly come to His temple, even the
> Messenger of the covenant, in whom you delight. Behold, He is coming,"
> Says the LORD of hosts. "But who can endure the day of His coming?
> And who can stand when He appears? For He is like a refiner's fire and
> like launderers' soap. . . . and I will come near you for judgment; I will be a
> swift witness against sorcerers, against adulterers, against perjurers, against
> those who exploit wage earners and widows and orphans, and against
> those who turn away an alien—because they do not fear Me," says the
> LORD of hosts. (Mal. 3:1–2, 5)

A refiner's fire has to be intense so it can burn away all impurities. Revival, likewise, is a powerful spiritual cleansing agent. When God revives His people, the filth of sin is stripped away, and the image of Christ remains.

Sins of the Nation in the Church

A church in the southern United States entered into a two-week series of revival meetings in the spring of 1994. At the beginning of the services, the members made a list of sins they saw exhibited in the nation. Their list contained forty-one specific sins. Then they prayed for their nation.

As they prayed, God began to deal with sin in their midst. One by one members began confessing their wrongdoings and seeking forgiveness and cleansing. Much of the confession began in the prayer room and with counselors. Some was shared with the entire congregation. The refining work of God began to go deep, and services continued for five weeks. At the conclusion of that time, the pastor reviewed the list of forty-one sins. He was amazed to realize that every one of the sins listed for the nation had been confessed by church members! Months later the church began to experience the joys and fruits of revival, but the pastor testifies that those five weeks of refining were some of the most painful and yet, rewarding days of his life and ministry.

Revival Is like Judgment Day

J. Edwin Orr was one of the twentieth century's foremost authorities on revival. The last sermon he ever preached, the day before he died, was titled: "Revival Is like Judgment Day."[8] When God comes into the midst of His people as a refiner's fire, the process of purification may be deeply disquieting for individuals and churches. Usually as we pray for revival, what we really want are the fruits of revival—the joy, cleansing, nearness to God, and the conversion of sinners. But before we can experience the rewards of revival, we must be "baptized with fire." However, as Orr assures us: "Of one thing a believer may be certain, that the Holy Spirit never leaves a seeking heart untouched. Skillful is all His surgery, tender all His healing."[9]

Richard Owen Roberts notes that repentance is the first word of the gospel.[10] John the Baptist predicted that when Jesus came preaching repentance, He would baptize people with the Holy Spirit and with fire (Luke 3:16–17). In response people would have to accept Jesus or fight against Him. God exposes the attitude of the heart when He comes in revival. No one can remain neutral. Once people hear what God requires, they must either obey or rebel against holy God. Individuals and churches cannot continue to do business as usual when God is calling them to revival and to be part of a spiritual awakening in the land. It is tragic when God comes to His own people and they refuse to respond to Him. Notice what happened in Jeremiah's day:

> "Why has this people slidden back, Jerusalem, in a perpetual backsliding?
> They hold fast to deceit, they refuse to return. I listened and heard, but
> they do not speak aright. No man repented of his wickedness, saying,
> 'What have I done?' Everyone turned to his own course . . . But My people
> do not know the judgment of the Lord." (Jer. 8:5–7)

Christians long for revival because they want their ambivalent friends, family, and neighbors to become believers. But whenever God brings revival, He first targets those who are already His. God examined His people in Jeremiah's day, and here is what He saw:

- They had turned away from God.
- No one repented of wickedness.
- They clung to deceit.
- People did whatever they wanted.
- They refused to return to God.
- They did not know God's requirements.
- They did not speak righteously.
- They were stubborn and proud.
- They were unwilling to admit transgressions.

These signs of spiritual illness were not unique to Jeremiah's day, nor do they describe only those who blatantly reject God. The prophet Malachi announced, "'Then you shall again discern between the righteous and the wicked, between one who serves God and one who does not serve Him'" (Mal. 3:18). When God comes, He causes a division between those who will follow Him and those who want to go their own way. Arthur Wallis observed: "If we find a revival that is not spoken against, we had better look again to ensure that it is a revival."[11] It should not come as a surprise when some people within the church oppose God's work of revival. According to Scripture,

"'This is the condemnation, that the light has come into the world, and men loved darkness rather than light, because their deeds were evil. For everyone practicing evil hates the light and does not come to the light, lest his deeds should be exposed. But he who does the truth comes to the light, that his deeds may be clearly seen, that they have been done in God.'" (John 3:19–21)

No one likes to be exposed as a sinner, yet that is the first thing we need God to do so we can come to the light, deal with our sin, and find cleansing and forgiveness. When the Holy Spirit comes on God's people in power, there will always be those who are unwilling to undergo the refining process and those who choose to cling to the deceptive comfort of their sins. Revival greatly disrupts the normal flow of a church, but it is imperative that revival comes.

Revival in Brownwood, Texas

Coggin Avenue was a traditional Baptist church in Brownwood, Texas. Not many years before God brought revival to this church, it was in a state of desperate spiritual need. Several pastors had left under difficult circumstances and after short tenures. Broken relationships were common among the members. Sexual immorality was being practiced by church members, even by some of the leaders. The church had almost no evangelistic impact on the community, and spiritual apathy was commonplace.

John Avant became the pastor of this congregation in the midst of its spiritual destitution. After a year and a half of hard work, John reached a point of frustrated exhaustion. He cried out to the Lord, "God, I can't do anything with these people." He had finally reached the end of himself. That was when God chose to act. God would receive the glory for what happened next.

Gradually people began to develop a hunger for the Lord. Over three hundred people went through the study *Experiencing God: Knowing and Doing the Will of God.* They began to experience a closer intimacy with the Lord. Then Avant led the church in a study of *Fresh Encounter: God's Pattern for Revival and Spiritual Awakening.* People were beginning to deal with sin in their lives, but the spark of revival was yet to be lit.

A godly man in the church ran for election as police chief on the platform "Revival is coming to Brownwood, and I want to be a part of it as your police chief." He won the election. A prominent citizen in town left his wife and was contemplating suicide. God dramatically intervened in his life and turned him around. He was reconciled with his wife and returned to the Lord. God began to work through him to see others come to Christ. Other marriages were restored, and the church began to see the power of God at work among its members.

One church member decided to have his convenience stores stop selling pornography, alcohol, and lottery tickets. Everyone was amazed when his overall sales actually increased. People didn't have to wait in line for lottery tickets and his sales sped up.

Then Pastor Avant met Fernando, a young Hispanic man who had been a drug addict and a convict. Fernando had become a Christian and returned to his hometown with a burden to minister to young people involved in gangs. He was already seeing dramatic results from his ministry. Lives were changing; dropouts were returning to school and enjoying success. The principals and teachers of the high schools had noticed the positive difference Fernando was making in the community.

John introduced Fernando to the members of Coggin Avenue and asked them to help fund his ministry. However, the charismatic church in town was already supporting Fernando's ministry, and it was almost unheard of for Baptist churches to cooperate with charismatics. Nevertheless, after hearing the testimonies of some of the kids, the church overwhelmingly voted to undergird the work. When the other sponsoring church heard what the Baptists had done, barriers separating the denominations began to fall. Several local pastors began meeting together to pray for revival in their town.

On January 22, 1995, God's Spirit brought great conviction of sin to Coggin Avenue Church. People came to the altar weeping and getting right with God. They began openly to confess sin and to seek forgiveness. Broken relationships were reconciled. During the first service on that Sunday morning, twenty-two people made public decisions for Christ. That evening, at a previously planned joint meeting between Coggin Avenue and their Hispanic mission, they were to baptize some young people who had come to know Christ through Fernando's ministry. By the end of the service, blacks, whites, and Hispanics were weeping and praying together. Racial barriers were falling.

At least two other nearby churches were affected by God's Spirit in unusual ways that same day. Churches from other denominations were beginning to experience revival as well. The charismatic pastor said to John, "We have a group in our church studying *Experiencing God*. It is led by a Presbyterian, filled with charismatics, and has a Church of Christ pastor in attendance, and they are studying Baptist materials. That's got to be revival!" Unity among God's people is often a fruit of genuine revival.

By mid-February widespread confession of sin swept the campus of Howard Payne University in Brownwood. Testimonies from that experience sparked similar movements of God's Spirit on dozens of other college and seminary campuses across the country.[12]

Conclusion

As long as Christians are content with their sin and the present level of their spiritual vitality, they will remain as they are, or they will continue to decline. However, the Holy Spirit is always working to open people's spiritual eyes to the reality of their spiritual condition. When they recognize their woeful condition, they must confess it and fervently turn from it. When God's people renounce their sin, the Holy Spirit's power is unleashed among them. Most of the great revival movements in history began when God's people grew weary of their sin and repented of it.

Such profound movements of God among His people compel us to ask the same question the saintly Robert Murray McCheyene regularly asked: "Is the desire of my heart to be made altogether holy?"[13]

QUESTIONS FOR REFLECTION AND DISCUSSION

1. Can you identify a time when you or your church disobeyed what God wanted?
2. Can you pinpoint ways you and your church have departed from God and turned to substitutes for Him?
3. How do you deal with sin in your life? How has your church responded to sin when it has occurred among its members?

4. Has your church sinned in a way that requires restitution? Has your church mistreated a former pastor or member? How can your church set matters right again?

5. Was your church birthed out of a church split? Have you been reconciled with your estranged brothers and sisters in Christ, or is there still bitterness and hard feelings between you?

6. What do you see as hindrances to revival in your life and in your church?

CHAPTER 11

Responding to Revival

Stifling God's Work in Korea

In 1906 a missionary named Swallen attended a meeting in Seoul, Korea. There he and other missionaries were inspired to hear of a great movement of God in the Kassia Hills in India where eighty-two hundred converts had been baptized in two years.[1] Swallen and his fellow missionaries returned to their mission station in Ping Yang convinced that if God was willing to do a mighty work in India, He would be just as desirous of working powerfully in Korea among them. The Methodist and Presbyterian missionaries began praying daily together at noon for revival.

After a month of praying, nothing unusual happened, and some thought the meetings should be suspended. Instead the missionaries increased the fervency of their intercession, and God united the various denominations into a solid phalanx of prayer. Four months passed. Then Swallen and another missionary named Blair went to an outstation for some routine meetings. During a service a wave of strong emotion began to sweep over the congregation. Swallen attempted to subdue the emotionalism by announcing the singing of a hymn. He tried several times to gain control of the gathering and to restore a sense of decorum but to no avail. Finally, "in awe he realized that Another was managing that meeting; and he got as far out of sight as possible."[2]

Revival is not a human work. Arthur Wallis notes: "Revival can never be explained in terms of activity, organization, meetings, personalities, preachings. These may or may not be involved in the work, but they do not and cannot account for the effects produced. Revival is essentially a manifestation of God."[3] It can be difficult to understand revival fully because people have no control over when or how it occurs.

Historically, people have often been caught by surprise when revival came, even when they had been fervently praying for it!

Possible Objections to Revival

Not everyone wants revival to come. Therefore, calls for repentance are not always enthusiastically received, especially among church leaders. Resistance to revival can come in several forms:

1. *Some dismiss revival as an Old Testament phenomenon.* They say, "God is not like that anymore," or, "That is a message from the Law, and God is a God of grace." But the God of the Old Testament is the same God of the New Testament. The Scriptures, from Genesis to Revelation, reveal Him and the ways He relates to people. God says, "I am the LORD, I do not change" (Mal. 3:6). James 1:17 claims, "the Father of lights [the Creator] with whom there is no variation or shadow of turning." Jesus relied heavily on the Old Testament for instruction. The early church did not have Scriptures other than the Old Testament for most of its history. The Bible says, "All Scripture is given by inspiration of God, and is profitable for doctrine, for reproof, for correction, for instruction in righteousness, that the man of God may be complete, thoroughly equipped for every good work" (2 Tim. 3:16–17). God did not suddenly become gracious in New Testament times, nor did His opposition to sin cease after the New Testament was written.

2. *Some people cannot comprehend God as a God of discipline and judgment.* They choose to focus instead on His grace and mercy. They exert positive thinking, hoping to bring about a positive result. They argue that the past should be forgotten. In Scripture God condemned those who went about saying, "Peace, peace," when there was no peace. In the middle of a sinful church, some will say, "We are a great church. Look at our growing attendance!" The writer of Proverbs tells us, "He who covers his sins will not prosper, but whoever confesses and forsakes them will have mercy" (Prov. 28:13). When known sin exists in a church and the Holy Spirit is bringing conviction, they are false prophets who proclaim, "Peace, peace, everything is wonderful."

3. *In order to protect the church's or an individual's reputation, some congregations will disobey the clear teaching of God on how to deal with sin.* What can appear to be respecting privacy can in fact be nothing less than pride or fear of people. Open sin that is covered over or ignored will inevitably shut down God's activity in a church. If we regard iniquity in our heart, God refuses to hear our prayers (Ps. 66:18).

Moreover, treating sin lightly can tempt others to sin. Sin can spread like a deadly disease left untreated. Sometimes God requires that sin be confessed openly in a congregation. To cover up such sins is corporate rebellion on the part of a church.

4. *Some choose to rely on human wisdom and reason, even when it is in direct opposition to God's Word.* Some in the congregation are highly opinionated, vocal, and intimidating. They may present their case to imply that anyone who disagrees with them is a fool. Sadly sometimes the pastor or other church leaders act this way. They may argue against God's ways even when confronted with a clear word from Scripture. They may try to redefine evil and call it good or say it is no longer sinful. Do not allow such people to intimidate you or your church from following what God says in His Word. A church and its leaders need to fear God and not people. "Let God be true but every man a liar" (Rom. 3:4).

Refusing to "Judge"

We know of a church that discovered one of its members was committing adultery. When the man refused to end the relationship, the church met to discuss what should be done. Church leaders shared how they had met with the man and pleaded with him to renounce his sin and to return to his wife. The man adamantly refused. The church leaders, therefore, recommended that the church withdraw the man's membership in the church and publicly denounce his actions.

While most members agreed that this was the proper biblical response, one couple grew angry and belligerent. They argued that the church was supposed to be a place of grace and that it should not judge other people's actions. They announced they would not remain in a congregation that was legalistic and uncaring. The church voted to remove the man's membership, and the couple left the church. Ironically, that couple later underwent a divorce themselves after the husband committed adultery. Here was a loud, angry couple challenging the church not to deal severely with sin. It only became apparent later why they did not want to remain in a Christian fellowship that unwaveringly denounced sin.

5. *Some want revival on their terms.* Christians know they and their church desperately need revival, but they will only welcome it on their conditions. Some distrust any form of emotionalism and fear it will creep into their church. These people believe they honor God by their stiff formality and well-orchestrated religious rituals. Order is viewed as a cardinal virtue. Yet revival is a sovereign act of God. He will do it His way. Generally the manner God chooses is designed to humble His people.

Jonathan Goforth noted: "If the Almighty Spirit moves in sovereign power on the hearts and consciences of men the outcomes must be above the normal."[4] Richard Owen Roberts claimed that revival is an "extraordinary" movement of the Holy Spirit producing extraordinary results.[5] You cannot cling to the status quo and experience revival. If you are praying for revival, prepare yourself for the extraordinary. Duncan Campbell asked those unsure if they wanted revival, "Are you in the place where God can hurt you with revival?"[6]

Revival Is God's Work

God is the One who revives repentant people. We can beseech God to revive His people, and we can ready our hearts for its coming, but we cannot cause revival to occur or pressure God to act or "pray it down." He brings revival under His conditions and on His timetable. Arthur Wallis claimed there were two foundational aspects to revival: God's sovereignty and the church's preparation. God is the sovereign ruler of the universe, and He will not yield His prerogative by reducing revival to a formula. In some cases Christians have prayed for only a short time before revival came. At other times people cried out to God for years. The timing of revival is one of the clear ways in which God retains His control over the church. When revival comes, its suddenness highlights the reality that no one can fully anticipate how and when God will act.

Although we cannot pressure God to act, the truth is that He wants revival more than we do. In fact, He is the One who instills in us the desire to be revived. God draws us to Himself. God initiates revival, and He brings it to pass when His people meet His conditions.

God said, "Return to Me, and I will return to you" (Mal. 3:7). How can you know when God is bringing revival? You will know you have truly returned to God when God draws near to you (James 4:8). The Asbury revival was described this way: "It was as if the campus had been suddenly invaded by another power."[7] To those at Asbury College, there was no question when God manifested His presence on their campus. During the revivals under Jonathan Edwards, people came under great fear as they realized Almighty, Holy God was in their midst and He knew every sin they had committed. Yet Edwards's biographer noted: "The sense of fear which Edwards describes was not an irrational hysteria, it was the effect of truth brought home powerfully to the conscience."[8] It was obvious when God's Holy Spirit was at work in people's lives during those revivals, for people could not hide it if they tried.

Charles Finney, who witnessed many powerful outpourings of God's Spirit, observed: "It would probably not be possible for one who has never witnessed such a scene to realize what force the truth sometimes has under the power of the Holy Spirit."[9]

If you and your church are missing God's presence and power, you can be sure you have not met God's requirements. When you experience God's coming in power, you will never be the same. If you remain unchanged, whatever happened was not an encounter with God. Simply saying a prayer does not mean you have returned to God. Signing a card, confessing transgressions before your church, weeping, or praying with your pastor does not mean you have returned to God. If you do not experience God's presence and know He has returned to you, get on your knees and ask Him what you still need to do in repentance.

God is waiting for you to draw near to Him. Repentance and revival, however, are not just reformed behavior. Revival has not taken place unless a change of heart and character has occurred. You cannot transform your own heart; God must do that: "'Then I will give them a heart to know Me, that I am the LORD; and they shall be My people, and I will be their God, for they shall return to Me with their whole heart'" (Jer. 24:7).

When your love for the Lord compels you to obey Him and when your heart's consuming desire is to please Him, that is the indication that the love relationship has been restored. Read the following verses from the book of Ezekiel and watch for ways God said He would revive and restore His people:

> "Therefore say to the house of Israel, 'Thus says the Lord GOD: "I do
> not do this for your sake, O house of Israel, but for My holy name's sake,
> which you have profaned among the nations wherever you went. And
> I will sanctify My great name, which has been profaned among the
> nations, which you have profaned in their midst; and the nations shall
> know that I am the LORD," says the Lord GOD, "when I am hallowed in
> you before their eyes. For I will take you from among the nations, gather
> you out of all countries, and bring you into your own land. Then I will
> sprinkle clean water on you, and you shall be clean; I will cleanse you from
> all your filthiness and from all your idols. I will give you a new heart and
> put a new spirit within you; I will take the heart of stone out of your flesh
> and give you a heart of flesh. I will put My Spirit within you and cause
> you to walk in My statutes, and you will keep My judgments and do them.
> Then you shall dwell in the land that I gave to your fathers; you shall

be My people, and I will be your God. I will deliver you from all your uncleanness. I will call for the grain and multiply it, and bring no famine upon you. And I will multiply the fruit of your trees and the increase of your fields, so that you need never again bear the reproach of famine among the nations. Then you will remember your evil ways and your deeds that were not good; and you will loathe yourselves in your own sight, for your iniquities and your abominations. Not for your sake do I do this," says the Lord God, "let it be known to you. Be ashamed and confounded for your own ways, O house of Israel!"

"'Thus says the Lord God: "On the day that I cleanse you from all your iniquities, I will also enable you to dwell in the cities, and the ruins shall be rebuilt. The desolate land shall be tilled instead of lying desolate in the sight of all who pass by.

"So they will say, 'This land that was desolate has become like the garden of Eden; and the wasted, desolate, and ruined cities are now fortified and inhabited.' Then the nations which are left all around you shall know that I, the Lord, have rebuilt the ruined places and planted what was desolate. I, the Lord, have spoken it, and I will do it."
(Ezek. 36:22–36)

These are some of the things God does when He brings revival:

1. He reveals to us the holiness of His name.
2. He cleanses us from all impurities and substitutes for His presence.
3. He removes our hardened heart and gives a tender one in its place.
4. He renews our spirit and gives us the desire to obey Him.
5. He saves us from sin's bondage.
6. He restores what was taken away during His discipline and judgment.
7. He removes our disgrace.
8. He causes us to view our evil behavior in the same light God sees it.
9. He rebuilds our broken lives.

What Does Revival Look Like?

Many people have preconceived ideas of what revival looks like when it comes. Here are three examples:

1. Some people see revival as a well-planned series of services. After much prayer and personal preparation, God's people gather to hear anointed preaching. Under that preaching, conviction comes, and people respond with broken and contrite hearts and return to the Lord.

2. Others think revival cannot be planned. They believe revival is always a spontaneous response to God's presence and holiness. During a service, with no advanced warning, the Holy Spirit suddenly brings deep conviction of sin, and "everything breaks loose" as people get right with God.

3. When a church has changed for the better, that constitutes revival to some. They may say: "Our church is not the same as it used to be. We have grown to love one another and to love the Lord more than we ever did before. People are serious in their desire to obey God's will. We are united with one heart and spirit. But it didn't used to be that way. I can't explain what happened. Somehow over the past two years our church has changed."

Which of the above is genuine revival? They all may be. The essence of revival is that God's people return to Him and He returns to His people. Revival could be diagramed in this way:

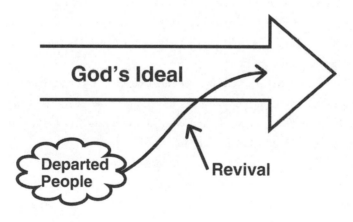

God has a standard for how He expects His people to function in a proper relationship with Him. When they are living as He intended, spiritual awakening is a natural by-product. Before revival, people who have departed from God live their lives far from His ideal for them. They have strayed from God's presence, His purposes, and His ways. Revival occurs when God draws His people to repent and return to Him. When people return and are rightly related to God, revival has occurred. However, that can happen in a multitude of ways. In fact, God can cause each experience of revival to be unique. He doesn't want us to look for a program, a method, or a set pattern. He wants us to look to Him.

This means one church's return to the Lord may be experienced as a process. Under the regular preaching and teaching of God's Word, the people—out of love for their Lord—hear God's call and return one step at a time. It is a progression, wherein, over a period of time, they have moved from where they once were to where God intends for them to be. That is revival. You could call it renewal or use some other term, but they have returned. Under the powerful, biblical preaching of Charles Haddon Spurgeon, the people in his Metropolitan Tabernacle experienced almost continual revival for several decades. People's lives were regularly being transformed, and converts were steadily received.

In another congregation the people could be going about their normal religious activity. Then one day they face a crisis, or they are confronted with a biblical truth in such a compelling way that God grips His people with conviction of sin. In a deeply emotional time, people may flood the altar at the close of a worship service. They weep, pray, and publicly confess sin. In a short period of time, God accomplishes what many thought could never happen. This might be a time when God has been calling, but He has faced resistance. Then in His sovereign choice, He decides to deal deeply with sin in a profound outpouring of His Spirit. This, too, is revival if the people have returned to a right relationship to the Lord. There is no one correct formula for how God revives His people.

As we studied revivals in Scripture, we saw that God also worked on scheduled days and times for covenant renewal. He can send genuine revival to a people who have sincerely sought Him in prayer and who join in a scheduled event to examine their spiritual lives and return to the Lord.

As you anticipate that God is working to send revival to the people where you fellowship or serve, don't expect God to work in only one way. He is sovereign. Expect Him to act any way He chooses. The fruits of revival can be the same regardless of whether you return to the Lord gradually over time or during a sudden dramatic event.

When Revival Comes

When God restores His people, He takes them into the mainstream of His mighty redemptive activity throughout history. Spiritual awakening waits on revival in the hearts of His people. You will know revival has come when God returns to His people. There will be evidence, including:

- the return of God's manifest presence
- new freedom
- new joy
- new peace
- true worship
- deep love for and faith in Jesus
- clean and clear conscience
- Christlikeness
- reconciliation (among individuals, couples, families, groups, churches, denominations)
- holiness
- moral changes based on love for God, not just a reformed behavior
- advance of the church, though the gates of hell try to prevail
- God's voice clearly speaking
- answered prayers
- power of the Spirit evident to all
- integrity lived out, like Jesus
- increased love for one another
- increased hunger and love for God's Word
- new burden for unbelievers

Responding to Revival

You may see other evidence of genuine revival. Be attentive to ways God will reveal what He is doing in your midst. When revival comes, a spiritual leader needs to proceed with great caution and much prayer to make sure nothing is done to quench the Spirit of revival. Here are some words of caution to consider when revival comes:

Immediately adjust your schedule to facilitate what God is doing.

At times God may initiate a work in our midst; but if we do not adjust our schedules in response, the work of renewal will be extinguished. Revival cannot be squeezed into our busy schedule or slated into our church calendar. Revival immediately takes center stage and relegates everything else to the side.

Duncan Campbell's passion for the Lord had waned during his seventeen years as a pastor. Though he was respected by his congregation and he administered the ministry of his church faithfully, he knew in his heart that there was no spiritual power in his ministry. He said, "Oh, the deceit of the human heart! I knew how unfit I was. . . . I knew barrenness . . . barrenness . . . in *my* spirit."[10] Campbell's sixteen-year-old daughter asked to see him in his study one day and said, "Daddy, when you were a pilgrim in the Faith Mission, after the First World War, you saw revival in Scotland. You saw revival! Daddy, how is it that God is not using you in revival today? Tell me Daddy, when did you last lead a soul to Christ?" Smitten by the innocent question of his daughter, Campbell confessed, "Thank God for faithful daughters! And I tell you, dear people, that shook me. Oh, it shook me! I knew! I knew! Campbell, a convention speaker . . . in his study, smashed and broken by a question from his daughter."

Haunted by his daughter's questions, Campbell knew he had to get right with God. He announced to his wife and daughter, "I'm going to my study and I want you to leave me alone. I'm going to seek a meeting with God." Campbell lay down on the rug in front of the fireplace and cried out to God. God met him early the next morning in an awesome, unforgettable experience that empowered and shaped Campbell's ministry for the remainder of his life. A power came to his preaching that had previously been missing. Wherever he went, revival came. Campbell had been a busy but powerless minister. Only after he set everything in his schedule aside except for seeking God's face did God do a transforming work in his life.

In a similar fashion D. L. Moody was challenged that God wanted to take him to a deeper dimension in his faith. While preaching in a camp meeting in June 1871, he noticed two women, Mrs. Cooke and Mrs. Hawxhurst, sitting on the front row praying fervently. After the service they informed the preacher that they had been praying for him. "Why don't you pray for the people?" Moody asked. "Because you need the power of the Holy Spirit," they replied.[11] Their comment haunted Moody. He claimed, "There came a great hunger into my soul. I did not know what it was. I began to cry out as I never did before. I really felt that I did not want to live if I could not have this power for service."

The next few weeks were momentous for the evangelist. He lost almost everything he had in the Chicago fire. Yet he continued to sense a deep need in his life to be fully consecrated to God and to be filled with the Holy Spirit. Moody had been unwilling to leave Chicago and to become a traveling evangelist. Finally, while walking down a busy street in New York, he quietly but fully surrendered his will to

God. Immediately he experienced an overpowering sense of God's presence. So overwhelming was it that he quickly found a room where he could meet alone with God. He later claimed that the room in which he retired seemed "ablaze with God," and he spent the next several hours basking in God's almighty presence. God came so near to him that Moody asked the Lord to stay His hand out of fear that His awesome presence might kill him.[12] As in Campbell's case, Moody's ministry was dramatically changed. In fact, after that encounter with God, Moody could not recall a time he preached when someone was not converted.

Churches, like these two spiritually sensitive men of God, must be willing to make any necessary adjustments so they are receptive to what God intends to do in their midst. They must yield their schedule to God so He has the time required to revive His people. Revival does not fit into neat, one-hour time slots. Services can often last for hours as people confess and weep before the Lord. Additional prayer times become necessary. People seek counseling until late into the night. Phone calls come at all hours from people seeking peace with God. The reason revival does not come to some churches is because they are unwilling to adjust so much as the order of the announcements to accommodate a fresh moving of God's Spirit among them.

Don't try to defend revival.

Revival will always have detractors. Just as religious leaders rejected Jesus when He came to them, so every revival in history has had those who denounced it and attempted to explain it away. Whether you are experiencing personal or corporate revival, do not let yourself become so distracted by answering your critics that you lose focus on your Lord. Just as Jesus did not attempt to convince His opponents of the validity of His message and ministry, so you ought not focus on those who do not believe.

Every person God has used in revival has been criticized and had their motives and methods scrutinized and second-guessed. After facing intense criticism during a time of revival, Charles Finney commented: "That the brethren who opposed these revivals were good men, I do not doubt. That they were misled and grossly and most injuriously deceived, I have just as little doubt."[13] Finney refused to take personal offense at those who opposed revival. Rather, their opposition confirmed his belief that they were of all people most in need of revival themselves.

The danger with criticism is that it can foster pride. Soon we are more intent on defending *our* reputation than we are determined to exalt God's name. The best defense against criticism is a profound sense of humility. Henry Scougal observed: "But the humble person hath the advantage, when he is despised, that none can think more meanly of him than he doth of himself; and therefore he is not troubled at the matter, but can easily bear those reproaches which would wound the other to the soul."[14]

If Satan cannot discourage you in the work of revival, he will attempt to distract you. Always stay in the light and what the light is accomplishing. Don't be distracted by prolonged, futile discussions with the darkness. Scripture indicates: "But wisdom is justified by all her children" (Luke 7:35). Allow God and the passing of time to prove that what you experienced was indeed from Him.

Be alert to potential problems that can hinder the continuation of revival.

These may include physical exhaustion, publicity, people seeking to control what is happening, impure motives, pride rather than brokenness in testimonies, emotionalism instead of genuine encounters with God, activity replacing relationship, people-centered rather than God-centered responses, rushed "repentance" that stops short of changed lifestyles, a dependence on methods instead of God, and a focus on decisions rather than conversions. Every revival has eventually come to an end, but if a congregation gets sidetracked from its focus, the time of renewal may be extinguished far sooner than God intended.

Don't try to steal God's glory.

Encourage people to testify to God's work in their lives, even when it is still in process. Don't glorify a corrupt past. Christian testimonies can inadvertently make celebrities out of people who previously indulged in a sinful lifestyle. The bulk of their testimony focuses on their sordid past while God's work hardly merits more than a footnote. Going into lengthy detail on our sinful past merely gives glory to Satan and his work. The focus ought always to be on God and how He set people free from their bondage of sin. People ought to point the glory to God and not to other people, the church, a course, or a method. God may have used others, but give God the ultimate credit for orchestrating your life events in order to revive you.

Don't overpublicize.

A well-known speaker and writer was said to have experienced a great move of God in his church. Sometime later he was asked what had happened to the movement.

His response was, "I reported it to death." Reports of God's activity often spread the flames of revival. Talking about God's activity is important, but avoid these pitfalls: (1) You may be tempted to steal God's glory and claim credit for the work. (2) Don't become so busy reporting the happenings that the revival fires die out for lack of attention. (3) Resist the temptation to exaggerate or sensationalize what happened in an effort to promote God and His work. Revival, by its nature, has an influence on surrounding areas. In fact, it is impossible to suppress the reverberating effects when the Holy Spirit comes in power. Rely on the Holy Spirit to guide you in knowing when and where you ought to share with others what God has done in your life and church.

Don't neglect your home church.

When people experience revival, our tendency is to put them on a speaking circuit so they are constantly away from their home and church telling others what happened. The danger, as time goes by, is that the speaker begins to live on yesterday's experience with God. You cannot give to others what you do not have. Sometimes when people are asked to give a testimony of God's working in their lives, they find they must go farther and farther back in time because they have been too distracted to experience God in the present. Some people are still giving talks to church groups about what God did in their lives twenty or thirty years ago, but they have nothing to report of His activity in their lives during the last year. God is always at work in our midst. We must watch that we are not so enamored with the past that we fail to join His activity today.

Enlist prayer partners.

If you have experienced a time of personal or corporate revival, enlist others to pray regularly with you to preserve and build on the work God began in your life and your church. With God every work He does is preparatory. There is always more He will do if we will faithfully respond to what He reveals to us. The best way to continue moving forward with God is to have people faithfully and regularly praying for you.

Keep your focus God centered, not people centered.

Be purposeful in the way you talk about God's activity. If you discover you are using a large percentage of personal pronouns—I, my, mine, me—it may indicate your life and your focus is self-centered rather than God centered. Revival is a radical reshifting of our lives where we return our focus and concern to Christ and away from ourselves. If we are not careful, the excitement and emotion of revival can tempt us to think we had an important role to play in the revival and that we are somehow more spiritual than those who are not experiencing revival. Henry Scougal observed, "It is a silly ignorance that begets pride; but humility arises from a nearer acquaintance with excellent things, which keeps men from doating on trifles, or admiring themselves because of some petty attainments."[15]

At the height of D. L. Moody's fame, an evangelist named "Uncle Johnnie" Vasser commented to Moody, "How glad I am to see the man that God has used to win so many souls to Christ."[16] To which Moody bent down and scooped up a handful of dirt and let it pour through his fingers. "You say rightly, Uncle John, the man whom *God has used*. . . . There is nothing more than *that* to D. L. Moody, except as God uses him!" Moody's genuine humility made him pliable in God's hands for revival.

Continue in God's Word.

If you have experienced personal renewal, stay regularly in God's Word so the Holy Spirit can deepen and continue the work He has begun in your life. If revival comes to your church, don't become so focused on the testimonies of others that you neglect going to the Scriptures yourself for a fresh word from God. Historically, revivals based on Scripture last much longer than those built on experience and testimonies. Scripture keeps us focused on God and His expectations. Testimonies can bring unbiblical views and teachings into a revival which can quickly quench God's work in that place.

Watch for God to broaden the revival to encompass the broader Christian community.

Be keenly aware that when God does a work in your life, it is generally for you to share. God created us to be interdependent. We need one another. When God entrusts you with a deep encounter with Him and a fresh insight into His Word, that is for you to bear witness to others. If your church experiences revival, invite others to join you. J. Edwin Orr once expressed his opinion that he did not believe God would initiate revival in certain denominations because they were too isolated, having few relationships with churches of other denominations. He observed that when God brings revival, He wants to refresh all His churches. Therefore, God often brings revival to individuals, churches, or denominations that have cultivated relationships with fellow believers from various backgrounds so the streams of revival quickly flow throughout God's kingdom when they are poured out by God's Spirit.

Wheaton College Revival, 1995

On Sunday night, March 19, 1995, about seven hundred students gathered on the campus of Wheaton College in Wheaton, Illinois, for a World Christians Fellowship. That night two students from Howard Payne University (Brownwood, Texas) shared testimonies about the emergence of revival on their campus the previous month. The service began at 7:30 p.m. and continued till 6:00 a.m. the next morning as student after student stood to confess their sins. As young men and women confessed, they were immediately surrounded by fellow students who prayed with them.

When it became clear that more confession still needed to take place, they agreed to meet again that evening at 9:30 p.m. That evening several large trash bags were placed along the front of the meeting room, and students were given the opportunity to throw away things that hindered their walk with the Lord or that tempted them to sin. Five bags were filled with drugs, alcohol, pornography, secular music, and even credit cards. At 2:00 a.m. God was still dealing with students. In order to give students time to rest, the meeting was concluded for the night, and another meeting was planned for the next day. These meetings continued for four nights as the Spirit continued to do His work across the campus.

During the sessions, time was given to worship and praise. Scripture reading and impromptu special music was interspersed between times of confession. On Wednesday leaders recognized the need for specific instruction from Scripture to keep the responses in a manner that honored God and His Word. Three school officials spoke on dealing with temptation, sin, and discipleship for Christian growth. By the end of Wednesday's session all students who desired to confess sin publicly had done so. Students formed small groups to hold one another accountable for the commitments they made. Students who were not already in a group were adopted by a group before they left the session.

Thursday evening's session was given to praise and thanksgiving for what God had done. Students shared testimonies of the victories they experienced or told about what God was teaching them. At the conclusion of that session, a call was issued for students to surrender their lives to full-time Christian service, and more than two hundred students responded. Testimonies from Wheaton began to spread to other colleges, universities, seminaries, and churches. God intervened in the daily life of

His people. Those God met with sought to respond to God's visitation in a biblical manner. The world continues to feel the impact of that encounter.[17]

Conclusion

Revival is a sovereign work of God. Yet He invites us to participate in it. Those who are sensitive to the Spirit's working can be invited into the middle of God's powerful, life-transforming activity. While we cannot orchestrate revival, we can prepare our hearts and lives so we recognize when God is at work. We can consecrate our lives so we can serve as holy instruments in God's hands. Let us strive to have lives that are ready when the Holy Spirit begins to work in and around us so we are able to participate fully in all He does.

QUESTIONS FOR REFLECTION AND DISCUSSION

1. What are some of the pitfalls to avoid when revival comes?
2. What should be done to encourage and sustain revival when it comes?
3. What are some ways to ensure we do not rob God of His glory during revival?
4. What are some ways believers mishandle revival when it comes?
5. Have you ever been part of revival? If so, how did you know it was God at work?

CHAPTER 12

Great Awakenings: The Fruit of Revival

A Testimony of the Moravian Brethren[1]

In the 1720s about three hundred people moved to the estate of Count Nicholas Ludwig von Zinzendorf to escape religious persecution. Most were Moravians, a religious group associated with the martyr John Hus. But the refugees included Lutherans, followers of Calvin and Zwingli, Anabaptists, and others. In the spring of 1727 internal conflict came close to destroying the religious community. Zinzendorf and three other elders drew up a covenant of brotherly union describing the way these Christians would live together. It recognized their differences but insisted on love and unity in the body of Christ.

On May 12, 1727, the entire community repented of their divisions, were reconciled with their brethren and entered a covenant to live in harmony to honor their Lord.

> "The Brethren all promised, one by one, that they would be the Saviour's true followers. Self-will, self-love, disobedience—they bade these farewell. They would seek to be poor in spirit; no one was to seek his own profit before that of others; everyone would give himself to be taught by the Holy Spirit."

God began to bind this body of believers together in love and unity. On August 13, 1727, they had a significant encounter with their Savior at a Lord's Supper observance.

On Sunday, 10th, Pastor Rothe was leading the afternoon meeting at Herrnhut, when he was overpowered and fell on his face before God. The whole congregation bowed under the sense of God's presence and continued in prayer until midnight. He invited the congregation to the Holy Supper on the next Wednesday, the 13th. As it was the first communion since the new fellowship, it was resolved to be especially strict with it and to make use of it "to lead the souls deeper into the death of Christ, into which they had been baptized." The leaders visited every member, seeking in love to lead them to true heart-searching. In the evening of Tuesday, at the preparation service, several passed from death to life, and the whole community was deeply touched.

"On the Wednesday morning all went to Berthelsdorf. On the way thither, any who had felt estranged from each other afresh bound themselves together. During the singing of the first hymn a wicked man was powerfully convicted. The presentation of the new communicants touched every heart, and when the hymn was sung it could hardly be recognized whether there was more singing or weeping. Several brethren prayed, specially pleading that, as exiles out of the house of bondage, they knew not what to do, that they desired to be kept free from separation and sectarianism, and besought the Lord to reveal to them the true nature of His Church, so that they might walk unspotted before Him, might not abide alone but be made fruitful. We asked that we might do nothing contrary to the oath of loyalty we had taken to Him, nor in the very least sin against His law of love. We asked that He would keep us in the saving power of His grace, and not allow a single soul to be drawn away to itself and its own merits from that Blood-and-Cross Theology, on which our salvation depends. We celebrated the Lord's Supper with hearts at once bowed down and lifted up. We went home, each of us in great measure lifted up beyond himself, spending this and the following days in great quiet and peace, and learning to love."

Among those present in the church when the communion was held were a number of children. One writes: "I cannot attribute the great revival among the children to anything else but that wonderful outpouring of the Holy Spirit on the communion assembly. The Spirit breathed in power on old and young. Everywhere they were heard, sometimes at night in the field, beseeching the Saviour to pardon their sins and make them His own. The Spirit of grace had indeed been poured out."[2]

Following that encounter with Christ, the Moravian Brethren were ingrained with a zeal for missions. They began a twenty-four-hour prayer watch for the causes of Christ's kingdom, which continued for more than one hundred years. During the following twenty-five years they sent out more than one hundred missionaries.

Once God revived this group of Moravian believers, their pure faith and gentle spirits invariably drew others to Christ. Among those were at least two men whose lives greatly impacted God's kingdom. Some of those missionaries met John Wesley, a passenger onboard a ship bound for America in 1735. In them Wesley saw a personal faith in God and a love for Christ as well as a calm assurance he did not have. When he returned to London, Wesley came to a personal faith in Christ in a Moravian chapel at Aldersgate. He went from there a different man and led the evangelical revival in England. Even William Carey, known as the father of modern missions, was greatly influenced toward missions by the testimonies of these Moravian missionaries.

Revivals and Spiritual Awakenings

Arthur Wallis observed: "Clearly it is the saints, not the sinners, that are primarily involved in revival. The quickening of the saints is the root, while the saving of the sinners is the fruit."[3]

Although authors define revival and spiritual awakening in various ways, we see a distinction between revival and spiritual awakening. Revival is for God's people, for Christians who have given their lives to Christ but whose faith has wavered and whose spiritual vibrancy has waned. Revival renews the flames of fervent love for Christ the believer once knew. Revival brings God's people back to Himself. Spiritual awakening applies to the unbelieving world. It involves the conversion of a great number of people over a brief period of time. It is evangelism on a massive and rapid scale. Spiritual awakenings generally occur after God's people have been revived.

Because revivals and spiritual awakenings go hand in hand, they are often considered to be the same thing. However, it is important that, in the excitement of seeing so many people put their faith in Christ for the first time, God's people do not neglect the equally miraculous and absolutely vital work of revival. Without the church first being brought back to spiritual vitality, there will not be a spiritual awakening.

Brian Edwards noted there is "little that is new" in revival. That is, all the elements of revival, such as preaching, singing, praying, testifying, and repenting are activities that ought to characterize the church at all times. Edwards notes that revival is not normative Christianity. It is restorative Christianity, bringing God's people back to where they should be. Says Edwards, "Revival is not normal any more than spiritual decline and backsliding is normal. These are opposite ends of the normal life of the church. Revival is supernormal and backsliding is subnormal."[4]

Likewise, spiritual awakening does not necessarily contain elements foreign to normal Christianity and church life. Christ has clearly commanded His disciples to go and make disciples of all nations (Matt. 28:18–20). Evangelism ought to characterize every church. What is unusual about spiritual awakening is its intensity and depth of impact in a short period of time. Jonathan Edwards believed revivals were God's method of periodically gathering in a large harvest of souls into the church. While Edwards faithfully preached and taught his congregation, he always prayed for the next great spiritual awakening God would send. Edwards did not slacken in his duties while awaiting the next harvest. Rather, Edwards vigorously prepared his people for the next divine visitation while diligently teaching those who had entered the church during the previous mighty movement of God.

Arthur Wallis notes, "Again and again the history of revival has been the history of God's intervention to retrieve what was hopeless." Wallis noted that revival "is designed to achieve what the quiet workings of the Spirit do not."[5] Spiritual awakenings are periods when God intervenes into a spiritually darkened world and brings large numbers of people to a saving faith in Him. Just as revivals impact believers in many ways ordinary religion does not, so spiritual awakenings produce in a short period and on a massive scale what ordinary missions and evangelism generally achieve over a much longer period of time.

God's Merciful Timing

God's ways are not our ways (Isa. 55:8–9). As the psalmist wisely asked the Almighty to "teach me Your way, O LORD" (Ps. 27:11), so it behooves God's people to learn and recognize the ways of their Lord. Why does God choose, in His sovereignty, suddenly to draw large numbers of people to Himself over a brief time period? Why is there a sense of urgency in times of revival and spiritual awakening? There are many reasons. For one thing God knows the future.

Pentecost

During the time of Pentecost in Jerusalem, thousands of people accepted the gospel message preached by Peter and the early church. The Christian movement was birthed and set in motion around the known world. But what did God know that the citizens of Jerusalem did not? Four decades later Roman legions would surround the city and level it, killing thousands of people. Judgment was coming on the city. Some of those saved at Pentecost might one day lose their lives at the end of a Roman sword. The people of Jerusalem did not have an indefinite period of time to turn to Christ. It was critical that the Holy Spirit produce a great ingathering at Pentecost.

The First Great Awakening

The First Great Awakening in America began around 1734 and lasted until 1770, the year of George Whitefield's death. Thousands of people across colonial America found salvation during that period. What did God know that Americans did not? They would soon be at war with the greatest superpower of their day, and the seemingly invincible British army would invade American soil. The land would be pillaged, battlefields would scar the countryside, and many of the young men converted in the revival meetings would be cut down on the battlefields. Unbeknownst to many of those saved during the First Great Awakening, this would be their last opportunity to be reconciled with their Creator before they stood before Him in judgment.

Layman's Prayer Revival

Between 1857 and 1858 a great awakening stemmed from the prayer meetings held in Manhattan, begun by a layman named Jeremiah Lanphier. An estimated one million people were converted within one year and added to the churches. Even as churches across America were celebrating the influx of new converts into their ranks, God knew that the most horrific war in America's history was just a few years away. More than 600,000 young men would die in the carnage of the Civil War, thousands of whom had only recently given their lives to Christ during the awakening of 1857–1858.

The Great Awakening of 1904–1905

In 1904 God initiated a great awakening in Wales under Evan Roberts. Within six months 100,000 people in Wales had been converted. That revival spread globally so that people around the world experienced revival, and thousands upon thousands of people were converted. Only God could have known that a decade later an appalling human slaughter would occur as millions of young men were butchered in the trenches of World War I.

Ruanda and Uganda Revival

During the 1930s and again in the 1970s two revivals occurred in Ruanda and Uganda.[6] Thousands of people were converted during these times of revival and awakening. While Christians around the world rejoiced that people in Africa were turning to the Lord, God knew of the genocide that would eventually occur between the Hutus and Tutsis in which hundreds of thousands of innocent people would be mercilessly slain. Thousands of Christians and church leaders would be brutally massacred during these uprisings.

How should the history of spiritual awakenings affect the way God's people live? First we should have a keen spiritual eye for the moving of the Holy Spirit. Christians ought always to stay informed about where God is working mightily in the world. Christians who choose to remain ignorant of world affairs are not taking their citizenship in God's kingdom seriously. When we become Christians, we simultaneously become citizens of the kingdom of God. That kingdom includes every Christian and Christian church in the world. Every believer becomes our brother or sister.

Second, when we see God working powerfully in a region of the world, we must ask the Lord, "What do you know about the future that is affecting what You are doing today?" Could it be God is aware of coming strife, epidemic, war, famine, or natural disasters that will obliterate large numbers of people? Could this awakening be the last opportunity for many people to come to a saving faith in Christ?

Third, wise Christians are always seeking the Lord's guidance to know how we should personally become involved in God's activity. When God was doing a massive work in Ruanda in the 1970s, churches in the west did not understand what was at stake. They rejoiced that those missionaries and church leaders assigned to that area of the world were experiencing success. Later, when the rivers were gorged with Christian corpses, many horrified western Christians wished they had done more to undergird God's work when they had the opportunity.

Today God is mightily at work in countries such as South Korea and regions in Africa. As we see God's handiwork around the globe, we must ask ourselves, "What does God know about the future that is motivating the work He is accomplishing today?"

Social and Educational Impact

Among the marked results of great awakenings, in addition to large numbers of converts added to the churches, are the enormous social changes that occur as many people turn to God. For example, the Second Great Awakening had an enormous impact in the United States and its social and moral climate. J. Edwin Orr cited H. H. Sweet, American historian who claimed that "the last two decades of the eighteenth century were the darkest period, spiritually and morally, in the history of American Christianity, the low water mark of its lowest ebb tide, when infidelity rode roughshod over the feelings of the disoriented majority."[7] At that time there were only two students at Princeton University who openly professed to be religious. Students at Williams College conducted a mock Communion service. The "filthy speech" movement was popular, encouraging people to use the most shocking profanity. Christians were so unpopular in Ivy League schools, which were permeated with deism, that they met in secret and kept their minutes in code. During this period Chief Justice Marshall wrote to Bishop Madison of Virginia and declared that the church was too far gone to be redeemed.

Christians became scandalized at the sinister spiritual climate pervading society. With the atheistic teachings of David Hume and Thomas Paine being widely embraced by college students and their professors, American society seemed to have fallen irredeemably far from God. The young people of that era were steeped in skepticism and a profound worldliness. Significantly many of the greatest movements of God have begun among young people. During the First Great Awakening in the 1730s, Jonathan Edwards noticed it was among the formerly party-going young adults that a renewed interest in spiritual things began.[8]

Likewise the Second Great Awakening may be traced to a spiritual stirring among students at Hampton Sydney College in Virginia in 1787.[9] Four students—William Hill, Cary Allen, James Blythe, and Clement Read, none of whom had been active Christians—met together because they were appalled at the moral condition of their school. At one point they locked themselves in a room and spoke quietly for fear of being discovered by other students. However, after some initial opposition, over half the student body placed their faith in Christ.[10]

Dwight Edwards, grandson of Jonathan Edwards, became president of Yale University during this period. He began a series of sermons entitled "Is the Bible the Word of God?" to challenge the atheistic teaching of his day. God's Spirit enveloped the student body, and many students were converted. In 1798 a revival swept Williams College that ultimately motivated a group of students to spearhead the formation of the first foreign missions agency in North America.

The Second Great Awakening eventually spread to the American West. A Presbyterian minister named James McGready went to Logan County, Kentucky, in 1798, arriving at a place called "Rogue's Harbor," the favored destination for criminals who fled over the mountains to the frontier to escape the law. The people of that community were a hardened group of pioneers with scant interest in religion. McGready decided to conduct a Lord's Supper service for those who had been unable to participate in Communion since coming to the frontier. Surprisingly thousands of people participated, and revival swept through the crowds. The camp meeting emerged on the American frontier at that time. Camp meetings became times, usually after harvest, when people gathered from all over the region at a large campsite to hear preaching and to partake in Communion. At Cane Ridge, Kentucky, as many as twenty-five thousand people gathered for the meetings. The crowd was so vast that as many as seven preachers would preach simultaneously in various sections of the gathering. Great numbers of converts as well as revived believers resulted from these annual gatherings. During the latter part of the Second Great Awakening, Charles G. Finney adopted many aspects of the camp meetings and brought them to cities in the East where God worked powerfully through his ministry. These practices were adopted by other churches and evangelists and developed into what became known as annual "revival meetings."

The results of the Second Great Awakening were extensive and long lasting. From 1800 to 1830 Presbyterians quadrupled their membership.[11] Baptist membership swelled from 64,975 to 517,523. There was also a major increase in the emergence of societies as a result of the awakening. As people were drawn into a love relationship with Christ, they naturally began to care about the same things their Lord did. Numerous societies for home and foreign missions were spawned. The American Bible Society was established in 1816. Various Sunday school unions were established to teach people the Scripture. Organizations such as the YMCA were established. Many of those who were converted during the awakening felt called into Christian ministry and subsequently enrolled in seminaries. Princeton Seminary and Yale Divinity School were formed at this time. Music was also affected by the awakening, bringing many camp meeting songs into the mainstream of church worship services. Significantly there was also a noticeable alteration in America's moral climate. Crime rates plummeted. Occurrences of drunkenness declined steeply. Families were restored. God's Spirit awakened a nation and brought it from the precipice of judgment back to Him.

In spiritual awakenings, the Holy Spirit works in powerful, mysterious ways to draw large numbers of people to Christ. Lewis Drummond notes, "A spiritual awakening always soars on the wings of the word."[12] Whereas sermons may have been preached before with little or no effect, when the Holy Spirit begins to move powerfully among people, an authority comes to the sermons, not from the orators but from the Spirit who anoints them. Duncan Campbell witnessed many people converted to Christ during the revival in the Hebrides. But Campbell said: "I never spoke to a single person in that village in an endeavor to help them find the Savior! We just left them to God and God did it! That is why you haven't a single backslider in that whole community. Oh, my dear people, when God does a work, He does it well!"[13]

Spiritual Awakening in Wales

The nation of Wales has been blessed with a series of revivals and spiritual awakenings over the years. During the 1857 Layman's Prayer Revival in New York, Christians in the British Isles watched and prayed that the same Spirit who was bringing hundreds of thousands of Americans to faith in Christ would revive their land as well. Humphrey Jones, a church leader from Wales, had been in the United States and witnessed the marvelous working of the Holy Spirit. Upon his return to Wales, he longed for God to do a similar work among his own people. Jones began challenging his countrymen at every opportunity that it would be through an "awakened" church God would convert the world.[14]

A pastor named David Morgan confided in Humphrey that he wanted to gather people to pray for revival, but he was concerned the endeavor would merely be a human effort and not divinely empowered. Humphrey replied: "You cannot do any harm . . . and if you try it, you will not be long before God will be with you."[15]

When the Spirit did descend in power upon Wales, Morgan explained what he learned about revival:

> Two things are necessary to be a successful preacher: first, *to pray much in secret*—to be there many times in the day, wrestling with God—to wrestle each time as if it were the last, and not to rise from your knees until you have a proof that the Lord has heard you. Ask the Lord in faith, and with great fervency, what to say to the people. Go straight from your closet to the pulpit each time (like Moses from the mount to the camp), then will the anointing follow your preaching, and every word you say will be received as from an angel from God. . . . I would wish to preach each time as if I had to die in the pulpit when I am done preaching—as if I had to go direct from the pulpit to judgment.[16]

Revival came to Wales through people such as Morgan and Humphrey. The power of the Holy Spirit's presence was palpable in the services. One preacher testified of a congregation, "They appear as if they had been shot by the truth." Not surprisingly the revival first erupted among young people. As God worked among the youth, the Spirit soon gained the attention of the adults. During one service a young girl went to the front of the church and implored the people to pray for her wayward father whose heart was hardened toward God. As the young girl tearfully interceded for her father, there was a commotion in the auditorium and it became apparent the girl's father was present. That day he felt drawn to the service and now, there in the auditorium, before his devout daughter, he was overwhelmed with conviction for his sin and he cried out to God for forgiveness.[17]

While there were strong preachers such as David Morgan, this revival did not showcase celebrity preachers. The Holy Spirit empowered His ordinary servants and His churches dramatically to impact their nation. "The power that accompanied the word was very great; it was a melting power, a power which riveted the attention of every one present." Everywhere people's thoughts were on eternity. In some towns drunkenness all but disappeared. The revival reached the coal mines. One mine reported that all but one of the miners had been converted, and that calloused, remaining sinner was being deluged with a torrent of earnest prayers for his conversion.[18] When spiritual awakening comes to a city or nation, even unbelievers recognize God is present and at work in their midst.

In the fall of 1904, a fresh awakening encompassed Wales that surpassed the one in 1859–1860. During six months 100,000 people were converted in a great spiritual awakening. There had been no organized campaign. There was no advertising, public relations, radio broadcast, or program for outreach. God did a sovereign work that captured the attention of the world.

After the Welsh Revival of 1859–1860, the next generation saw the cycle continue that characterizes God's people; and by the turn of the century, church membership was again declining. People were apathetic to spiritual matters. Church services were stiff and formal. Once again God's people needed revival.

In 1904 God was evidently at work in many places throughout Wales. The nation was like a tinderbox God prepared for the quick spread of revival fires. This time God chose a young man named Evan Roberts to ignite the flame. Roberts had worked in the coal mines as a young man. He was burdened for revival in his land. For thirteen years he prayed for an outpouring of God's Spirit. Prayer meetings with different groups of God's people became a major emphasis in his life. Early in 1904 Roberts accepted God's call on his life to preach, and he went to school to prepare.

While attending a service led by Seth Joshua, Roberts heard Joshua pray: "Lord, bend us." The Spirit touched Evan's heart with that statement. He bowed his head and pled with God, "O Lord, bend me!"

God gave Roberts a burden to return to his home church in Loughor for a week of services with the young people. Following a Monday night prayer meeting on October 31, 1904, seventeen people remained after the service to hear Evan's message. His sermon had four points:

1. You must put away any unconfessed sin.
2. You must put away any doubtful habit.
3. You must obey the Spirit promptly.
4. You must confess Christ publicly.

That night all seventeen responded to his appeal. They decided to continue meeting. Attendance increased nightly. The Spirit was poured out on the area as God's people returned to Him. Unbelievers were dramatically converted—seventy thousand in two months, eighty-five thousand in five months, and more than 100,000 in the six months following that October meeting.

These were life-changing commitments. Taverns closed for lack of business. Sporting venues and dance halls had to cancel events because people were flocking to the churches instead. Crime dropped drastically, leaving the police little to do. People paid old debts and made restitution for thefts and other wrongs. Reportedly, there was even a work slowdown in the coal mines as the pit ponies had to learn the sanctified language of the converted miners![19] News of the revival spread to other countries, and Christians internationally were stirred to prayer. Soon God was at work across the globe bringing people to Him.

An Undiluted Gospel

J. Edwin Orr claimed that "defective evangelism" had become a "national scandal." He asked, "Is it not possible that many ills of the Christian life are due to handicapped beginnings in spiritual birth? That unfortunates, whose professed conversions were marred by a lack of understanding of what was involved, might find their spiritual life full of trials and woes not experienced by the children of God who were well born?"[20] In times of spiritual awakening, the gospel message is not watered down. Discussion of sin and its consequences is not avoided. The undiluted message of salvation has a powerful effect on people being drawn to Christ by His Spirit.

Spiritual awakening occurs when, over a short period of time, large numbers of people (or a high percentage of people in an area) experience new birth to spiritual life. Spiritual awakenings are not merely occasions of mass decisions for Christ. Decisions may or may not reflect a new birth. In a spiritual awakening people's lives are radically changed. Often a spiritual awakening results in a changed society, affecting a city or a even a nation. Major social reforms have often accompanied spiritual awakening. When people cast off the old life of sin and accept new life in Christ, their perspective on their own lifestyle and the way society behaves is completely altered. "If anyone is in Christ, he is a new creation; old things have passed away; behold, all things have become new" (2 Cor. 5:17).

Based on Scripture and the record of history, here are some changes you might observe during spiritual awakening:

- Bars and taverns close for lack of business.
- Police and law enforcement personnel see dramatic decreases in crime.
- Businesses receive money and merchandise from thieves, employees, and shoplifters returning stolen goods.
- Christians and churches begin serious efforts at helping the poor and needy in the community through orphanages, ministries to the homeless, and other ministries.
- Laws change or are enacted to protect the oppressed and to uphold justice.
- Reconciliation takes place between races and ethnic groups.
- Foul language is replaced by civil and wholesome talk.
- Evil practices, such as prostitution, cease and often are outlawed.
- Private and public acts of immorality decrease dramatically.
- Marriages are restored, and family life is strengthened.

Spiritual Awakening at Pentecost

Prior to Jesus' coming, the spiritual condition of Israel had declined dramatically. For over four hundred years, God's people had not heard a word from the Lord through His prophets. The Pharisees developed a legalistic spirit based on keeping the letter of the law without considering its spirit. There was no teaching regarding a personal and real relationship with the Lord. Temple worship became an academic action rather than a response of the heart. God's people desperately needed revival. "But when the fullness of the time had come, God sent forth His Son" (Gal. 4:4). God was preparing to call His people to repentance and revival. When Jesus first began to preach, His message was: "'Repent, for the kingdom of heaven is at hand'" (Matt. 4:17). Many did repent and return to the Lord. Revival was beginning among God's people.

During Christ's arrest, trial, and crucifixion, His disciples deserted Him. The days between Jesus' resurrection and glorious ascension provided time for renewal of the disciples. The risen Christ used these days to prepare the disciples for the mighty works God was going to do through them. "He also presented Himself alive after His suffering by many infallible proofs, being seen by them during forty days and speaking of the things pertaining to the kingdom of God" (Acts 1:3). Jesus pointed them to the Scriptures and explained everything they said about Him. "Beginning at Moses and all the Prophets, He expounded to them in all the Scriptures the things concerning Himself" (Luke 24:27). The Father was putting everything into place for the imminent outpouring of His Holy Spirit.

When the Holy Spirit came on the day of Pentecost, He empowered the early church to carry out the assignment He gave them. Without a divine assignment there was no need for Pentecost. At this point the disciples had already been revived. Now they were poised for a spiritual awakening that would catapult the church into becoming a force to be reckoned with. As a newly empowered people, they were beginning to experience the fullness of life God intended for His church.

> When the Day of Pentecost had fully come, they were all with one accord in one place. And suddenly there came a sound from heaven, as of a rushing mighty wind, and it filled the whole house where they were sitting. . . . And they were all filled with the Holy Spirit and began to speak with other tongues, as the Spirit gave them utterance.
>
> And there were dwelling in Jerusalem Jews, devout men, from every nation under heaven. And when this sound occurred, the multitude came together, and were confused, because everyone heard them speak in his own language. Then they were all amazed and marveled, saying to one another, "Look, are not all these who speak Galileans? And how is it that we hear, each in our own language in which we were born? . . . We hear them speaking in our own tongues the wonderful works of God." So they were all amazed and perplexed, saying to one another, "Whatever could this mean?" (Acts 2:1–2, 4–8, 11–12)

When God's people fully surrender themselves to the work of the Holy Spirit, God will draw a watching world to Himself. Peter answered the questions of the crowd by preaching from the Old Testament about the coming of the Holy Spirit. He then proclaimed Jesus as the Christ. The message was brief, but God was working through him, so the results had God-sized dimensions.

> "Therefore let all the house of Israel know assuredly that God has made this Jesus, whom you crucified, both Lord and Christ." Now when they heard this, they were cut to the heart, and said to Peter and the rest of the apostles, "Men and brethren, what shall we do?"
> Then Peter said to them, "Repent, and let every one of you be baptized in the name of Jesus Christ for the remission of sins; and you shall receive the gift of the Holy Spirit." . . .
> Then those who gladly received his word were baptized; and that day about three thousand souls were added to them. (Acts 2:36–38, 41)

This biblical account is our purest example of what God will do in spiritual awakening when His people are rightly related and fully surrendered to Him. God displayed His power through the believers as they spoke foreign languages they had not learned. After only a brief message, people "were cut to the heart" by the convicting work of the Holy Spirit. Three thousand people accepted the message, repented, were baptized, and received the gift of the Holy Spirit. The church began with 120 believers, and God added three thousand in a single day. That is spiritual awakening!

This is God's pattern—revival among God's people and then spiritual awakening among unbelievers. The early church's spiritual awakening continued in the first century:

> They continued steadfastly in the apostles' doctrine and fellowship, in the breaking of bread, and in prayers. Then fear came upon every soul, and many wonders and signs were done through the apostles. Now all who believed were together, and had all things in common, and sold their possessions and goods, and divided them among all, as anyone had need. So continuing daily with one accord in the temple, and breaking bread from house to house, they ate their food with gladness and simplicity of heart, praising God and having favor with all the people. And the Lord added to the church daily those who were being saved. (Acts 2:42–47)

The people in the early church were filled with awe as they observed the miraculous way God was working. Their lives were changed. They lived unselfishly with joyful and sincere hearts. They praised God and enjoyed the favor of everyone. This sounds like the kind of church that would draw unbelievers. The close relationship these early Christians enjoyed with the Father bound them together in love, and their Christlike love for one another attracted the people of Jerusalem. So the spiritual awakening continued. Here is what God was doing through His people:

- "Many of those who heard the word believed; and the number of the men came to be about five thousand" (Acts 4:4).
- "Believers were increasingly added to the Lord, multitudes of both men and women" (Acts 5:14).
- "The word of God spread, and the number of the disciples multiplied greatly in Jerusalem, and a great many of the priests were obedient to the faith" (Acts 6:7).
- "Then the churches throughout all Judea, Galilee, and Samaria had peace and were edified. And walking in the fear of the Lord and in the comfort of the Holy Spirit, they were multiplied" (Acts 9:31).
- "It became known throughout all Joppa, and many believed on the Lord" (Acts 9:42).
- "When the Gentiles heard this, they were glad and glorified the word of the Lord. And as many as had been appointed to eternal life believed. . . . And the disciples were filled with joy and with the Holy Spirit" (Acts 13:48, 52).
- "So the churches were strengthened in the faith, and increased in number daily" (Acts 16:5).
- "This became known both to all Jews and Greeks dwelling in Ephesus; and fear fell on them all, and the name of the Lord Jesus was magnified. And many who had believed came confessing and telling their deeds. Also, many of those who had practiced magic brought their books together and burned them in the sight of all. And they counted up the value of them, and it totaled fifty thousand pieces of silver. So the word of the Lord grew mightily and prevailed" (Acts 19:17–20).

Conclusion

Today's world has millions upon millions of people who have never heard the name of Christ. Many societies oppress their people and inflict grievous suffering on innocent victims. Natural disasters occur that extinguish thousands of lives in a moment. This world needs more than evangelism; it needs a global spiritual awakening. The world will not be won incrementally. Too many people will enter eternity without Christ if the church continues to reach people one by one. The Spirit of God yearns to bring in a massive harvest of souls as He has done in times past. God is not content that anyone should perish.

There has not been a great awakening in America for over a century. Society has deteriorated morally. Crime and violence have escalated. Countless marriages have failed. Suicide has become epidemic. God's people must be faithful to witness, to teach, and to minister; but it is incumbent upon every believer to pray regularly and fervently that God would send another great awakening that would bring millions of people into God's family and turn the nation back from its impending destruction. Any Christian who has a heart like God's must feel compelled to pray every day for God to send one more great awakening.

QUESTIONS FOR REFLECTION AND DISCUSSION

1. What is the difference between revival and spiritual awakening?
2. What strikes you most about the accounts of spiritual awakenings?
3. How do the events in the Gospels and Acts provide a model of what revival and spiritual awakening should look like?
4. What kinds of changes might God make in our community if we were to experience revival and spiritual awakening?

CHAPTER 13

The Role of Prayer in Revival

Crying Out to God

William M'Culloch was a faithful pastor but not a talented preacher. As a public speaker he was said to have "virtually no gifts."[1] His voice was reportedly "thin" and "weak," and he was slow of utterance. People claimed that he was "able, judicious, and faithful, yet no way distinguished as a popular preacher."[2] However he loved his people, and he had a burning desire to see them experience the same revival he had been reading about occurring in America under leaders like Jonathan Edwards and George Whitefield.

M'Culloch would customarily rise at five o'clock each morning to study and prepare for his preaching and teaching ministry until eight o'clock in the evening. He faithfully taught his people God's Word and lovingly ministered to them. But, like many pastors before and after him, he was discouraged that Sunday after Sunday the words of Scripture seemed to have little impact on his people.

On February 18, 1742, M'Culloch preached on Jeremiah 23:6 in hopes the verse would stir his people. However, as he drew his sermon to a close, the people routinely prepared to go home. The sight of his flock's continued indifference to God's Word broke M'Culloch's heart. He cried out to God from the pulpit, "Who hath believed our report, or to whom is the arm of the Lord revealed? Where is the fruit of my labor among this people?"[3]

The church began to fill with the sounds of anguished weeping as deep conviction for sin swept over the congregation. Immediately the people experienced a deep hunger to get right with God. Daily services ensued and lasted for almost seven months. Every evening the pastor saw a steady stream of people coming to his parsonage to receive counsel and instruction on how to find peace with God.

Large crowds began attending the meetings in his town of Cambuslang. At times there would be eight or nine thousand on a Sunday. M'Culloch invited George Whitefield to speak during Communion services. Whitefield estimated that as many as twenty thousand people gathered to hear him at one service.[4]

Despite M'Culloch's efforts to teach, preach, and exhort his people, his longing, borne out of many hours on his knees in private prayer, rather than his orating at a podium finally sparked the outpouring of God's Spirit. Today many want to see revival come, but they are not prepared to cry out to God in prayer with the fervency and humility required. Jonathan Goforth noted, "The history of revival shows plainly that all movements of the Spirit have started in prayer."[5] The following are five key roles of prayer in revival.

Praying as a Priority

Matthew Henry said, "When God intends great mercy for His people, the first thing He does is to set them to praying." It has also been said, "Satan laughs at our toil, mocks at our wisdom, but trembles when we pray."[6] E. M. Bounds wisely stated: "Talking to men for God is a great thing, but talking to God for men is greater still."[7]

Studying revivals throughout history will reveal that they are not identical. Revivals in Wales, New England, Kentucky, Korea, India, Ruanda, and South Africa had characteristics unique to the people and the social environment in which they occurred. However, in every revival the consistent common denominator is fervent, faithful, persistent, righteous prayer. As Brian Edwards observed: "No church can ever expect revival unless it is praying for it."[8] However, though Christians generally recognize the need for prayer, it continues to be one of the most neglected of all Christian practices. Time after time Christians are reminded that God has worked mightily in response to His people's fervent praying, yet still people find it difficult to do, or they are unwilling to make prayer a priority. Church prayer meetings remain the domain of the faithful few.

Praying in Korea

During the revival in Korea, the people of one church became so burdened for revival in their community that they began to meet at five o'clock each morning to pray for it. They met for six months before revival came. Referring to their commitment to pray, Jonathan Goforth challenges us: "Do we really believe in God the Holy Spirit?

Let us be honest. Not to the extent of getting up at five o'clock through six months of cold weather to seek Him!"[9] Christians of South Korea are renowned for their dedication to prayer. Is it any wonder God has worked mightily in their nation in recent decades? Many people from North America have traveled to South Korea to visit its massive churches to gain insight into their phenomenal growth. Yet even though they have repeatedly been told it is due to prayer, most westerners have not sought to duplicate the prayer efforts of their Korean brethren.

Octavius Winslow suggests: "When a professing Christian can pray, and yet acknowledge that he has no nearness to the throne, no touching of the scepter, no fellowship with God—calls him 'Father' without the sense of adoption—confesses sin in a general way, without any looking up to God through the cross—has no consciousness of possessing the ear and the heart of God, the evidence is undoubted of a decline in the state of religion in the soul."[10] Prayerless Christians are clear evidence of the urgent need for revival.

Charles Finney was often castigated for his introduction of "new measures" in revival meetings. Finney believed that by using these "new measures" or methods in conducting revival meetings, great results would occur. Yet Finney's ministry was fundamentally characterized by prayer. At one point early in his ministry, Finney declared "the burden of prayer almost crushed me."[11] While Finney became the most famous revivalist of his day, less known was that he enlisted the help of a man named Father Nash who was a powerful prayer warrior. Nash would go in advance of Finney to a city and begin praying for it. By the time Finney arrived for the meetings, the Spirit of God was already moving mightily in that place.[12] Finney, himself, would often rise at 4:00 a.m. to pray. He felt that when he was not strong in prayer, neither was he powerful in the pulpit.

Evan Roberts, who was used so powerfully for six months in the Wales Awakening of 1904, retired from active preaching while still in his twenties and devoted the remainder of his life to prayer. Those who have been used mightily in revival have not only *believed* prayer was a priority but also *made* praying a priority in their daily lives.

Praying with a Burden

Knowing we ought to pray for revival is part of the equation. But if we do not have a burden for those in need of revival and we do not grieve over the fact that God's kingdom is not yet ruling in every heart, church, and nation, then we will inevitably become lax in our praying. The burden we have for revival does not come from within our own noble souls but from the heart of God. When we pray for revival, we are not praying in order to convince God He should move among His people. He longs to do that far more than we could ever imagine. Arthur Wallis noted: "Let us not think, as we plead for revival, that we move God to share our concern and burden about the matter. We feel as we do because God has stirred us to share but a fraction of His concern. Our longing is but a feeble, pale reflection of His own."[13]

Zeal for God and His people led Phinehas to take dramatic action against those committing immorality in the Israelite camp (Num. 25:1–13).

A burden for the restoration of God's people was what compelled Elijah to stand alone atop Mount Carmel and defy 850 false prophets to a showdown while the king looked on. Love for God and His people compelled Nehemiah to risk his high position in court in order to see God's people lifted up. Love for God and His people motivated Queen Esther to risk her life and plead with the king. A burden for his people made the prophet Jeremiah cry out, "Oh, that my head were waters and my eyes a fountain of tears, that I might weep day and night for the slain of the daughter of my people!" (Jer. 9:1).

The reason some people have a deep longing for revival is because they know what God's judgment and the consequences of sin involve. Just as Jesus wept over the city of Jerusalem because He knew they would face certain judgment (Matt. 23:37–39), so those who pray for revival do so because they know that certain judgment is coming if God's people do not turn from their sin and return to the Lord. A burden for revival can become all consuming as you understand what is at stake and what is being lost. Duncan Campbell said, "We say we want revival, but are we willing to pay the price?"[14] When you truly have a burden for revival, you will pay any price, rise at any hour, set aside any amusement, and risk misunderstanding from others in order to plead on your knees for God to revive His people.

Praying in Righteousness

Arthur Wallis claimed, "If there is no revival of righteousness, there is no revival at all."[15] Scripture promises: "The effective, fervent prayer of a righteous man avails much" (James 5:16). Fervent prayer is important. Righteous praying is crucial. God does not hear the prayers of the unrighteous (Isa. 1:15). If He does not hear, He will not respond. The Scripture says that when God hears our prayers, He always responds (Matt. 7:7–8).

Righteous praying is praying in total agreement with God's heart. It is prizing what God values and despising what God hates. Righteous prayer is devoid of any selfish or sinful motive. Often Christians pray with wrong motives. Pastors can pray that revival come primarily so antagonistic church members ease up or so the attendance and offerings increase. People ask for revival because they want to put their church on the map. Praying can also be self-centered, which automatically renders it unrighteous. Righteous praying values, above all else, God being glorified and His will being carried out on earth exactly as it is in heaven. Such a prayer must flow from absolute surrender to God's will. If the people praying will not completely surrender their own lives to Christ's lordship, then it is futile for them to pray that God's kingdom be extended into other people's lives.

Praying in righteousness involves praying after you have allowed the Holy Spirit thoroughly to cleanse you of sin in your own life. It is first inviting God's scrutiny of your life before you begin to pray for the sins of others (Ps. 139:23–24). This is why revival precedes spiritual awakening. Once God's people have been cleansed, they are in a proper place to pray earnestly as righteous men and women for unbelievers in their land. Praying in righteousness also means you are so aligned with your Father's wishes that you place your life on the altar for God to use you. If you are unwilling to be a part of God's answer, then you are not yet praying according to His will.

Praying in Faith

William Chambers Burns declared: "The Gospel has lost none of its power. It is we Christians who have lost our power with God."[16] He added, "The work of God would flourish by us, if it flourished more richly in us."[17] Those times when God has moved mightily among His people have been when His people truly believed that He would.

Faith at Midnight

Duncan Campbell was conducting revival meetings in the small rural town of Arnol in the Hebrides Islands off the coast of Scotland. The meetings had not begun well, and God's people sensed that some kind of breakthrough was needed. Several of them gathered with Campbell to pray at the home of Donald and Bella Smith.[18] Sometime after midnight Duncan Campbell asked Smith to pray. Smith had not yet prayed aloud during that meeting. After praying for a while, Smith said, "Lord, I do not know how Mr. Campbell or any of these other men stand with you, but I know my own heart. I know that I am thirsty. You have promised to pour water on him who is thirsty. If You don't do it, how can I ever believe You again? Your honor is at stake. You are a covenant-keeping God. Fulfill Your covenant engagement." As he spoke these words, the house shook. Many of those inside supposed it to be an earthquake, but later reports confirmed that no one else in the surrounding area around the house had felt a tremor. Two people in that meeting were not Christians and had begun dozing at that late hour. Both were shaken awake and converted that night. As the prayer gathering concluded, people left the house only to discover that the entire town was awake, and many people were silently walking to the church building. Some were carrying chairs and wondering if there would be adequate room for them. The time was past midnight. The revival in Arnol had begun!

Referring to Smith's prayer, Campbell later exclaimed: "I love to believe that angels and archangels were looking over the battlements of heaven saying to one another, 'There is a man who believes God!'"[19] Faith is more than desire. As Campbell explained: "Desire is one thing; confident expectation that the desire will be fulfilled is quite another thing."[20]

God keeps His promises. He is absolutely faithful to His Word. Too many Christians neglect to claim God's promises for their own lives and for their church, so they never see them fulfilled. Regarding claiming God's promises in faith, Arthur Wallis stated, "This is a spiritual lever that never fails to move the hand that moves the world."[21] Time and time again when people have investigated the antecedents of a great moving of God, they have invariably traced the divine work back to someone or some group who thoroughly believed God would keep His promises.

Praying Believing

In 1872 D. L. Moody sailed for Great Britain. He was little known across the Atlantic, and he was unsure of what the Lord had for him when he arrived. A congregational minister invited him to preach at Arundel Square near the Pentonville Prison in a lower middle-class neighborhood in England. The people's response to Moody's preaching during the Sunday morning service was less than enthusiastic, and Moody wondered if he had made a mistake in agreeing to come. However, Moody was unaware that a young woman hurried home after the service to report to her bedridden younger sister, Marianne Adlard.[22]

When she told Marianne who had preached at their church that morning, Marianne excitedly pulled out from under her pillow a newspaper clipping reporting on Moody's work in Chicago. "I know what that means! God has heard my prayers!" Marianne exclaimed. Ever since she had read of Moody in the newspaper, she had pleaded with God to use Moody to bring revival to her church. As that evening's service began, the atmosphere was one of unusual excitement. At the close of Moody's sermon, he asked anyone who wanted to accept Christ to stand so he could pray for them. So many people rose to their feet that Moody assumed they must have misunderstood what he had said. He had them sit back down, and he carefully explained that those wanting to accept Christ as their Savior should adjourn to another room where people could counsel with them. That room filled up with people seeking God. Moody preached during the week to that congregation and ultimately more than four hundred people were added to the church. When asked later what had brought the spiritual breakthrough, Moody believed it was the faithful prayers of the invalid young lady who claimed God's promises for her beloved congregation.

Notice how Jesus instructed His disciples:

"So Jesus answered and said to them, 'Have faith in God. For assuredly, I say to you, whoever says to this mountain, "Be removed and be cast into the sea," and does not doubt in his heart, but believes that those things he says will be done, he will have whatever he says. Therefore I say to you, whatever things you ask when you pray, believe that you receive them, and you will have them.'" (Mark 11:22–24)

Jesus identified the quality of praying that regularly sees results. It is no half-hearted, lukewarm praying filled with qualifiers and escape clauses should God not grant what is being requested. Bold, confident praying is done with the expectancy that God will hear and He will answer. People who pray this way are not surprised when God answers them, for they fully expected as much. It is not prayer that tells God what to do. It is praying that has come to understand God's will and then boldly asks God to do what is in His heart to accomplish. God delights to find people who truly believe He will do what He has promised.

Today God is looking for people of faith like the centurion who told Jesus he was satisfied that a mere word from the Lord would bring healing to his ailing servant (Luke 7:1–10). Jesus "marveled" at the faith of this Gentile who clearly recognized God's power. We can only wonder if our praying ever causes God to marvel at the audacity of our faith.

Praying as One Body

One final characteristic of effective revival praying is that it is corporate and unified. Jesus declared, "Where two or three are gathered together in My name, I am there in the midst of them" (Matt. 18:20). God has chosen especially to honor the prayers of like-minded people who pray in unity. During the 1859 revival in Wales, someone observed, "A powerful spirit of prayer has laid hold of the churches."[23] A great spirit of unity and singleness of purpose characterized God's people as they prayed together for revival.[24] During the Korean revival in 1907, the mission leaders prayed together, Presbyterian and Methodist, until there was no distinction or feeling of competition. Once the church and mission leaders were unified in their desire for the Holy Spirit to bring revival, revival came.[25] Tens of thousands of people were converted, yet little was done for evangelism other than prayer.

Today's church sorely neglects corporate prayer. Little praying is done during the worship service, though Jesus declared His Father's house was to be a house of prayer (Luke 19:46). When people do pray in church gatherings, the prayers are not often characterized by impassioned cries to God for mercy and forgiveness. Rather, they often consist of a string of Christian clichés that say little and ask for less. During the great revival in Manchuria, many people were revived and confessed their sins. However, there were those who sought to appear spiritual before others even though their hearts were far from God. During one meeting a prominent leader in the church was praying a long, eloquent prayer but saying little. Goforth, in exasperation, went up to the man and stopped him, declaring, "Please, let's not have any of your ordinary kind of praying."[26] What might Goforth think if he visited many of our churches today?

A noteworthy example of corporate praying that led to revival and a great awakening was the layman's prayer revival in New York City in 1857–1858. J. Edwin Orr, the foremost revival historian of his era, labeled this movement of God "The Event of the Century."[27]

The Prayer Revival of 1857–1858

With little in the way of human planning, a nationwide revival broke out among God's people beginning in 1857. In the awakening that followed, nearly a million people accepted Christ as their Savior and became involved in churches in a single year. A similar move of God in our day would result in more than thirty million people turning to Christ.

The years immediately preceding 1857 saw tremendous growth and prosperity for America. The population was booming. Businesses flourished, and many people grew wealthy. Materialism captured the minds and hearts of Americans, choking out their interest in God and His kingdom. Churches were declining in numbers, strength, and influence.

The growth of New York City began to force the wealthy residents out of the downtown area. They were replaced by unchurched masses of common laborers crammed into tenement buildings. Many churches decided to move to "more fruitful" locations. In a state of decline, the North Dutch Church decided to remain where it was and to attempt to evangelize the unchurched masses surrounding them.[28] They employed a businessman, Jeremiah Lanphier, as a lay missionary. Lanphier was described as "tall, with a pleasant face, an affectionate manner, an indominatable energy and perseverance; a good singer, gifted in prayer and exhortation, a welcome guest in any house, shrewed and endowed with much tact and common sense."[29] He began to visit homes, distribute Bibles and tracts, and advertise church services. Facing a discouraging response, he found comfort in prayer.

One day Lanphier prayed, "Lord, what wilt thou have me to do?" He sensed God's direction to begin a weekly prayer service for workers and business people over the noon hour. He began on Wednesday, September 23, 1857, with only six people attending. The second week twenty participated, and forty came the third week. The hunger and thirst after God became evident, and they began daily "union prayer meetings" the fourth week. People of all classes of society and from every denomination attended.

God had praying people in place when the financial crash of 1857 hit, just weeks after the prayer meetings began. "Merchants by the thousands all over the country were forced to the wall, banks failed, and railroads went into bankruptcy." In New York City alone, thirty thousand people lost their jobs. Added to the economic crisis, the nation was gripped by regional tensions over slavery. America's future was bleak indeed.

In the midst of disaster and with a desperate hunger for God, people flooded the prayer meetings by the thousands. The meetings spread throughout New York City and then across the nation. Businesses closed over the noon hour to allow their employees time for prayer. Newspapers devoted front-page coverage of "revival news," and revival spread rapidly across the country. Religion became the common topic of conversation.

When the revival/awakening was at its peak, fifty thousand people were being converted every week. Within a year nearly one million people had been saved. "Bishop McIlvaine, in his annual address before the Diocesan Convention of Ohio, said . . . 'I rejoice in the decided conviction that it is "the Lord's doing;" unaccountable by any natural causes, entirely above and beyond what any human device or power could produce; an outpouring of the Spirit of God upon God's people, quickening them to greater earnestness in his service; and upon the unconverted, to make them new creatures in Christ Jesus.'"[30]

Praying for Revival in Our Nation

God is sovereign over every nation. Throughout history He has raised up and blessed nations, and He has likewise punished nations that gave themselves to wickedness and evil. God holds nations accountable for their actions as He does individuals. Read the following truths from the psalmist and identify ways you can be praying for your nation:

> The LORD brings the counsel of the nations to nothing; He makes the plans of the peoples of no effect. The counsel of the LORD stands forever, The plans of His heart to all generations. Blessed is the nation whose God is the LORD, the people He has chosen as His own inheritance. The LORD looks from heaven; He sees all the sons of men. From the place of His dwelling He looks on all the inhabitants of the earth; He fashions their hearts individually; He considers all their works. No king is saved by the multitude of an army; a mighty man is not delivered by great strength. A horse is a vain hope for safety; neither shall it deliver any by its great strength. Behold, the eye of the LORD is on those who fear Him, on those who hope in His mercy, to deliver their soul from death, and to keep them alive in famine. Our soul waits for the LORD; He is our help and our shield. For our heart shall rejoice in Him, because we have trusted in His holy name. Let Your mercy, O LORD, be upon us, just as we hope in You. (Ps. 33:10–22)

Many people wonder if God will ever judge America for its sins. The truth is, God is *already* judging America. No nation in history has been able to scorn God's standards and to blaspheme His name and not suffer the consequences. Our day is no different. To whom much has been given, much is expected. God's judgment on America is not yet final. But it will steadily increase until people either repent or perish. God's judgments are not vindictive or petty. They are designed to bring people back to God. If wealth, ease, and security cause people to turn their backs on God, then God will deal with those idols the same way He has dealt with idols and idol worshippers throughout history.

Revival: Our Only Hope

Every great nation or empire in history has eventually fallen. God is extraordinarily patient, but a time comes when people become so wicked and so depraved that holy God must make them reap what they have sown. Our only hope as a nation is for revival to sweep our churches and for spiritual awakening to cover the land. If our nation is to return to the Lord and fear Him once again, God's people must repent. God's message to us is surely the same as it was to the people of King Solomon's day: "If My people who are called by My name will humble themselves, and pray and seek My face, and turn from their wicked ways, then I will hear from heaven, and will forgive their sin and heal their land'" (2 Chron. 7:14).

If we are to see revival, we must meet God's requirements. We must deal ruthlessly with our consuming pride and humble ourselves before the Lord. Then we must pray and seek His face. Prayer is communing with the person of Christ. Prayer is entering into the throne room of the universe to stand before the Lord God Almighty. When God's people take prayer seriously and reverently enter the presence of Holy God, they will recognize their sin and fall with broken and contrite hearts before His majesty.

Watchmen and Prophets

Are you willing to adjust your lifestyle significantly enough to be the kind of prayer warrior God will use to change your family, your church, your city, your denomination, and your nation?

God is looking for men and women of prayer who will intercede for their city and people. Notice what God said through His prophet Isaiah: "I have set watchmen on your walls, O Jerusalem; they shall never hold their peace day or night. You who make mention of the LORD, do not keep silent, and give Him no rest until He establishes and till He makes Jerusalem a praise on the earth" (Isa. 62:6–7). The fate of a city rested in the hands of the watchmen. Those who became careless or who slept at their post could cost men, women, and children their lives.

You do not volunteer to be a spiritual watchman. It is an appointed position. God looks at your heart to see if you can be trusted with such an immense assignment. He looks for those who will stay spiritually alert. He wants those on the walls of their family, their church, their nation, who will not grow weary from watching, who will not become discouraged, but who will be found at their assigned post at all times. Being a spiritual watchman means you maintain your spiritual concentration so you detect the movings of the enemy or of God's Spirit. You are alert to threats your church, family, or nation is facing. You are quick to sound the alarm when you see danger approaching. How blessed is the family who has a parent standing watch on the walls of their home. How fortunate is the church who has faithful watchmen praying on their behalf.

There is one other aspect to spiritual watching. God also appoints people to speak a word to His people on His behalf. The prophet Amos declared: "Surely the Lord GOD does nothing, unless He reveals His secret to the prophets" (Amos 3:7). When God is working, He looks for someone who can speak a word on His behalf to His people. Prophets are unique in some ways, but they can also be extremely ordinary people. Amos said of himself, "I was no prophet, nor was I a son of a prophet, but I was a sheepbreeder and a tender of sycamore fruit. Then the LORD took me as I followed the flock, and the LORD said to me, 'Go, prophecy to My people Israel.' Now therefore, hear the word of the LORD" (Amos 7:14–16). Amos was an ordinary businessperson, but God chose to use his life to give a divine message to the people. Jeremiah was just a youth and certainly did not see himself as a prophet when God called him (Jer. 1:6). The twelve disciples were business people when God called them and appointed them to proclaim His message.

We live in a day when people urgently need to hear a word from the Lord. God's judgment could be imminent. Ours is an age that cries out for spiritual watchmen as well as prophets who will declare a word from the Lord. If your heart is devoted to God and you are prepared to stand watch for the spiritual welfare of those around you, don't be surprised if God gives you the words to speak that the people around you desperately need to hear.

QUESTIONS FOR REFLECTION AND DISCUSSION

1. How would the Lord evaluate your present prayer life? What adjustments do you believe He wants you to make?
2. Is prayer a priority in your life? What is the evidence? If it is not, how can you make it a priority?
3. Do you presently have a burden to pray for revival? If not, why do you think you do not care more about seeing revival come to your life and to your church?
4. Could your prayers be described as "righteous prayers"? How is God seeking to align your heart and values to match His as you pray?

5. Have you been praying in faith? Do you pray expecting God to answer? How do your actions reveal your faith that God will answer?

6. What is the evidence in your life that you believe in corporate prayer? Are you presently praying with anyone regularly from another denomination or ethnic group or social class? Do you regularly pray with others from your church? Does God want you to enlist others to meet together to pray?

7. Has God entrusted you to be a spiritual watch person? If so, how faithfully have you been performing that assignment?

CHAPTER 14

Corporate Hindrances to Revival

In churches today people are discussing our generation's need for revival. Numerous books are being published on the subject. Prayer conferences are being held regularly around the country for the sole purpose of crying out to God for revival. Organizations focused on revival are being established in record numbers. Yet we are not seeing widespread spiritual awakening in North America. Churches must humbly approach God and ask Him why.

Hindrances to Revival

One of the major reasons revival has not yet come—despite multitudinous praying, conferencing, and organizing—is because of corporate hindrances. Corporate hindrances are church practices that hinder rather than facilitate revival. Tragically, despite enormous efforts by churches to experience a fresh outpouring of God's Spirit, those same congregations hinder the work for which they are praying. By allowing unbiblical theology as well as secular methodology to permeate their activities, church practices can actually quench the Spirit's work rather than promote it. In this chapter we'll consider eight obstacles to revival prevalent among churches today.

Misleading Terminology

A seemingly innocuous issue such as the language we use in church can disorient Christians to the Holy Spirit's work. Without noticing it, churches often adopt the world's approach to classifying sin. Thus, "adultery," the sin of giving your heart and body to someone other than your spouse, becomes "an affair." People no longer "commit" this sin; they "fall into" it.

Another current trend is to reclassify sin as weakness or bad habit. Rather than committing the sin of lust, one is said to have an addiction to pornography. However addictive and enslaving habitual sin can become, its roots still lie in sin. Society commiserates with an addict: God judges sin. Society encourages addicts to seek therapy and counseling but not necessarily to repent of sin. We know the Bible condemns greed and materialism, but we are encouraged to pray continually for God's blessings and to believe that, if we will believe, God will grant us whatever we ask of Him.

In addition to opting for euphemisms where sin is concerned, the church has developed clichés used so often people assume they are biblical. From the pulpit, for example, we may hear, "I knew God wanted me to preach on this subject, but I really wrestled with Him about it." The allusion is usually to Jacob's experience of wrestling with God (Gen. 32:22–32). Such grappling with God is viewed in positive terms, such as holding onto God until He blesses you. However, the scriptural account of Jacob's tussle with God is not presented as a model for modern believers. Not only is it the only such account in the Bible, but Jacob walked with a limp the rest of his life because of his presumption. It is always better to use biblical terms for Christian experiences. Scripture does not generally speak in terms of wrestling with God but rather of obeying or disobeying God's will. When Jonah grappled with doing what God told him, he ended up as fish food. By glamorizing our unwillingness to obey and trust our Lord, we exalt our stubbornness rather than Christ. God's strength is beyond contesting. "Wrestling with God" just seems more palatable than admitting we were disobedient.

Christian clichés are inundating the church. While these can sometimes capture profound truths in simplistic language, they can also inadvertently dilute God's message and inoculate people from a word from God. Bumper stickers urging us to "let God be God" suggest that in some way we control God's divinity in our lives. Or, "God is my copilot" portrays God as someone who submits to our whims and wishes with us firmly in control at the wheel. While clichés can often sound compelling and even profound when shouted from the pulpit, they are inculcating God's people with a dangerously simplistic and misguided view of God.

Misdirected Appeals

Churches often unwittingly challenge people in an unbiblical manner. Preachers extend altar calls wherein people who have not been walking in obedient fellowship with God are invited to rededicate their lives to His will. In this process people may come before the church and acknowledge they have disobeyed God's will. They will affirm their fresh resolve to obey God. Often members of the congregation will be invited to come and encourage those who have expressed their desire to try harder to obey God. These same people may rededicate themselves over and over because their last resolution did not hold for more than a few days. Some people are caught in a spiraling cycle of rededications and increasing guilt.

Such a process is unbiblical. The crux of the gospel message is not a call to rededication but a call to repentance. John the Baptist preached repentance (Matt. 3:2). Jesus preached repentance both in His earthly ministry and as the resurrected Lord (Matt. 4:17; Rev. 3:19). If people's previous commitment did not keep them faithfully walking in obedience to Christ, recommitments are no more likely to make them faithful. The proper response to disobedience is not a commitment to try harder but brokenness and repentance for rejecting the will of Almighty God. God looks for surrender, not willpower. Yielding indicates our absolute dependence on God. Resolutions place the focus on us and our efforts. If I can just try harder this time . . . but repeatedly breaking our promises to God is a serious matter. Ecclesiastes warns that it is better not to make a vow to God at all than to make a promise and then break it (Eccles. 5:1–5). Yet churches inadvertently encourage those who have brazenly broken their commitments to God to come time and again to make new promises that they inevitably break as well. When people fail to follow through with what they promised God, they should return with tears of repentance. Rather than asking church members to applaud rededication, pastors should call on people to grieve over the way they stubbornly resist God's will.

Mistaken Compassion

When the Holy Spirit works in people's lives by convicting them of their sin, churches often do not know how to respond. Many Christians are uncomfortable with spiritual brokenness. The tears and anguish of sinners under conviction by the Holy Spirit make us feel awkward. Rather than allowing people to respond to God's prompting, we often quickly intervene to alleviate their misery. Seeing someone weeping under conviction, we feel compelled to assure them that things are not as bad as they think. We try to comfort one whom God is making uncomfortable. One reason God's people are not consecrated is because we do not allow people thoroughly to repent. Before sinners can experience true joy, they must undergo thorough, heartfelt repentance.

In our quest to be seeker sensitive, the modern church has largely eliminated opportunities for sin to be openly confessed. In the past churches extended "altar calls" or "invitations" at the close of the service when people were invited to come to the front of the church to pray or to receive counseling from a minister. Today's churches have largely abandoned this practice. Out of sympathy for those who feel uncomfortable with this approach, we dismiss the congregation at the point when they are under the most intense conviction.

God's Word is living and active and able to judge people's thoughts and intentions (Heb. 4:12). When God suddenly confronts people with His convicting Word, it is a powerful and unsettling experience. When people come under conviction that they have sinned against Almighty God, the most compassionate thing their minister can do is provide them with an immediate opportunity to be made right with God. We have often witnessed the impact God's holy, convicting Word has upon people. When this occurs, people do not find relief by filling out a card and placing it in a box at the back of the auditorium or by making an appointment to meet with the staff later that week.

One other caution is for those ministers who have deleted altar calls from the service out of their own pride. Unfortunately some churches view altar calls as a public evaluation of the sermon. If no one "walked the aisle," then it was a weak message. If week after week no one comes forward, many ministers awkwardly feel as if they are being given a nonconfidence vote. So they either make the altar call extremely brief (We'll sing two verses, and if no one comes, we'll close.). Or they water down their altar call so much they are able to save face when no one comes forward (You may not need to respond to God today, or you may just want to pray where you are without coming forward. We'll sing a verse and then close if no one comes.). The minister may offer so many qualifiers and loopholes people sense it would disrupt the service if they actually did make a public decision. Preachers need to approach the pulpit with the profound conviction that there is nothing more powerful in the world than a word from God. If they are going to deliver a message from God to the people, they need to *expect* it will have an impact, and they need to preach their message with a profound sense of confidence.

Misplaced Priorities

The structure of many worship services mitigates the Spirit's working. Under pressure to end a service on time, preachers and worship leaders often leave little time for people to respond to what God has just done in their midst. Altar calls, if offered, are so brief people have insufficient time to make it to the front of the auditorium before the time is brought to an abrupt end. One of the most deadening practices in modern churches is to schedule the giving of announcements at the close of the service. We have been in many services where the Spirit clearly moved among the people, convicting some and comforting others. Then, as people were still wiping tears from their cheeks and returning to their seats, a church minister began the litany of announcements, reminding people of the pot-luck dinner for the senior adult department next Tuesday and encouraging people to sign up for the coming father/son fishing trip. The holy moment people were experiencing is soon quenched.

We have been in worship services where God clearly visited His people in a powerful way. But soon after the service concluded, the church janitor was already turning down the auditorium lights to encourage people to exit the place where they just encountered God. Many larger churches feel pressured to quickly usher people out of the auditorium at the close of the service because there is a second or third service and people are already waiting to enter the auditorium. Churches with live telecasts on television or radio feel constrained by time pressures to have their services begin and finish promptly. The pastor cannot adjust his sermon or speak extemporaneously without making the intricately timed program be thrown off kilter. The mighty moving of the Holy Spirit may not fit in neatly to the printed order of service. In many of the larger churches in which we have spoken, we will be given a detailed schedule listing to the minute how long the sermon is to be along with detailed time allotments for the prayers, announcements, and songs. Various colored lights will shine from the sound booth upon anyone who transgresses their time quota. The reality is that in many carefully crafted and professionally conducted church services, nothing clearly authored by the Holy Spirit has occurred in a long time.

Misleading Revival Terminology

Many churches fail to understand revival terminology. The word *revival* describes the process of God's people returning to Him. This involves God's sensitizing and cleansing His people's hearts. Revival does not refer to bringing unregenerate people to faith in Christ. Yet most contemporary "revival" services have a distinctly evangelistic tenor. Church members are encouraged to bring their non-Christian friends to the revival services. When several unbelievers become Christians, the meetings are proclaimed to have been a success.

Revival is for God's people. Preaching evangelistic messages to God's people will not necessarily revive Christians who have grown spiritually lethargic. Rather, when spiritually deadened Christians hear the preacher describing how someone must be "saved," they will conclude that they have already taken that step so the sermon and the meetings have no relevance for them.

Historically revival meetings emerged in America from the camp meetings on the western frontier. After the fall harvest farmers would gather from all over the territory to receive Communion. Preachers would preach for a week to prepare God's people to participate in the Lord's Supper. Then, during the second week, with God's people now spiritually prepared, the preachers would exhort unbelievers to receive Christ into their lives. This pattern was brought into cities by revivalists such as Charles G. Finney. For years churches would schedule fall revival meetings where the first week was focused on consecrating church members. During the second week church members were encouraged to bring their unbelieving friends to hear the gospel preached. Over time two-week meetings were viewed as too burdensome for most churches so the meetings were compressed into one week. Then revival meetings were further compacted to Sunday through Wednesday evening meetings, or Friday through Sunday. Of course, with so little time to meet, it was hoped the church members had already been sanctified ahead of time so the limited number of services could be devoted to converting unbelievers. Today many larger churches are having one-day "revival services." On a designated day the church will have a special evangelistic emphasis and call it an "old-fashioned revival."

The word *revival* has become synonymous with rebirth. Now when you see the word *revival* on a church sign, it is anyone's guess what is meant. The problem with the shifting focus is that God's people are left confused. It is good for a church to hold an evangelistic meeting for the purpose of reaching unbelievers. It is also fine for a pastor to preach an evangelistic sermon during a church service. However, Christians need opportunities to be revived. If Christians are not being salt and light, the world around them doesn't have a chance. If all of the church's energies are so directed at evangelizing nonbelievers that it neglects the renewal and growth of God's people, Christians will continue to remain spiritually comatose. God's people need regular times of refreshing where they are drawn back into an intimate walk with their God. This is the true meaning of revival.

A second issue has already been mentioned. The word *repentance* is often misunderstood. That term is often viewed negatively in a society where everything is expected to be phrased in a positive light. Yet "repentance" is one of the most positive words in the English language. The word implies hope for sinners who recognize their sin and want to return to God. It describes the turning away from sin and a turning to God. It is the ability to repent that gives all Christians hope. As Octavius Winslow proclaimed: "We state it distinctly and emphatically, that whatever the departure of a backsliding child of God, it is recoverable: not a step has he lost but may be retraced; not a grace decayed but may be restored; not a joy has fled but may be won back."[1]

Misdiagnosed Symptoms

Churches are often tempted to deal with symptoms rather than root causes. Rather than addressing the condition of people's hearts, churches attempt to change their behavior. If people are not attending particular programs or activities, church leaders attempt to make the activities more attractive, or they put guilt trips on delinquent members. If members are not inviting their unbelieving friends to attend church with them, training in evangelism is offered. If needs in the church are going unmet, staff is hired to fulfill that assignment.

Church programs are a tool, nothing more, like musical instruments in the sanctuary and copy machines in the church office. We are no different from the world if we attempt to manipulate people's behavior and fail to address the heart condition behind the activity. People who have a vibrant, joyful walk with God won't be able to suppress their witness from those around them. Those who are living daily under the lordship of Christ will readily volunteer to meet the needs of fellow church members. When church members chronically fail to demonstrate even the most basic Christian behaviors, they do not require a tongue-lashing or another training course. They need a fresh encounter with the living God.

The greatest seasons of Christian volunteerism have come immediately following times of revival. The largest evangelistic harvests have occurred during seasons of revival. But when God's people are living carnally and are spiritually anemic, another evangelistic service will not provide a remedy. Such people must be reminded of the height from which they have fallen and the beloved Savior whom they have forsaken. When people's hearts are made right, their behavior and service for God will also be correct. Jesus stated, "He who has My commandments and keeps them, it is he who loves Me" (John 14:21).

Misguided Relationships

Just as in a family, so church members must realize that dissension within the body dishonors God. Congregations are to colabor with one another and to make themselves vulnerable to the others by praying and confessing their sins to one another. Matthew 5:23–24 indicates that Christians should forgive anyone with whom they have a conflict. Today when a church splits, the local association does nothing to bring reconciliation but rather counts the splinter group as a mission start.

Churches have a collective responsibility to seek reconciliation just as individuals have been commanded to do. If a church refuses to forgive, then its individual members will assume it is acceptable for them to withhold forgiveness as well. If a church, as a body, repents of its unforgiveness toward another church or toward a person, its members will learn to forgive as well. God's healing and transforming power will be powerfully released in a congregation when it takes God's command to forgive seriously.

Missing Prayer

Jesus claimed the church was to be a "house of prayer" (Matt. 21:13). Modern church buildings are often places of recreation (gyms/ball fields), refreshment (coffee bars), business (bookstores), learning (classrooms/library), banquets (fellowship hall), and worship (auditorium). But fewer and fewer churches even offer a place for reflection and prayer. Moreover, the Sunday worship service has become so jam-packed, prayer is little more than verbal bookends to the service. At times public prayers appear merely to provide opportunities for the musicians to sneak on and off the stage. By the time the announcements are made, visitors greeted, songs sung, and sermon preached, there is scant time for talking to God.

Another casualty of modern time pressures is the pastoral prayer. There was a time when this portion of the service was sacred and much anticipated. The minister cried out to God on behalf of the people. One of the reasons church members have anemic prayer lives is because they never hear true, searching, heartfelt, reverent prayer from their spiritual leaders. Many prayers in churches today are nothing more than a shallow string of clichés that say little and which are often patently unbiblical. Public prayers regularly ask God to "be with us" and to "be with the missionaries" as if He were not omnipresent and committed to His promise never to leave or forsake us. We ask God to give us a good day as if the entire worship experience was designed for us and what we receive. At times worship leaders "invite" God to join their worship service as if God were the guest rather than the owner of the house of worship. We must never forget that God is the center and focal point of our worship. If He is not present, we have nothing to worship!

In a typical church service you would discover that all of the corporate praying combined wouldn't total five minutes in an hour-long service. Surely a few moments of selfish requests is not what God meant by His house being a place of prayer. If churches cannot fit prayer into their already packed schedules, they should not be surprised that there is also no room for revival.

Conclusion

Our land desperately needs revival. We would be foolish not to look inward to our-selves and our church practices to see if we are not hindering the very thing we are seeking. Tragically, churches longing for revival may be inadvertently contributing to their congregations' spiritual demise. By adopting secular methods or popular but unbiblical fads, or by striving to accomplish misplaced priorities, churches can actu-ally hinder the work of God they claim to be seeking. If churches are not experienc-ing revival, they must take their practices and place them before God's plumb line laid out in Scripture. Just because methodology is "effective," "efficient," "traditional," or "contemporary," it cannot continue to be embraced if it is not thoroughly biblical.

Time of Reflection and Prayer

This chapter can tempt us merely to identify all the shortcomings of our church and to become critical. This will not help us or God's people. Take time to consider the way your church is presently functioning. Do so not with a critical spirit but with a heartfelt desire to see your church become all God wants it to be. When God makes you aware of a need, it is not an invitation to be judgmental but a divine summons to intercession.

If you are studying this book in a group setting, rather than discussion, devote your meeting time to pray fervently and humbly for your congregation. Ask God to alert you to any area where you need to intercede. Have you been part of the prob-lem? How might God work in your life so your church can become more honoring to God?

CHAPTER 15

Worship and Revival

When revival comes, it revolutionizes the way we worship God. Every account of revival in the Bible and testimonials throughout history relate that after God revived His people, the way they worshipped Him was transformed. God's people gathered in eagerness, expecting Him to work powerfully among them. Ritual, routine meetings were replaced with vibrant, dynamic, reverent worship. Biblically you cannot encounter God and remain the same. When Isaiah beheld God enthroned in His splendor, the prophet's life was forever changed. John met the risen Christ on the Isle of Patmos, and the godly apostle was dramatically impacted by the encounter. True worship both leads to a genuine encounter with God and results from such an encounter. People ought not to be leaving church worship services unaffected. Too often they are doing just that. Worship services, when conducted in an unbiblical manner, can actually deaden people's spiritual senses. Ironically, despite a renewed interest in worship among churches today, revival still has not come. Churches must ask themselves, with all the worship we are doing, why has revival not come? The following are ten modern worship practices that can hinder revival in churches today.

Modern Worship Practices

True Versus False Understanding of Worship

In many churches today worship services consist of people gathering to sing songs and to hear a preacher exhort them on moral living. It is not generally a life-changing encounter with the living God. The word *worship* comes from the Greek word *proskeneo*, which means "to bow down, to prostrate oneself." It is what people did when they entered the presence of the Persian emperor who demanded to be treated as if he were a god. To enter the king's presence uninvited or to approach him without showing proper reverence was to invite instant death. No one dared show lack of awe and respect to the sovereign. Those entering the king's presence would prostrate themselves, bowing their faces to the ground in an effort to demonstrate their total, abject submission. This act of submission and reverence came to define the word *worship*.

Likewise, the Christian understanding of worship was heavily influenced by Old Testament teachings and practices. In Old Testament times the center, the focus, the beginning, and the end of worship was God. Only He could forgive sins or give life. The Jewish people went to great lengths to offer sacrifices to God in atonement for their sins. The sacrifices had to be perfect, without blemish, so they were pleasing and acceptable to God (Mal. 1:6–8). Old Testament worship was not based on what satisfied people, as the pagan religions were, but upon the foundation of what was acceptable to God.

The ultimate act of worship performed each year was on Yom Kippur, the Day of Atonement. The high priest could enter the holy of holies in the temple to offer a sacrifice on behalf of God's people on only one day each year. The high priest would undergo a lengthy preparation process to purify himself before he dared to enter into the most sacred place (Lev. 16). To enter God's awesome presence was so terrifying that tradition says a rope and a bell were tied to the priest. If the people waiting outside the sacred place could no longer hear the bell jingling, it meant God found the high priest's offering unacceptable and summarily struck him dead. His fellow priests could then pull him out by the rope so they did not run the fatal risk of entering God's fearful presence to remove the corpse.

Biblical worship was centered on God's people relating to a holy, awesome God. It was not meant for unbelievers, for they are unable to worship God. Worship was designed so God's people could demonstrate their adoration and praise for their Creator and Lord. The measure of acceptable worship was not whether the people enjoyed themselves or how they felt as they worshipped but whether or not God was pleased with what people offered Him. The concern was not whether the worship service met people's needs, or whether it was boring, or whether the people's favorite songs were sung, or whether the service ended promptly, but whether Almighty God found the worship by His people acceptable measured against His demanding standards. After Jesus' death on the cross, there was no longer a need to offer sacrifices for the atonement of sin. Now, the apostle Paul said, Christians must "present your bodies a living sacrifice, holy, acceptable to God, which is your reasonable service"

(Rom. 12:1). To properly worship God today, our own lives must be an acceptable sacrifice offered up to Him.

Modern worship services often fall short of God's ideal. People rarely prepare themselves spiritually before entering the church auditorium for worship. They may have stayed up late the night before watching a movie so they are bleary-eyed as they arrive. They may have been watching news or sports highlights on television before they came to church. People's minds are often filled with all manner of concerns other than thoughts of God as they drive into the church parking lot on Sunday morning.

As people enter the church auditorium, there is generally not a hushed expectancy. Rather, the noise of people greeting and talking with one another can resemble the cacophony of sounds found in a college football stadium at halftime. As people begin to sing songs to God, their hearts and minds may be filled with unrepented sin. They may be experiencing conflict with the person sitting in front of them. When people leave the service the same way they entered it, they may feel good about having attended church that week, but they have not encountered Almighty God.

Contrast this to a description of worship by Henry Scougal: "It is impossible to express the great pleasure and delight which religious persons feel in the lowest prostration of their souls before God, when, having a deep sense of the Divine majesty and glory, they sink, if I may so speak, to the bottom of their beings, and vanish and disappear in the presence of God."[1] David Matthews claimed that during the Welsh Revival in 1860, the worship services were so profound and glorious people could remain in church for ten hours, yet it seemed as if they had only been there for five minutes.[2] Repeatedly those who experience revival claim that when people have a genuine encounter with God in revival, they are stricken by their sinfulness in the presence of an absolutely Holy God. Jonathan Goforth claimed that during the revival in China, conviction of sin would become so great among the people they cried out to God for mercy. In one such meeting Goforth recounted: "When I looked up it seemed to me as if every last man, woman, and child in that church was in the throes of judgment."[3] The record of revival testifies that when God's people truly worship Him, they feel deeply convicted of their sin, are awed by God's majesty, and are forever changed.

Deadness Versus Expectancy

In times leading up to periods of revival, there is a recurring complaint of deadness in the worship services, in the prayer meetings, and in church activities. Once revival comes, however, the people gather with expectancy that God will do a fresh work among them. Sadly many churches go through religious motions week after week, year after year without any sense of expectation that God will do anything unusual in their midst. This should grieve us all, but sadly for many this is all they have ever known. Octavius Winslow observes, "Rocked to sleep by a mere formal religion, the believer is beguiled into the delusion that his heart is right, and his soul prosperous in the sight of God."[4]

Today countless churches faithfully open their doors every Sunday and conduct another routine service. Those who attend are comfortable because they know what to expect; the music is to their taste, and the seats are soft. The preacher tells a few funny stories and ends with an innocuous platitude. They see friends and receive a lesson from the Bible. People come to such churches for a variety of reasons, but one thing is certain: they do not arrive expecting God to do anything miraculous during the service. Their church has become like a panacea; they feel better after going. Longtime members measure their attendance in decades, yet they cannot remember the last remarkable thing God did in their congregation.

C. L. Culpepper, who witnessed the Shantung revival, told how God sent Marie Monsen, an evangelical Lutheran missionary from Norway, to challenge the Baptist missionaries. With her penetrating questions such as, "Have you been born of the Spirit?" Monsen shook the complacent missionaries to acknowledge their spiritual lethargy and impotence. Said Culpepper, "It became apparent that God raised her up to expose the spiritual apathy and weakness that existed among the Christians of North China."[5] Once they were awakened, status-quo religion was no longer acceptable. Once God began reviving His people, they developed the predisposition that God would do a great work in every service.

During the 1970 Asbury Revival, students saw that everywhere they went to recount their meeting with God at Asbury College, God would do a similar work in that place too. Time and time again the revival would spread as those who experienced it in one place, shared it with people in other locations. J. Edwin Orr once said, "The fame of revival spreads the flame of revival."[6] During one service students were convinced the Spirit wanted to do something unusual, yet the first part of the meeting was rather uneventful. Then during the offertory people began flooding to the altar to pray. God had chosen one of the most mundane portions of the service to intervene in His people's midst. During that revival people did not know when or how God would work in a service, but they knew *that* He would act.

Prior to many revivals the people's sense of expectancy came as a result of fervent prayer. According to Colin and Mary Peckham, people in the Hebrides Islands began praying earnestly for revival. They prayed so passionately and faithfully that they sensed God would surely come. Duncan Campbell often clarified that he did not bring revival to those islands, but revival was already there when he arrived due to the people's prayers. Campbell was only the spark that ignited the kindling God's people had carefully laid through their fervent praying. Earnest praying brings a strong sense of expectancy to God's people that He is preparing to do something powerful in their midst.

The questions for today's churches are: what do people expect as they enter the church auditorium to worship? Do they anticipate a good musical number? A humorous opening monologue by the pastor? A boring sermon? A moving drama? Or do they enter the sanctuary with the hushed expectancy that God is about to encounter them? When people expect God to powerfully encounter them during a worship service, members come early to pray for the upcoming service. The preacher prepares to extend an altar call so those whose lives God touches that day can respond. Counselors are prepared. The schedule is kept flexible so the church can respond to whatever God chooses to do that day. If God's people are not entering the church building with a sense of expectancy, it may be because they do not understand why they are there in the first place.

Self-Centered Versus God Centered

Western society is chronically self-centered. We are aggressive consumers who expect quality service and all of our needs to be met promptly, thoroughly, and enthusiastically. After all, the customer is always right. With the media bombarding us with slogans and jingles assuring us we deserve the best, a media-driven generation finds it difficult not to bring this consumer mind-set into church. This self-focused attitude has been compounded in recent years by the seeker-sensitive focus of many congregations. Now many worship services are designed so a non-Christian visitor is made to feel at home. One church we know placed flags over the crosses hanging on the auditorium walls so they would not offend visitors! While churches must be sensitive to those God brings to their services, many congregations have transformed their worship times into evangelistic events. We have deviated from what worship services were meant to be—a time and place for God's people to express their adoration and praise to Him. The focus of worship is not meant to be centered on God's *people* but on *God*.

Today, however, Christians assume the measure of a good worship service is whether or not *they* enjoyed it. If the service goes too long, or the preaching is dull, or none of their favorite songs are sung, they claim they "didn't worship" or they "didn't get anything out of the service today." The truth is, they were there not to get but to give. Rarely does a church member leave a worship service asking the question, "Was God pleased with our worship of Him today?" Many worship leaders speak of "an audience of one," but most services are designed to please the audience composed of hard to please church members who "pay the bills."

Church members are fickle; they want worship leaders to "help them worship" while we simultaneously barrage them with critiques and suggestions about our tastes and what makes us most comfortable. Worship leaders are not there to make worship palatable for us. Their role is to help us approach God in an acceptable manner. Nowhere is this self-centered attitude any more prevalent today than in the songs being sung. While some contemporary Christian music contains solidly biblical lyrics, many songs cultivate an extremely self-centered approach to worship and to the Christian life. A. Daniel Frankforter has studied the number of first-person pronouns used in modern choruses and suggests it testifies to a "stunning egocentrism."[7] He notes that the seeker-sensitive approach to worship seeks to make everything "friendly" to the visitor in attendance. Frankforter suggests that people attending worship services need much more than friendship.[8] Many lyrics in modern choruses suggest that all Christ thought about as He went to the cross was me. In truth, Jesus' thoughts were on the Father. Song after song lists what Christ does for *me*. We are reminded through the lyrics that even when we chronically fail Him and disobey Him, He is always there for us. For a Christian consumer, this is as we would expect, but to a biblical worshipper such self-centered worship is ultimately dissatisfying and certainly dishonoring to God.

Today's society is enormously influenced by the media. We are no longer prepared for lengthy, weighty discourses on great doctrines of the faith. We want sound bites with plenty of multimedia clips and PowerPoint presentations to hold our interest. We have all preached in services where longtime members rose and left the service promptly at noon whether the service was over or not. Having put in their hour of church for the week they did not feel obligated to spend one minute longer than what they felt was absolutely necessary. Preaching to such congregations is a challenge, to say the least. Such congregations desire self-help, feel-good sermons, not denunciations of their sins. Pastors who attempt to address the congregation's transgressions can soon find themselves looking for another flock to shepherd.

Self-centered churches desperately need revival. Such congregations typically spend an inordinate percentage of their money on themselves. They construct increasingly grandiose buildings and stage elaborate media productions, but their giving to missions or evangelistic efforts is often sadly wanting.

When self-centered churches experience revival, their focus changes from what pleases them to what satisfies God. God's standards rather than their tastes become the measure for their activities. However, because society is pathologically self-centered, many churches have embraced worldly attitudes without being aware of how far they have departed from being God centered in their outlook.

Performance Driven Versus God Honoring

Excellence is the driving force for what many churches do. Everything done during the worship service must be performed professionally and in a first-class manner. "After all" they proclaim, "God deserves our very best!" God *does* deserve our best. However, professionalism is often mistaken for excellence. In confusing the two, many churches have made costly compromises. The godliest people in a congregation are not always the most talented singers or piano players. In an effort to field the most professional-sounding worship team possible, worship leaders are tempted to enlist people whose walk with God is shallow at best. Churches that invite people to sing on their worship teams who are known adulterers or whose business ethics are notoriously corrupt, demonstrate a profound ignorance of what worship is about. At times worship leaders hire non-Christians to play in the worship band because they are professional musicians. This is excused as a brilliant outreach ploy to get nonbelievers into the church building. At other times, church members who covet the limelight will bask in the attention of the congregation as they croon away with microphone in hand. While such singing may be technically excellent, it surely is not pleasing to God.

Jesus told the woman at the well that worship acceptable to God was done in Spirit and truth (John 4:24). Some worship leaders will drive their worship teams to practice rigorously each week to ensure their harmonization and timing are perfect, but they neglect to nurture their worship team's relationship with God.

The modern drive for professional-quality performances in worship services has many modern manifestations. Megachurches compete to have the largest musical extravaganzas during special seasons such as Christmas and Easter. Churches hire musicians from the local symphony, dramatists, or ballet dancers for their special performances. Advertising for these events is filled with words like *biggest, best, greatest, spectacular* as if they are promoting the newest Broadway play. All of this is done under the well-intentioned but misguided effort of attracting unbelievers. Jesus equipped His disciples to *go out* to spread the gospel, not to huddle together to devise clever ways to draw unbelievers into their building.

Pastors are not immune to efforts of the church for excellence. Churches who broadcast their services on the radio or television are concerned more with their preacher's attractive appearance and oratorical voice than they are with his prayer life or godliness. We know a pastor who served his congregation faithfully and with integrity for almost a decade. He led them to retire their debt early and regularly to baptize new converts. Yet when the minister contracted an illness that affected his appearance, church leaders became embarrassed, so they abruptly dismissed him. Today many churches have pastors who sport Hollywood looks, an ultramodern facility with the latest programming, and musical and dramatic productions that are the talk of the town; yet of many of these churches the risen Christ would say, "Behold, I stand at the door and knock. If anyone hears My voice and opens the door, I will come in to him and dine with him, and he with Me" (Rev. 3:20). Could this be the reason that although in America there are more churches as well as television, radio, and Internet ministries being offered than ever before, the United States and Canada continue to experience relentless moral and spiritual decline?

Shallow Repetition Versus Profound Truth

Daniel Frankforter argues that worship leaders must "constantly guard against the temptation to fabricate facsimiles of religious experiences for their followers."[9] There is a danger in equating emotionalism with worship because encounters with God *are* profound and can foster a deep emotional response. If people are moved emotionally while singing a hymn or hearing a tragic story during the sermon, that is not necessarily because they have worshipped. Preachers and worship leaders strive to get an emotional reaction out of people during each service. Music is one of the most emotional experiences people have. Music speaks directly to the heart; that is why people write songs. Worship leaders seek to employ music so it exercises the greatest impact. Often this means simple choruses will be sung over and over again, as many as eight to ten times. As Frankforter notes, "Their purpose is not to proclaim truth but to induce dazed stupefaction."[10]

Jesus said we would know the truth, and the truth would set us free (John 8:32). Understanding and experiencing truth sets us free, not mindless repetition of the same song. It can seem bewildering why, when there is a wealth of good music available to be sung each Sunday, that the thirty minutes devoted to singing in each service is invested in singing only three songs. It is the belief of many song leaders that by singing the same words repeatedly, the truth of their lyrics will sink slowly into people's hearts, much like a good water soaking on your lawn provides nourishment to the roots of your grass. But one might ask, "If you have to sing the words of a song eight times before the profundity of its lyrics impresses you, perhaps the lyrics are not as vivid as you suppose they are." Clearly it is the driving beat of many modern choruses and the simple tunes producing emotional responses in the singers and not the profound truths the worshippers are contemplating as they sing. The result of much of this style of worship is a church membership who are biblically and doctrinally illiterate and who constantly clamor for another worship experience.

Perfunctory Versus Presence

Stephen Olford warned, "Complacency is the deadly enemy of spiritual progress."[11] Lewis Drummond observed: "Traditionalism—business as usual—will rarely precipitate a profound moving of the Spirit."[12] Yet many churches continue to practice the same annual routines and rituals despite the fact they are not producing spiritual fruit among their members. Churches will often bravely face the reality of dwindling congregations and conclude that people are simply not interested in church any more. Yet many church leaders do not ask the difficult questions, such as: "Why is it that when people attend our worship services, they don't find anything that interests them or makes them want to return?"

In times of revival, even the secular media becomes interested in what is happening in the churches. Francois Carr has described revival as "God in the midst of His people."[13] While theologically we understand God is always present with His people (Jesus claimed He would never leave us or forsake us, Matt. 28:20), yet in times of revival, people become keenly aware of God's manifest presence in their midst. This aspect of revival has engendered much speculation and debate. How can people attend worship services week after week and not "feel" anything special? Then suddenly, it seems as if God has filled the auditorium with His presence, and you cannot go into the auditorium without sensing you have entered a sacred place.

During the Asbury Revival, President Kenlaw observed, "It was just as though Jesus walked in and He has been here ever since."[14] Kenlaw also noted; "In these past days there is a sense that God separated us from the world and shut the world out so that he could speak. God has our attention."[15] Theologically we know God was in the auditorium at Asbury College during previous chapels, but at this time God chose to make His presence palpably obvious to everyone who entered the building. Students would remain in the auditorium throughout the night, not wanting to leave the place where they felt God's presence so powerfully. One of the most common descriptions of revival is the overwhelming awareness of God's presence in the meetings and on those who lead them. It seemed as if God chose to reveal His presence to people wherever Duncan Campbell traveled throughout the Hebrides Islands. In one meeting Campbell claimed, "The very atmosphere seemed to be charged with the power of Almighty God."[16] During the Welsh Revival of 1860, it was said, "We felt at this time as if the glory of the Lord was passing by, whilst we were in the cleft of the rock."[17]

Worship cannot fabricate or summon God's presence in a worship service. God is not at our beck and call. However, it is possible for God to be in our midst and for us not to recognize Him. Once, when Jesus' disciples failed to recognize His activity in their midst, He asked: "Do you not yet perceive nor understand? Is your heart still hardened? Having eyes, do you not see? And having ears, do you not hear?" (Mark 8:17–18). The problem in most worship services is not that we must plead with God to join us in our worship service but that we must open our spiritual eyes to recognize that He has been with us all the time.

Note the profound sense of awareness of God's presence described by C. L. Culpepper during the Shantung Revival: "We were scheduled to meet for the last time Saturday morning, and I had been asked to lead the service. I began to read the 32nd Psalm, and when I had read two verses, every one stood and began to praise God in unison. It seemed the whole room was filled with the glory of the Lord, and love and joy was in every heart. . . . No one wanted to go home because it seemed that heaven had come down, and we wanted to praise God and rejoice."[18] Later, as Culpepper met with two other men, God made His presence profoundly evident to the veteran missionary, to a degree he had never experienced before. Culpepper described it this way: "For the next half hour I was completely enraptured in Him. Human words and man's mind cannot understand nor explain what I heard and saw. The experience is as vivid as if it happened yesterday. The Lord became more real to me than any human being had ever been. He took complete control of my soul— removing all hypocrisy, shame and unrighteousness—and filled me with His divine love, purity, compassion and power."[19]

Clearly these were no ordinary encounters. Culpepper notes that much of the singing during these services was heartfelt and sincere but poorly done. The type of instruments used and the hymns sung seemed irrelevant to the events taking place. The only thing that mattered was that God was unmistakably present and He was dealing with His people. When God is obviously present, many of the issues churches normally spend large amounts of time, energy, and money on become obviously immaterial.

Daniel Frankforter suggests that much of what's happening in contemporary worship today is an effort to find adequate substitutes for lacking the sense of God's presence in worship. He notes: "Pressure is building on congregations to fabricate easily marketed similes of worship—to buy amplifiers, hire rock bands, outfit clergy with clothing from Gap, substitute amateur theatricals for exegetical sermons, scrap sacraments in favor of support groups, and jettison troubling biblical texts for the smarmy cream of pop poetry."[20]

Today's church can offer a wide array of facsimiles for God's presence. When the prophets of Baal on Mount Carmel began to realize their god was not making an appearance at their worship time, they responded by getting increasingly louder and more emotional (I Kings 18:26–29). But the noise and hype and excess were no substitutes for God's coming. We can imagine the prophets of Baal anxiously gesturing for technicians in the sound booth to raise the volume on the drums and guitars. Likewise, many worship leaders may sense they need to captivate their congregation's attention and imagination with something emotionally gripping, but at the end of that experience, God's people go away in the same spiritual condition they entered. People encountered a church service, but they did not meet the living God.

Responsiveness Versus Repression

Christ is the Head of the church. He is its Lord, and He exercises His authority as He wills. The role of spiritual leaders is to hear from God and to move their people on to God's agenda.[21] God may have an extremely different intent for a particular service than the pastoral team might assume. The issue is how responsive God's people are to His activity in their midst.

For example, many preachers would not adjust their sermon in any way, regardless of what happened in the service before they rose to speak. The soloist may have sung an extremely moving song before the sermon about Christ's suffering on the cross. Even as many people are wiping tears from their cheeks at the close of the music and exclaiming "amen!" at the profound message in song they just encountered, most pastors who prepared an opening joke would still proceed to tell it. Many worship leaders and preachers appear unwilling to adjust their plans, or they seem oblivious to the Holy Spirit's working in a different direction at that moment.

The Holy Spirit and Ice Cream

Richard was speaking at a large church where the Holy Spirit was clearly working. At the close of the service, many people came to the front of the auditorium in tears to pray about what God said to them. People were kneeling shoulder to shoulder across the vast platform area. Couples were fervently praying together as they yielded their marriage and home to the Lord. One man was lying prostrate on the ground crying out to God. As people continued silently to leave their seats and make their way to the front of the auditorium to pray, Richard turned the microphone over to the senior pastor so he could shepherd his people through this divine encounter. Incredibly the pastor's first words to his shaken congregation went something like this: "Well, hasn't this been good? But as you know, tonight we are having an ice cream fellowship, and our hospitality committee is already over in the fellowship hall with the ice cream ready. So I am going to close tonight's service in prayer, and then let's all make our way over as quickly as possible. We can visit with one another over there." A brief prayer was offered, and then the church staff quickly led the exodus to the dessert tables.

While fellowship is an important, biblical part of church life, God had something far more important in mind for this congregation that evening. The busyness of church activity can short-circuit a special visitation of God. While extending altar calls long after people have ceased to respond is an abuse of God's people, cutting them short when God is still working is an affront to Him. Worship leaders ought prayerfully to arrange worship services each week. However, if they are sensitive to the working of the Holy Spirit in their midst, as soon as they recognize God at work, they will immediately adjust everything they are doing to support, rather than suppress, what the Holy Spirit is doing.

Preeminence of Singing Versus Powerful Preaching and Praying

Postmodern culture seeks to be far more participative than earlier generations. This is reflected in the record numbers of mission trips and volunteers for ministry projects. This generation is dissatisfied with merely hearing about missions or ministry; they want to *do* ministry. This same participative mind-set is also affecting the way churches conduct their services. In the past, services would include some singing, but the focal point was the sermon. For many people today, however, sitting and listening to a sermon is extremely nonparticipatory. Many listeners will tune out after twenty minutes or less and discreetly begin checking messages on their handheld devices.

In response to this reality, churches have made various attempts to keep the congregation engaged. Many sermons today rarely exceed twenty minutes. Preachers will also barrage the congregation with outlines to be filled in, PowerPoint presentations, video clips, and object lessons in the hope of keeping the people's attention. Another trend is to place greater emphasis on the congregational singing than on the sermon. People assume that during the singing portion of the service, everyone is involved. But the sermon is only a monologue. Today's young adults also identify far more easily with music than they do with sermons or lectures.

While church leaders need to be sensitive to the realities of the culture in which they are ministering, it is dangerous for churches to minimize something Scripture insists should be a priority. Paul confessed: "For since, in the wisdom of God, the world through wisdom did not know God, it pleased God through the foolishness of the message preached to save those who believe" (1 Cor. 1:21). God has chosen uniquely to honor His word as it is preached. While preaching styles vary from one age to the next and across differing cultures, the ministry of exhorting people to heed God's Word is an activity God continues to honor and empower.

In our travels we have participated in many services where the preached word was treated like an unwelcome relative during the holidays who had to be found a seat somewhere around the dinner table. Each of us speaks regularly in various churches and conferences. We have had numerous experiences when the singing portion of the service extended well past its allotted time so there was no time left for a sermon to be preached. Richard spoke at a conference that focused on personal revival. The worship leader became so engaged in the songs he was leading that he continued to sing and to testify long after Richard was supposed to have begun preaching. Finally, still enraptured in his worship, the song leader closed the meeting in prayer and dismissed the people. After being reminded by those in the congregation that he had neglected the sermon, the worship leader sheepishly invited Richard to say a few closing words.

Why would song leaders lead congregations to sing for forty-five minutes and then feel they could allow only ten minutes for the minister to preach? Why would worship leaders sing the same familiar choruses repeatedly but then feel disturbed if the visiting speaker took more than thirty minutes to unfold God's Word? They believe the greatest thing people can do is worship God. By this they mean singing. The problem with this is twofold. First, their definition of worship is limited to singing. It is the emotional experience people receive as they sing that these worship leaders are striving for and which in their mind represents authentic worship.

However, through the preached word God's power and wisdom are revealed (I Cor. 1:23–25). There is no substitute for preaching. Many pastors today have moved to a teaching approach making extensive use of PowerPoint and handouts to be filled in as they lecture. There is a valuable place for teaching, but teaching cannot replace preaching. Neither can singing. Notes Brian Edwards, "Historically the church has prayed its way to the outpouring of God's Holy Spirit, but it can never sing its way into revival."[22]

In many churches the preaching has become so powerless that people prefer the greater emotional appeal of singing. Jonathan Edwards claimed that during times of revival, it seemed as if the preaching of sermons was all new to them.[23] The preaching was being delivered with power once again. When church leaders try to revive their people through singing, they will discover that without proper teaching, preaching, and praying, they will have less and less authentically to sing about.

Traditionally there have been two primary kinds of revival: Word centered and experience centered. Word-centered revivals are generally led by pastors and are anchored on preaching. Experience-centered revivals are led by laypeople who participate through sharing their testimonies and singing. While both are legitimate forms of revival, Word-centered revivals are less vulnerable to abuse and extravagance, and as a result they tend to last longer. One reason the 1904 revival in Wales did not continue longer was because Evan Roberts did not emphasize preaching during the services and the meetings consisting of much singing and testifying, were open to abuses that eventually quenched the Spirit's work.[24]

One other aspect of modern church life has negative implications for revival. Ironically, a great hindrance to revival today is praise choruses. While God has mandated us to praise Him, in many church services today, praise is all that is done. In an attempt to be positive and upbeat, congregations sing only songs praising God for what He has done and will do for them. But revival will not come unless God's people repent of their sin. For that to happen, people must be led to reflect on the state of their walk with God. They must reach a point of brokenness over anything that separates them from an intimate walk with God. This requires other kinds of singing. The church at Laodicea praised God that they had need of nothing while the risen Christ was declaring, "You are wretched, miserable, poor, blind, and naked" (Rev. 3:17). Praise should follow, not replace, repentance. After we have confessed our sin and returned to God, *then* we can joyfully and enthusiastically praise Him with a clean heart.

Order Versus Ardor

For many people the greatest fear of revival is the loss of control. When people are overcome by the convicting power of the Holy Spirit, they can become quite emotional. Historically people have cried out and wailed before God after they encountered Him. Listening to people in the midst of a profound encounter with God can be unsettling. Often people may also desire to speak to the congregation and to confess their sins. This has the potential for revelations of subject matter the pastor is uncertain he wants to bring before the church. As a result, many worship leaders keep tight control of the service and immediately suppress any expression of emotion before it "gets out of hand."

While it is irresponsible for church leaders to try to work their people into an emotional frenzy, it is also unhealthy for church leaders to suppress the Holy Spirit's work in an effort to maintain control over the service. Jonathan Goforth said, "As well expect a hurricane, an earthquake, or a flood, to leave nothing abnormal in its course, as to expect a true revival that is not accompanied by events quite out of our ordinary experience."[25] Church leaders who want to remain in control during revival will not experience it. Martin Lloyd Jones has said, "A revival is not the Church deciding to do something and doing it. It is something that is done to the Church, something that happens to the Church."[26] To experience revival you must be willing to relinquish control to the Head of the church.

When God begins to revive His church, He will often rearrange the order of the service. At the beginning of the Asbury Revival, the dean was scheduled to preach in chapel. However, he sensed he should forgo his sermon and allow some students to give their testimonies. Out of these testimonies the flame of revival burst forth.[27] It may well be that the reluctance of many church leaders to step aside in deference to the Holy Spirit is largely the reason the Holy Spirit is not doing more in our services today. We pray and ask God to bless what we are doing for Him. He waits for us to relinquish our plans so we can experience what He has wanted to do in our midst all along.

Times of revival can seem to have little order. In reality, during times which can seem chaotic, God is reordering His people's priorities and lives so they are pleasing to Him. Testimonial times by people can invite all manner of abuse. When this process is under the Holy Spirit's hand, however, a spirit of reverence and awe will prevent anarchy. In describing a fervent time of revival, Jonathan Goforth noted, "Though it was the most complete disorder it seemed to be the most perfect order."[28] While there have certainly been times when revival led to emotional extremes and excesses, during many revivals the demeanor of the people displayed great reverence and submission to the Spirit. During the Welsh Revival of 1860, the people were described as not exhibiting unusual emotion, but "a deep, profound, and awfully solemn impression prevails."[29] Regarding the Shantung Revival, despite the great emotion and the numerous confessions of sin expressed, it was noted, "One could sense that the Holy Spirit controlled their confessions because no one accused or implicated others."[30] God has a way of completely dismantling His people and remaking them into His image while keeping control of the process the entire time. This can be frightening to church leaders who want to remain in control. Yet God chooses to do His greatest work when His people yield to His sovereignty and respond to His leading.

Seeker Friendly Versus God Friendly

While it is commendable when churches are sensitive to their guests and make the services flow smoothly, there is a fundamental reality that what is pleasing to an unbeliever is not necessarily acceptable to God. Many worship leaders have felt compelled to model their worship services after popular rock concerts or television variety shows so non-Christian visitors are attracted to them. However, it is a dangerous and misguided practice to seek to use the world's ways to accomplish God's work. The world likes to be entertained. God desires to be worshipped. People are self-centered. God commands us to be God centered. The world applauds self-sufficiency; God promotes interdependence. Upbeat music can make people want to dance; God's Spirit makes us want to be holy.

As A. Daniel Frankforter observes, "Entertainments center us on ourselves and our pleasures, but Christian worship is meant to indict our egocentrism and lift us out of ourselves to become a people for others."[31] He further notes: "In practice, however, it is very difficult for a church to rely on the powers of the world without capitulating to them."[32] Sin by nature is self-centered. Redemption makes people God centered. Worship is designed to take our eyes off ourselves and on to our Creator. It is a masterful work of Satan's deception when he convinces God's people they have been liberated from their sinful nature even as they attempt to worship God in a completely self-centered and worldly manner. Biblical worship leaves the worshipper with profound thoughts of God. Pseudo worship leaves people with thoughts of how much they enjoyed the service.

Conclusion

Worshipping God is the noblest activity Christians can do. It is our opportunity to honor and adore our Creator and Savior. Worship ought to be a grateful response to what God has already done in our lives as well as an opportunity for God to accomplish a fresh work in us. Yet careless, unbiblical church services can hinder revival. If we relate to God in unbiblical ways and we speak of God and treat Him in a manner unbecoming to His nature, we can delude people into assuming that by participating in worship services they are pleasing to God. We can deceive ourselves by assuming that because we enjoyed the worship service, God must be pleased with it too. True worship frees us from our self-centered attitudes. It turns our focus away from ourselves and our earthly concerns, and it turns our gaze heavenward to the One who deserves our constant focus. It ought to serve as a warning to us that, with the resurgence of interest in worship among God's people, with large worship gatherings, a plethora of new worship styles, and many popular new worship bands, revival has not come any nearer. We must carefully examine our present worship and ask the Lord to give us His opinion on whether what we are doing is pleasing to Him. If we will not critically assess our current worship practices, we may one day be as shocked as the people of Judah when Almighty God asked of them, "When you come to appear before Me, who has required this from your hand, to trample My courts?" (Isa. 1:12).

QUESTIONS FOR REFLECTION AND DISCUSSION

1. Consider the manner in which you worship God. Is it honoring to Him?
2. Does the way you worship God transform you as you encounter Him?
3. In what ways are the world and its values affecting the way you worship God?
4. How might you better prepare yourself before entering a time of worshipping God?

CHAPTER 16

Counterfeits to Revival

A rthur Wallis notes: "When the Devil cannot carry the position by a frontal assault, he will use a flank attack or employ fifth column tactics."[1] Satan has innumerable weapons in his fiendish arsenal. He can launch a direct attack against God's people using persecution, ridicule, violence, and much more. But Satan is also a master deceiver. The blood of the first-century martyrs was the seeds of the church. When the Roman Empire attempted to stamp out Christianity through violence, the church only became stronger. Far more sinister was when Emperor Constantine made the church respectable, and soon many unbelievers wanted to obtain ecclesiastical positions. Often it is not the attacks on revival that harm it most but those who claim to be its allies and spokespersons.

James Davenport and the First Great Awakening

The First Great Awakening, during the eighteenth century, was a magnificent period in which God raised up some of the greatest religious leaders in American history. God used Theodore Freylinghuysen, Gilbert Tennant, Jonathan Edwards, and George Whitefield to bring a mighty revival to America during the decades preceding the American Revolution. Jonathan Edwards was one of the greatest religious writers and thinkers in American history. Few people have matched the oratorical ability of George Whitefield. His was the era of revival giants.

In this spiritually fruitful period, however, Satan was feverishly working to douse revival's flames being ignited throughout the land. James Davenport was swept up in the revival fervor. However, unlike leaders such as Whitefield and Edwards, Davenport claimed to receive direct revelations from the Holy Spirit. He boasted that he did not need Scripture or instruction from other people because God told him all he needed to know. Davenport viewed himself as more spiritual than any of his contemporaries, having once preached for twenty-one hours straight.[2] When Davenport entered a town, he would demand that the local preachers give him an account of their walk with God. Rarely did they meet his exacting standards. Davenport turned many of his followers against their local ministers and government officials when these leaders rejected his proclamations. Heeding Davenport's warnings, Ola Winslow went to the church house with his axe in hand. He chopped out the family pew, where his family had sat weekly since the church was built, and took it to the attic of his house.[3] Davenport's proclamations became increasingly spectacular. At one point he announced that people needed to reject their worldliness, so he had them bring their wigs, jewelry, cloaks, britches, hoods, gowns, and rings along with many evangelical books and burn them in a large fire.[4] Eventually he proclaimed that God revealed to him that the end of the world was imminent.[5] Davenport was eventually humbled, and he meekly apologized for the manner in which he had conducted himself and how he deeply hurt the cause of revival. But the damage was done. Said Jonathan Edwards, "Without question, the rise of the fanatical element coincided with the decline of the spiritual power of the awakening. Those who spoke most loudly of being led by the Spirit were the very persons responsible for quenching the Spirit's work."[6] Often when God raises up a Whitefield, Satan counters with a Davenport.

Satan in the Midst of God's Work

Satan hates God's people, and he prowls about like a roaring lion seeking those he can destroy (1 Pet. 5:8). Scripture warns that Satan "transforms himself into an angel of light" (2 Cor. 11:14). People generally assume they can trust an angel of light, yet the prince of darkness can appear as the most trustworthy of divine messengers. Christians must diligently seek to discern whether those speaking a word from the Lord are His legitimate emissaries.

One would think that in the midst of a mighty moving of the Holy Spirit, God's enemies would be in full retreat. But that is when they are most dangerous. From our greatest height we fall farthest. When God's people are most open to spiritual influences, we are vulnerable to allowing spiritual darkness into our lives. Jonathan Edwards was well aware that, in the midst of God's mightiest victories, Satan would launch his most bitter counterattacks. It seemed inconceivable that in the midst of the mighty outpouring of the Holy Spirit to set people free from their sins, a respected church leader could grow so hopeless that he saw no escape but to violently take his own life. We should not be surprised to find the false and counterfeit contiguous to the true and godly. The following are some of the common counterfeits that tend to arise during times of revival.

COUNTERFEITS TO REVIVAL

1. Signs and Wonders
2. Emotionalism
3. Evangelism
4. Unity
5. Music
6. Institution Building

---

1. Signs and Wonders

One might assume that signs and wonders provide incontrovertible evidence of God's activity. Many Christians today unwittingly accept and follow television evangelists or self-proclaimed miracle workers who erroneously assume miracles are always a sign of God's affirmation. Yet miracles have never been foolproof signs that someone was God's messenger.

Jonathan Edwards was careful to use Scripture to evaluate the unusual events that occurred during periods of revival. He observed: "But as the influences of the true Spirit abounded, so counterfeits did also abound: the devil was abundant in mimicking both the ordinary and extraordinary influences of the Spirit of God, as is manifest by innumerable passages in the apostles' writings."[7] Because Satan can appear to duplicate the work of God, it is imperative that God's people know how to discern the legitimate from the counterfeit.

When God sent Moses to deliver the Israelites from bondage in Egypt, God empowered him to perform many miracles. Yet initially the Egyptian sorcerers appeared to be capable of performing the same feats (Exod. 7:11–13, 22; 8:7). There came a point, however, where God's power clearly exceeded the might of the magicians (Exod. 8:18–19). Nevertheless, the powers of darkness were able to replicate, to an extent, God's miracles.

Television evangelists are notorious for claiming someone was healed during a service or on a live broadcast. The test of authority for such ministers is not how spectacular the miracle appears to be but how biblical is their teaching. The reason many of the current miracle-working television evangelists draw large crowds is because there are many people, as there were in Jesus' day, who crave miracles. These people incorrectly assume that the presence of the supernatural is evidence of great faith. Televangelists encourage people that if they will claim a miracle from God and truly believe, whatever they ask will be granted. Yet Jesus condemned those who pursued miracles from God rather than God Himself. He declared: "An evil and adulterous generation seeks after a sign, and no sign will be given to it except the sign of the prophet Jonah" (Matt. 12:39). Jesus made it clear that people who constantly need signs in order to prop up their belief are people of weak faith. True faith does not need to be constantly tested and undergirded with miracles. Those with commendable faith believe because of their relationship with God, not because they live on a steady diet of the miraculous. Shadrach, Meshack, and Abednego were only moments from being thrown into a fiery furnace. Yet they proclaimed, "Our God whom we serve is able to deliver us from the burning fiery furnace, and He will deliver us from your hand, O king. But if not, let it be known to you, O king, that we do not serve your gods, nor will we worship the gold image which you have set up" (Dan. 3:17–18). Their faith was based on God and His Word, not on whether God delivered them from danger or death. These men would have understood what the writer of Hebrews meant when he explained that faith "is the substance of things hoped for, the evidence of things not seen" (Heb. 11:1). Many of the greatest revivals of history have not been dominated by miraculous healings or unusual occurrences but by miraculous conversions and the restoration of those who came humbly back to a close relationship with Christ. If people are not careful, they can idolize the miracles of God rather than worship God himself.

2. Emotionalism

Jonathan Edwards witnessed the First Great Awakening. He was undaunted by expressions of emotion. He observed: "We ought not to limit God where He has not limited Himself. Therefore it is not reasonable to determine that a work is not from God's Holy Spirit because of the extraordinary degree in which the minds of persons are influenced."[8] Edwards had witnessed people come under such deep conviction of sin that they cried out in dread of God's judgment and fell to the floor as if dead. Yet Edwards never believed such emotional expressions were irrefutable evidence of conversion or to the Holy Spirit's working. Edwards would carefully examine such individuals to hear their confessions and diligently teach them how fully to respond to what God had said to them.

Feelings can exert a powerful influence in people's lives. Once emotions are aroused, they can spread like an epidemic throughout a congregation. While not adverse to emotional expression during church services, pastors like Edwards were careful to look beyond dramatic occurrences to discern people's spiritual condition. Weeping was not identical to confession, emotionalism did not necessitate a work of the Holy Spirit, crying out or falling to the ground did not indicate people had placed their faith in Christ. Problems developed because some people sought the form of an encounter with God without the substance. Arnold Dallimore comments on the revival meetings in George Whitefield's time: "The practice of creating noise and confusion in church services was developed. This arose from the fact that the Spirit of God had wrought an overwhelming conviction in many hearts, causing sinners to cry out. But certain persons, feeling these extreme experiences were a necessary element of revival, sought to imitate them, shouting and falling to the floor in the midst of the services."[9]

Religious leaders have always realized they could manipulate the emotions of people. By telling a compelling story, shouting and pounding on the pulpit, gesturing dramatically, singing emotional songs, taking a service late into the evening when people are tired, or leading people through a tragedy, leaders can elicit deep feelings in a congregation. Because people who experience a profound encounter with God feel deeply about it, many charlatans strive to reproduce the emotions while bypassing the encounter with God.

C. L. Culpepper claimed: "Excess? Extravagance? Yes, whenever a work of grace is going on, Satan is ever present among the sons of God. He seeks to destroy their work first by ridicule and second by duplicating it."[10] While emotion can be duplicated, a profound encounter with God cannot. The key is to evaluate every emotional experience in worship against the Scriptures. Often during revivals characterized by emotional responses, leaders would take those overcome with emotion to a separate room where they could receive counsel and be guided to make an appropriate commitment to Christ. People need to be helped to move beyond merely *feeling* about what God said to *believing* and *acting* on what they heard.

3. Evangelism

One of the most subtle counterfeits to revival today is evangelism. We have already established that revival is for God's people. It is what happens when spiritually lethargic Christians return to their love relationship with Christ and their spiritual life is reenergized. Evangelism is crucial, but it is not identical to revival. Evangelism invariably results from a revived people, but it is not a synonym for revival. Because new conversions are so closely linked with revival, they are often mistaken for the same thing.

Many churches today have one focus: evangelism. Every sermon is aimed at bringing unbelievers to faith in Christ. As we have seen, churches often hold evangelistic meetings and call them revival meetings. If there are many converts during that week, the "revival" meetings are considered a resounding success, even if God's people habitually continue to sin and to remain spiritually lukewarm. Pastors and church staff members who are evangelistically oriented regularly preach on evangelism and make evangelistic visits. As a result, their church experiences a growing number of baptisms. However, many churches that have focused exclusively on evangelism have suddenly imploded when the weak foundation upon which the church functions is exposed. Church leaders may suddenly be exposed indulging in immorality. Divisions and power struggles can develop. Pride can permeate the church life as it strives to reach new records of converts and attendance. While it is commendable for churches to want to reach their communities for Christ, a growing attendance is not the same as a revived church.

During the great Welsh Revival in 1859–1860, it was observed: "It is very probable that there is much chaff among the wheat."[11] While the crowds swelled during the period of revival, not all the people who were attending were truly born again and being motivated by the Holy Spirit. This occurs in most revivals. While this phenomenon does not discredit revival, it does compel church leaders to be extremely cautious in evaluating what is occurring within the crowds of people who are attending. Jesus never placed His trust in the crowd. One minute they could be shouting, "Hosanna! Blessed is He who comes in the name of the LORD!" (John 12:13), and the next day they could be screaming, "Crucify Him!" (John 19:6). Church leaders must resist the temptation to be enamored with numbers. They must look beyond the increased attendance and even the numerous professions of faith and examine whether there has truly been a transformation of people's hearts.

4. Unity

Another subtle yet sinister counterfeit to revival is unity among Christian denominations. Jesus prayed "that they all may be one, as You, Father, are in Me, and I in You; that they also be one in Us, that the world may believe that You sent Me" (John 17:21). As is the case with many aspects of quasi revival, unity is a good thing, and it is something God desires. But it is not a substitute for revival.

Historically, when God brought revival, the result was unity among God's people. During the Brownwood revival, churches from widely differing denominational backgrounds began working together preceding the outbreak of revival. This unusual cooperation and unity gave evidence that God was at work among His people. During the Laymen's Prayer Revival of 1857–1858, people from every Christian denomination were praying together. Revival brought unity to Christians in New York. Out of that revival a spiritual awakening spread across the nation. Typically when revival occurs, it flows out of the church or denomination where it began and quickly engulfs other portions of God's kingdom. Unity is therefore a significant component of revival.

Unity is a precursor and a product of revival but it is not revival. Some well-meaning church leaders believe that if they can just gather people from various denominations to a prayer rally or to conduct a joint ministry or to sign a declaration, then revival has come. The reality is that they may be witnessing a key work of God's Spirit in preparing for revival, but revival itself has not yet occurred. If people are satisfied merely with the outward semblance of unity between God's people, they may not keep pushing for the reviving of people's hearts. A revived people will naturally seek to live in unity with their brothers and sisters in Christ. But people working in unity have not necessarily had their intimate walk with God renewed and refreshed. Moreover, at times Christians can misguidedly seek unity at the cost of doctrinal integrity. These people assume that unity is the supreme goal and worth jettisoning biblical beliefs and practices. History has shown, however, that more than unity, God's people need revival. When God's people are revived, unity is a natural by-product. When unity becomes the end, doctrinal compromises lead to spiritual stagnation.

5. Music

Music speaks powerfully to our hearts. As a result, people can confuse singing with revival. While music has historically played an important role in revivals, it is but a tool and an expression of revival, but it is not revival.

Richard was once speaking at a church whose congregation consisted primarily of young adults. The Holy Spirit moved powerfully. When an invitation was extended for people to come to the front of the auditorium to pray and surrender themselves afresh to God's will for their lives, people began streaming to the front. One young man approached Richard and being brokenhearted began to recount how he had been disobedient to God's will, but he would resist no longer. As they began praying together, the volume of the worship music suddenly rose considerably. Apparently the members of the band were excited to see such a wonderful response from the people. They concluded that an upbeat praise song was in order. The drum was pounding. The guitars were squealing. The singers were belting out praises to God for the mighty work He had done. They reached the refrain and began hopping up and down in their exuberance. The music by this time was so loud that Richard could not hear what the young man was praying. They had to wait until the band was finished before they could resume praying.

The problem was not that the band liked playing loud music or that they wanted to praise God. At issue was their belief that the normative response whenever God does a work in His people's midst is immediately to respond at full volume. There is a time and place for singing praises to God. This was not one of them. People were still coming forward and praying. Some were waiting for counselors. In the band's enthusiasm they were actually squelching the move of God they were celebrating. More than hopping for joy, people needed to take steps of faith; more than hearing brain-jarring praise music, they needed to hear the still small voice of God. While the band may have left the service that day "pumped" at the fact that "God showed up," they were unaware that rather than helping God's people respond to God, they may have been the greatest hindrance.

Music can powerfully affect our emotions. But encountering a song is not identical to encountering God. Praising God is also not a substitute for repenting before God or asking His forgiveness. One of the reasons we occasionally ask the pianist to play a song during the altar call that people do not recognize is because many people enjoy singing, and they will instinctively sing along if they know the words. It could be, however, that on this particular day God wants them to pray, to talk with a staff member, or to weep. But hearing the words of a familiar song immediately compels some people to begin singing and to miss the unique experience God had for them.

A tendency among many contemporary music bands is to have people leave the auditorium each Sunday with a loud, upbeat praise song. While at times this may be appropriate, such an attitude often displays a lack of confidence in the work of the Holy Spirit. As visiting speakers in many different churches, we have often been unable to hold a conversation with anyone after the service due to the loud music being played. Attempting to pray at the close of the service with such intrusive music is futile. At times the worship band seems to be more concerned with people watching and listening to them as they leave the auditorium than for people to fellowship with one another or to pray about what God just said to them.

Many worship teams today act as if allowing people quiet time before God would indicate they had somehow fallen down on the job.

Music is a powerful, legitimate worship tool. Songs with biblical lyrics and worshipful music can be used by the Holy Spirit to impact worshippers deeply. But music can also become a subtle counterfeit to a true encounter with God. Whether the music comes from a harp, a pipe organ, a guitar, or a drum set, God can use any music to reach His people. However, when music becomes the end and not the means of worship, it is idolatry. Worship leaders must use it carefully and always under the Holy Spirit's guidance.

6. Institution Building

Whenever God moves among His people, we face the temptation of institutionalizing what He has done. People like to take control, even of God's activity. But when people attempt to take control of a divine work, it inevitably dies. Arthur Wallis observed the danger of people attempting to substitute with their administration and publicity what God had formerly accomplished by His power: "It became necessary to substitute human arrangement, which could be worked without the Spirit's power, for the divine arrangements, which were dependant on that power."[12] Duncan Campbell concluded: "I do not believe that the devil is greatly concerned about getting between us and work. His great concern is getting between us and God. Many Christian workers have buried his spirituality in the grave of his activity."[13] Busyness and church programming can create the illusion of a revived people, when in fact the congregation is frenetically active but spiritually dead.

If you had visited the temple in Jerusalem in the first century, many things would have impressed you. The beautiful architecture would have taken your breath away. The magnificent structure could be seen from miles away as people approached the city. It was one of the most magnificent edifices in the known world. As you reached the outer court of the temple, you would have been caught up in the hustle and bustle of the crowds trafficking through its courts. Like many modern churches, with a foyer filled with cafes, information booths, sign-up tables, and missions displays, the temple in Jerusalem was teeming with people prepared to provide whatever you needed to worship God. Large receptacles for people's offerings overflowed with donations. Many elaborate prayers were being offered publicly. Yet it would all have been an illusion. If you had dared to enter into the inner place of the temple, behind the veil, you would have discovered it was empty. The ark of the covenant, symbolizing God's presence, was no longer there. The glory of God had departed, and the people did not know it. They continued to come and engage in religious activity, assuming they were pleasing God. Yet when God sent His own Son to the temple, the people did not recognize Him, and some plotted to kill Him. As a result, Jesus prophesied that soon not one stone would be left atop another in that magnificent place of worship.

When people experience revival, they naturally begin to witness and to serve with renewed energy. Periods of revival are busy times. But again service and activity are the fruit of revival; they are not revival. At times a church may be languishing, then they call a new pastor, and he promptly introduces new programs and ministries. People notice the renewed activity and claim, "That pastor has revived the church." The mistake is, of course, assuming busyness equates a renewed spiritual state. The reality is that many Christians today are working extremely hard in their church and are present every time the church doors open, yet they are languishing spiritually.

Far from being the evidence of revival, busyness can actually prevent God's people from experiencing renewal. Zealous activity is often a false panacea to cover anemic spirituality. If we can just stay busy enough, we don't have to address our lethargic faith or the sin that torments us. Busy people can take such pride in the beauty of their church facility and, with the hum of religious activities, they see no reason for revival. Besides, when could the church possibly find time on its busy calendar to schedule a series of revival meetings even if it did need them? Many congregations erroneously assume a burgeoning calendar of events, and the hustle and bustle filling its multifunctional facilities testifies to spiritual vibrancy. In fact, churches become so preoccupied with improving the efficiency and marketability of their institution they forget they are a spiritual body to be fashioned by Christ. Their people are busy and productive but spiritually destitute.

WARNING SIGNS

1. Self-Centered Rather than Christ Centered
2. Lack of Repentance/Holiness
3. Unbiblical
4. Experience Driven
5. Extremes

Warning Signs

Christian leaders need spiritual discernment to recognize the difference between revival and man-made or satanic counterfeits. The following characteristics accompany counterfeits to revival.

1. Self-Centered Rather than Christ Centered

Genuine works of God always glorify Christ, not a person. Christians tend to make celebrities of people. If people were delivered from a sinful past, the church loves to put them on stage and listen to their testimony. The more salacious their history, the better. However, the limelight can become addictive as people begin to enjoy being the center of attention. Pastors and worship leaders especially must be cautious that, as they testify to God's work in their church, they don't become filled with pride. God will not share His glory. When we direct people's attention to ourselves rather than to God, the power and glory will depart. Today announcements about a new revival occur regularly somewhere in the country. However, many of these announcements talk far more about the preacher or leader than about God. That is a sure sign that God is not the author.

This was largely the crime Moses committed before God's people. While Moses had obviously played an enormous role in God's deliverance of the Israelites, no one believed Moses parted the Red Sea or sent manna from heaven. But when God instructed Moses to speak to the rock so it produced water, notice what he did:

> And Moses and Aaron gathered the assembly together before the rock; and
> he said to them, 'Hear now, you rebels! Must we bring water for you out
> of this rock?' Then Moses lifted his hand and struck the rock twice with
> his rod; and water came out abundantly. (Num. 20:10–11)

Moses presumed upon God. His word choice said it all: "Must we bring water out for you?" Moses spoke as if his effort as much as God's delivered the people. Rather than humbly obeying God's instructions exactly as he was told, Moses modified God's Word, striking the rock rather than speaking to it. He acted as though God's Word was merely advice and God's power was available to be summoned as Moses required. Despite all Moses did in God's service, no one is allowed to deflect God's glory without consequence (Isa. 42:8). Because of his presumption, Moses forfeited his right to enter the promised land. No one worked harder to enter Canaan than Moses. Yet God made it clear He will humble *anyone* who tries to take credit for His work.

When someone acts as if he or she is responsible for a divine work occurring, warning bells should sound immediately in the minds of alert Christians. When testimonies or sermons draw attention to people but not to God, you can conclude that the Holy Spirit is not speaking through the person at the microphone.

While Jonathan Goforth was speaking in a series of meetings during the Shantung Revival, he was tempted by feelings of pride. As he sat on the platform preparing to speak, he looked out on the large crowd and began to have thoughts about how God was marvelously using him. Suddenly Goforth realized Satan was tempting him to take credit for the revival. Instantly Goforth realized the peril he faced. God would not continue to use his life in revival if he ever entertained the thought that he was responsible. Goforth renounced any such thought, and God used him mightily for years afterward.[14]

Pride is one of the most insidious and deceptive hindrances to revival. It camouflages itself to look like piety. Pride can disguise boasting to look like giving a testimony. Public praying can be a vehicle for self-aggrandizing. Henry Scougal confessed his ongoing battle with pride: "Those varieties I have shut out of the doors are always getting in by the windows . . . and though I should come to think meanly of myself, yet I cannot endure that others should think so too."[15] Yet Scougal wisely recognized: "That which makes any body esteem us, is their knowledge or apprehension of some little good, and their ignorance of a great deal of evil that may be in us; were they thoroughly acquainted with us, they would quickly change their opinion."[16] The presence of pride in times of revival provides incontrovertible evidence that sin and Satan have found an inroad. The time of revival may have begun legitimately enough, but it may have been hijacked by Satan through his tried-and-true method of appealing to people's insatiable pride.

2. Lack of Repentance/Holiness

Another clear sign that a movement is not of God is when it does not lead people to repentance and to holy living. In modern times people have attempted to label various events as revival that did not involve repentance. People have described periods of music, laughing, or healing as revivals. Yet no one felt any conviction over their sin. People who burst into joyful laughing during a worship service but who do not feel grieved over their sin have undoubtedly experienced something, but it is not revival. Experiencing healing is not the same as experiencing revival. Sometimes Jesus healed people even before they believed in Him (John 5:1–15). Dancing in the aisles or weeping during a worship service is not the same as revival. You can't experience true revival without feeling conviction for your sin. When looking for evidence of true revival, repentance is the unmistakable sign.

3. Unbiblical

Francois Carr notes: "Genuine revival always brings a hunger and thirst for the word of God."[17] God is clearly reviving His people when they desire to hear and obey God's Word. The most effective way to measure the authenticity of revival is to evaluate all that is said and done against Scripture. God always remains true to His Word. Satan tempts God's people to compromise or adjust God's Word in their efforts to serve Him (Matt. 4:1–11; Luke 4:1–13).

Robert Murray McCheyne urged ministers: "Get your texts from God—your thoughts, your words, from God. . . . It is not great talents God blesses so much as great likeness to Jesus. A holy minister is an awful weapon in the hand of God. A word spoken by you when your conscience is clear, and your heart full of God's Spirit, is worth ten thousand words spoken in unbelief and sin."[18] While times of revival may make use of testimonies and singing, the heart and force of every revival comes from the Holy Spirit's use of God's Word. Jonathan Goforth declared, "The Sword of the Spirit, which is the word of God, is the only weapon which has ever been mightily used in revival."[19] Testimonies have no authority, regardless of how compelling they may be. Music, no matter how emotionally appealing, is not equal to Scripture. Every genuine revival will have Scripture at its center and will be conducted in a manner that is thoroughly consistent with God's Word.

4. Experience Driven

A final sign that what appears to be a revival is not authentic is when it is centered on experience rather than the Word of God. God used Evan Roberts powerfully during the 1904 awakening in Wales. Yet at the close of Roberts's public ministry, he began to fear that much of what occurred during the revival had actually been the activity of Satan.[20] During one meeting Roberts had a strong impression of the number 146. He asked a pastor what that number meant. No one knew. Afterward they discovered that 146 people had been converted that day. Roberts rejoiced that God had apparently demonstrated His foreknowledge. "However, something changed after that service, for the keenness of the Spirit was absent. So far, Mr. Roberts had been filled with one passion only, to see souls saved. After that, as he discovered later, he became interested in numbers, and began to look for them."[21] Later Roberts was conducting a meeting where he remained behind in a back room to pray before he went out to preach. Suddenly the entire room seemed to be filled with a brilliant light. Sensing it was God's encouragement, he went out to preach boldly, and many people were converted. Later that week he was preparing to preach in a different city. As he waited alone in a room, the room was suddenly filled with darkness and a sense of evil. Roberts prayed but did not sense victory. Later Roberts concluded that the experiences both of light and darkness had come from the enemy. "The strategy of the enemy to bring defeat at that important meeting was to switch him from the basis of faith and direct his attention to impressions and feelings. To begin by trying to discourage him with darkness was useless, for his faith would remain unshaken. The unusual light accomplished the enemy's purpose. He confessed that after the experience of the supernatural light he began to look for more manifestations and his position of faith was thus weakened. The experience of darkness came after he had already weakened himself by turning from the basis of faith to that of impressions."[22]

Even a revival leader like Evan Roberts had to be on his guard against basing his efforts on experience rather than on God's Word. The Bible calls us to believe and to obey by faith. Mystical and dramatic experiences are like eating cotton candy. They provide fleeting pleasure but soon leave us hungering for more. Some base their Christian life on a series of experiences, and as a result their Christian life is like a roller coaster with exhilarating highs and devastating lows. God's Word calls for faith and produces solid, mature Christians and healthy churches.

When experience is the focus of revival, those involved can mistakenly conclude that for others to experience revival, they must do things the same way and undergo the same experiences. During the revival in Uganda, Christians became seriously divided between those who believed that true revival had to occur in exactly the same way they had experienced it and those who believed there were various ways of being revived. At times Christians can become judgmental when others do not experience God the same way they do. Revivals can be cut short when people begin to focus on the means of revival rather than on the Author of revival.

5. Extremes

Beware of some, like James Davenport, who seek to join a work of God and then move it to extremes. These are generally people who have not seen God work in their own ministries so they attempt to hijack the divine activity taking place elsewhere. They are not content to see God work in the church; they want to control His activity and to have people within the movement look to them for spiritual guidance.

This element does not trust the Holy Spirit to guide His people. They may bully people into an emotional frenzy, or they may seek to orchestrate a movement through the use of dreams, visions, or signs. Conversely, some appoint themselves as theological and biblical "police." These people do not trust the Holy Spirit to guide His people through Scripture so they personally seek to correct any misunderstanding of Scripture or condemn any practice or behavior they believe is improper. Individuals have established Web sites or written pamphlets condemning what others are doing. This type of person is always clamoring for people's attention and adherence and is perpetually confounded that so many people turn to others for their guidance instead of to them. One of the most suspicious signs of such people is, despite the fact they claim to be the most biblical and orthodox of any of their contemporaries, God does not choose to use them, or their ministry, to initiate revival. These people are consigned, instead, to stand on the sidelines critiquing what others are doing. Revival is meant to restore Christians and churches who have lost their first love. Genuine revival does not bring people to extremes; rather it brings people back to Jesus. If a leader seeks to lead people farther and to greater extremes than the Spirit originally did, he ought to be treated with caution.

These are some of the surest signs of counterfeit versus genuine revival. Be vigilant to watch for them in your life and in your church.

QUESTIONS FOR REFLECTION AND DISCUSSION

1. Have spiritual counterfeits entered into your life or church? If so, what are they?
2. How do you measure people's claims to ensure they are biblical?
3. How do you keep an open heart to a fresh work of God when there are so many counterfeits today?

CHAPTER 17

Why Revival Tarries:
Preparing for Revival

Richard was once preaching at an older, formal church. The pastor, in briefing him before the Sunday morning service, alerted him that the people in the congregation were loving and sincere people but they were mostly white-collar professionals who were uncomfortable "walking the aisles" at the close of the service. The pastor told Richard to close the service in whatever manner he felt comfortable but not to be disappointed if no one came forward.

At the end of the service, Richard realized the people had been extremely attentive and they should be given the opportunity to respond publicly to what God said to them. Richard extended an invitation for people to come to the front of the large auditorium to pray while the music played. People began silently, steadily to come. The older auditorium was rectangular in shape with a balcony across the back. People began leaving the balcony and making their way down the long auditorium to pray at the front. A good group of people were already at the front praying, with more on their way. God was at work, and Richard felt the pastor should guide his people to respond, so he turned the microphone over to him. The pastor immediately brought the music to a halt and asked ushers to come forward to take the morning offering. One usher actually passed someone in the aisle as he was coming to the front to pray. The congregation was told to be seated. Those who had been praying quickly dispersed while those who were making their way to the front discreetly stepped into empty pews and took a seat. The moving of the Spirit came to an end. The program continued.

Later the pastor asked Richard what his impressions were of the morning service. Richard commented that the people seemed willing to come forward to respond to God but the leaders on the platform squelched God's work that morning. People apparently did not see the front of the auditorium as a safe place because they could be left stranded there before they hardly had an opportunity to pray. That night Richard asked if he could lead the entire invitation time at the close of the service. At the beginning of his sermon, Richard alerted the people that he was going to extend an altar call again, but this time he would leave it open until everyone had time to pray and to return to his seat. When the invitation was given at the close of the service, people began to come forward in droves. When the front was filled with people, Richard announced that the service would continue in reverent silence for several more minutes until people finished responding to God. Then Richard sat next to the pastor on the front pew. The pastor was ecstatic. He discreetly pointed out to Richard a businessman praying on his knees. The pastor indicated that he had never seen this man pray in public before. Then he pointed to a woman who was praying. The pastor said, "You have *no* idea how significant it is that she is doing that." Person after person came humbly and brokenly responding to God that night in ways they never had before.

This pastor had been faithfully preaching God's Word, and his people had been under conviction for their sin. The pastor, however, had made some incorrect assumptions about his people, hindering them from responding to God as they desperately needed. When that artificial barrier was removed, the church felt the fresh moving of the Holy Spirit in its midst.

In an earlier chapter we examined corporate hindrances impeding revival. In this chapter we want to ask the simple question, "Why does revival tarry?"[1] Second, we will look at ways to recognize the signs when the Holy Spirit begins to move softly and gently through your life or your church in renewal.

Why Revival Tarries

More organizations, books, and conferences may be devoted to promoting revival today than at any other period of history. Yet America and other parts of the world, such as Western Europe, continue to wait for revival to come. The urgent question is, why does revival tarry?

Revival involves God's people returning to Him. In Scripture, God has clearly set forth His guidelines for this to happen. People may have *left* God on their terms, but *returning* to God is always under His conditions. We have known people who willfully sinned and turned away from their relationship with God. When they faced the consequences for their actions, they realized they needed to return to God. Yet these people tried in vain to come back to God on their terms. Some who refused to obey God's instruction to enter the ministry wanted to have a close walk with God once more, but they still did not intend to do what God told them about serving Him. Others were serving as pastors when they sinned grievously. Now that they are ready to return to God, they insist they should be reinstated into all of their former positions without accepting any ongoing consequences for their sin. Richard Owen Roberts states: "It is absurd and erroneous to suppose that when you have repented of sin all the consequences of your sin cease. There are multitudes of sins that carry an automatic penalty with them, and no level of repentance can change that."[2] We cannot negotiate our repentance or our return to God. We have nothing with which to bargain. We entirely rely on God's grace and mercy for our relationship with Him to be restored.

Notice in the following verses what God says He looks for in those who return to Him:

> But from there you will seek the LORD your God, and you will find Him if you seek Him with all your heart and with all your soul. (Deut. 4:29)

> "Now it shall come to pass, when all these things come upon you, the blessing and the curse which I have set before you, and you call them to mind among all the nations where the LORD your God drives you, and you return to the LORD your God and obey His voice, according to all that I command you today, you and your children, with all your heart and with all your soul, that the LORD your God will bring you back from captivity, and have compassion on you, and gather you again from all the nations where the LORD your God has scattered you." (Deut. 30:1–3)

> If My people who are called by My name will humble themselves, and pray and seek My face, and turn from their wicked ways, then I will hear from heaven, and will forgive their sin and heal their land. (2 Chron. 7:14)

> Seek the LORD while He may be found. Call upon Him while He is near. Let the wicked forsake His way, and the righteous man his thoughts; let him return to the LORD, and He will have mercy on him; and to our God for He will abundantly pardon. (Isa. 55:6–7)

> Then I will give them a heart to know Me, that I am the LORD, and they shall be My people, and I will be their God, for they shall return to Me with their whole heart. (Jer. 24:7)

Then you will call upon Me and go and pray to Me, and I will listen to you. And you will seek Me and find Me, when you search for Me with all your heart. (Jer. 29:12–13)

Draw near to God and He will draw near to you. Cleanse your hands, you sinners; and purify your hearts, you double-minded. (James 4:8)

Throughout these verses God is consistent in what He wants.

First, we must return to Him. This implies our recognition that we are the ones who departed. It signifies our acknowledgment that the departure was our choice and a result of our sin.

Second, we must return with our whole heart and soul. No lukewarm, half-hearted return will do. Many backslidden Christians bemoan the fact their walk with God is not what it should be. Yet they do not care enough to pay the price necessary for a return to divine fellowship. Returning involves more than talking. It means reconciliation with God is the most compelling and consuming desire in your life. When you return to God in this manner, no obstacle will stop you, no consequence will be too severe, no humiliation will deter you from being thoroughly restored to God.

Third, we must repent of our sin. As James says, "Cleanse your hand, you sinners" (James 4:8). Returning to God implies more than beginning to attend church services again. It requires that we repent of our sin and return to God with clean hands (Ps. 24).

We have had many people say to us, "I did return to God, but I still don't feel like my relationship with Him is as it should be." The key, of course, is to view our return from God's perspective. We have not returned to God merely because we claim we have. We have not truly returned to God until He accepts our manner of returning. The book of James gives sure proof that we have returned to God: God will return to us (James 4:8). If we do not yet sense God's nearness, then our returning to Him is incomplete. Regardless of how much we feel we have made our way back to God, it is insufficient until we are sure He has drawn near to us. Whether we are seeking personal revival or helping our church experience renewal, this is the pattern for revival and enjoying fellowship with God once more.

Recognizing the Early Signs of Revival

During the beginning of the eighteenth century, Western society was riddled with the secular philosophy of John Locke and Thomas Hobbes. The wealth that was pouring into England from its colonies was creating enormous fortunes and cultivating a pervasive sense of materialism among society. This was an age when many sensed that the church had lost its ability to call society back to God and His standards. Yet in the midst of that darkened time, Arthur Wallis observed, God was at work. In 1703 three babies were born who would one day become giants of revival: Jonathan Edwards, Gilbert Tennent, and John Wesley.[3] Eleven years later George Whitefield was born. While people in the church cried out to God in revival, they had no idea that some of the young children playing in the church courtyard were God's answer to their prayers.

So it is with the movements of revival. While revival often appears to come suddenly and unexpectedly, studies of revival reveal that God put numerous antecedents in place before revival came. Wallis suggests there are two foundation stones for every revival: God's sovereignty and people's preparedness.[4] It is God's prerogative to decide when revival will occur, but He also works in the hearts of people to fulfill His requirements.

For example, an early indication that revival may be coming is an increased hunger in the hearts of God's people to hear, understand, and obey God's Word. At times a noticeable increase in attendance in the worship services or in the prayer meetings will occur without advertising or special promotion. Scripture indicates that "no one can come to Me unless the Father who sent Me draws him" (John 6:44). Even our returning to God is the work of the Holy Spirit in our lives. When you sense you or others are being drawn to return to God, you are witnessing an early sign of revival.

Martin Lloyd Jones declared, "The trouble, as I see it, with the Church today is that she does not realize, as she should, that her primary need, and her urgent need at the moment, is the need of life itself."[5] When people begin to have an uneasy stirring in their hearts that something important is missing in their lives, this restlessness is often the Holy Spirit's working to draw people back to Christ.

Brian Edwards notes that times of revival are the exaggerated ingredients of what God always expects from His people. It is not necessarily the spectacular that ushers in revival but an increase in the ordinary. Prayer meeting attendance begins to increase. Church volunteers grow in number. An increasing number of people request additional and deeper Bible study. Perhaps most importantly, more and more people come under conviction of their sin.

Often the outbreak is set off by a dramatic occurrence such as when students shared testimonies in the Asbury and Brownwood revivals. At first glance dramatic testimony can appear suddenly to plunge an entire congregation into a period of revival. But as you examine these moments, you soon discover that the testimonies were merely sparks to light the abundant kindling already laid. Already many were meeting to pray for revival. People were coming under conviction of sin. Marriages were restored. The Spirit was drawing people together into Christian unity. As you study these events, you realize the testimonies, the powerful sermons, or the crisis that instigated the revival was just one in a series of events God put into place to bring His people back to Himself.

Scripture exhorts those who have backslidden to "break up your fallow ground, for it is time to seek the LORD" (Hos. 10:12; Jer. 4:3). Fallow ground is soil left untended by a farmer, and now it has grown hard and impervious to seeds sown. For a crop to be produced once again, the soil must be ploughed and turned over. As long as it remains hard, no amount of seeds cast upon it will take root. Breaking up the soil is the key to further fruitfulness.

People can attend church services week after week, and yet the sermons they hear have no effect even though they address specific needs they are facing. In response the Holy Spirit will seek to break up the soil of people's hearts until they are responsive once again to the convicting word and work of the Spirit. For example, if people become calloused by the pursuit of wealth, God may allow a stock market crash, such as during the Laymen's Revival of 1857–1858 to shake people out of their materialistic stupor. God may allow people to lose their jobs so He removes their idol and gains their attention. The sudden deaths of two young people preceded the revival in Northampton under Jonathan Edwards. The American Civil War caused thousands of God's people to cry out to Him in repentance for the sins of the nation and led to thousands of soldiers coming to faith in Christ. God has innumerable ways to break up the fallow ground of His people's hearts. While this can be a slow, painful process, the Spirit of God will continually work to prepare the hearts of His people.

When the founder of the Salvation Army, General Booth, wanted to encourage his daughter in her endeavors for the Lord, he urged her to keep her eyes on the tide and not on the waves.[6] The wise general knew Satan would afflict God's people and the waves would come in only to recede again. But he also knew the tide was certain and, regardless of what individual waves might do, the overall course of events would change dramatically with the tide. We must have the spiritual eyes to recognize the general movements of God and not grow discouraged at isolated setbacks that inevitably come with kingdom work.

Jesus urged His disciples to open their spiritual eyes to recognize God's activity occurring all around them (Mark 8:17–21). So we will miss God's work around us if we do not remain spiritually alert. The Holy Spirit's handiwork will be evident in many ways, for example when:

- an unusual number of people come to the front of the auditorium to pray at the close of the service
- growing numbers of people are meeting to pray
- conversions are taking place
- people are experiencing profound conversion experiences
- our hearts are strangely stirred by a verse of Scripture we read one morning
- the pastor's sermon seems to be aimed directly at you
- the singing in the worship times is unexplainably heartfelt and enthusiastic
- people begin giving sacrificially and joyfully
- people seem unusually, reverently attentive to the preaching
- a growing number of people are meeting for Bible study
- people who had been estranged are reconciled
- people begin to confess their sins

Of course these are not necessarily proof revival has come. They may, however, indicate the Holy Spirit is working and preparing the soil for a coming revival. If God alerts you to recognize His work, then you must make whatever adjustment is necessary to join Him in what He is doing. Do not mistake preparation for revival itself. However, when you see the gentle stirring of the Holy Spirit in your life or in the midst of your church, take heart! God is not finished with you yet, and He is ever working to draw you and your congregation into a close walk with Him.

QUESTIONS FOR REFLECTION AND DISCUSSION

1. What evidence do you see that God is preparing your life for a time of renewal?
2. What evidence do you see that God is working to bring revival to your church, denomination, or nation?
3. What would it mean for you or your church to seek the Lord "with all your heart"?
4. What adjustments do you need to make in your life so you are fully prepared to respond to God's activity in your life?

CHAPTER 18

Becoming a Catalyst for Revival

W hat can I do to bring revival to my church?" We have been asked this question a multitude of times by people from around the world. Many people recognize that their church desperately needs a fresh moving of the Holy Spirit in its midst, but they have no idea how they can help bring it about. Occasionally pastors tell us how their people are spiritually lethargic and disinterested in hearing from God. Their deacons or elders resist changes they try to make. In despair these frustrated pastors ask if they should go elsewhere to a church where people are receptive to the Spirit's working.

Often laypeople claim their pastor preaches pop psychology but not the life-changing Word of God, that there is little spiritual growth among the members, that sin is tolerated, and the world's values and methods have infiltrated the church programming. They say they have shared their concerns with their pastor, but he countered by pointing to the numerous recent baptisms or their state-of-the-art facilities. These frustrated church members wonder if they should find another church where the Word of God is preached and the Spirit of God is evident.

In both cases the church has a problem, and people want to do something about it. But what can one person, one pastor, or a small group of people do to lift a church out of its spiritual lethargy? Can congregations sink so far into a spiritual coma they are beyond resuscitating?

Revivals are God's sovereign work. Yet He uses people to accomplish His purposes. When God wanted to save His people from inevitable judgment and destruction, He declared:

"So I sought for a man among them who would make a wall, and stand in the gap before Me on behalf of the land, that I should not destroy it; but I found no one. Therefore I have poured out My indignation on them;

I have consumed them with the fire of My wrath, and I have recompensed their deeds on their own heads, says the Lord God." (Ezek. 22:30–31)

Does God need people to accomplish His work? No. He has myriads of powerful angels ready and eager to do His bidding. However, throughout history God has chosen to work through weak, ordinary human instruments. If God were always to use His magnificent angels to achieve His purposes, people would inevitably begin to worship and admire angels. Instead, God uses frail human servants so, when He accomplishes a mighty work, God clearly deserves the glory.

Much has been written about the type of people God chooses to use. We can be sure of one thing: God's standard is different from the world's (I Sam. 16:7). The world assumes people of spiritual influence must be charismatic leaders, inspiring communicators, and effective administrators. While these attributes may be helpful, they can also be a liability. Brian Edwards observed: "We have our leaders today, but rarely do they have the mark of God's Spirit upon them. They have become leaders by denominational progression or by their force of character, or by their organizing ability and their capacity for hard work."[1] Biblically and historically God has used ordinary people to accomplish His work.

CATALYSTS FOR REVIVAL

1. Ordinary People
2. People with a Passion for God
3. People Committed to God's Word
4. People Committed to Prayer
5. People Committed to Working with Others
6. People Willing to Pay the Price
7. People Filled with the Holy Spirit
8. People Who Give God the Glory

Catalysts for Revival

I. Ordinary People

One of the relentless critiques leveled at revival has centered on how ordinary and imperfect many of its leaders were. Evan Roberts was used powerfully by God to bring spiritual awakening to Wales, but within six months he was worn out and withdrew from the public. Charles Finney was criticized for his adoption of "new measures" in revival meetings. D. L. Moody was so uneducated some people came to his meetings merely to mock his poor grammar. Yet, as Thomas Phillips notes, "The weakness of the instrument is no argument against the reality of the work."[2] The exceedingly evident frailties and mistakes of revival leaders highlight the fact these people were engaged in a work far greater than themselves.

Brian Edwards suggests that historical accounts rarely give a detailed physical description of revival leaders.[3] This may be because their appearance, style of dress, or other external features were deemed irrelevant to the effectiveness of their ministry. J. Edwin Orr observed during a revival lecture that the only distinguishing mark of James McGready, who was used powerfully to bring revival to the American frontier in the early 1800s, was that he was one of the ugliest men west of the Alleghenies. Orr claimed that McGready was so homely he drew attention to himself wherever he went. George Whitefield was nicknamed "Dr. Squintum" because he seemed to be squinting when he looked at people. Some of those used mightily in revival almost passed up their divine assignment because they assumed they were too ordinary for God to use in revival.

John Livingston was asked to preach at a large gathering at the Kirk of Shotts on June 21, 1630, during a special Communion service because the original speaker took ill. Livingston saw the great throng of people and knew there were more experienced pastors and orators in the audience, so he seriously contemplated fleeing the scene rather than embarrass anyone. He later confessed, "Considering my unworthiness and weakness and this multitude and expectations of the people . . . I was consulting with myself to have stolen away somewhere and declined that day's preaching."[4] Yet the Holy Spirit assured him that he was God's appointed messenger for that day. Livingston preached from Ezekiel 36:25–26, and five hundred people were converted.[5] The reluctant preacher discovered that, when it comes to delivering a message from God, what matters is not how important you are but how anointed you are.

William Chambers Burns, a young missionary appointee from Scotland, agreed to provide pulpit supply in his native land while waiting to sail to China. Burns is described this way: "Young, inexperienced, measured and slow of speech, gifted with no peculiar charm of poetry or sentiment or natural eloquence or winning sweetness."[6] Thus far he does not sound like the kind of person to be entrusted with the most modest ecclesiastical assignment. Yet the same commentator also observed,

"He bore so manifestly the visible seals of a divine commission, and carried about him withal such an awe of the divine presence and majesty, as to disarm criticism and constrain even careless hearts to receive him as a messenger of God."[7] God chose Burns to be His instrument to bring revival to the church in which he was the interim pastor while the church's famous minister, Robert Murray McCheyne, was traveling abroad. Does God use skilled and famous people for His work? Certainly. However, history is replete with examples when God chose an ordinary man or woman to accomplish His heavenly purposes.

2. People with a Passion for God

Revival is not a regular, routine occurrence. Too many churches try to schedule it on the church calendar like Vacation Bible School. Revival comes when people grow desperate for it. It happens when God's people become sickened with their worldliness and foolish rebellion against their Creator and they return to Him with all of their heart, mind, soul, and strength. For revival to occur today, God's people must seek it with an entirely new level of urgency.

Seeking revival is seeking after God. Duncan Campbell once asked: "How many today are really prepared to face the stark fact that we have been out maneuvered by the strategy of hell, because we tried to meet the enemy on human levels by human strategy? In this we may have succeeded in making people church-conscious, mission-conscious, or even crusade conscious, without making them God-conscious."[8] It was said of Robert Murray McCheyne, "He sought after God as fervently and assiduously as miners seek after gold."[9] As a result, McCheyne's church experienced showers of revival. A multitude is not always needed to launch a movement of revival, but there must be a catalyst. A handful of people must urgently and desperately seek after God. When a church has even a small group of people who are earnestly seeking after God, the entire church will soon feel the impact.

When Evan Roberts, a college student, returned to his home church to share his passion for God with his fellow church members, the pastor did not even allow him to address the congregation during a regular church service. Instead the pastor informed the people Mr. Roberts had something to say and those interested in hearing him could remain behind at the conclusion of the weekly prayer service. Seventeen people lingered. Roberts shared four basic requirements he believed God was looking for in His people. These were:

1. You must put away any unconfessed sin.
2. You must put away any doubtful habit.

3. You must obey the Holy Spirit promptly.

4. You must confess Christ publicly.[10]

Roberts urged his meager audience to covenant to keep these obligations to God. It was an inauspicious beginning to an enormous work of God. The young Welshman exhorted his fellow church members to share his passion for God. Within six months 100,000 of their countrymen had been born again and added to the churches.

If you can go for weeks and not feel burdened for God to bring revival to your own life or to your church or nation, cry out to God to place His loving, broken heart over yours. God is not willing that anyone perish. It must break the heart of any child of God to know millions eternally perish each year because God's people are not what they should be. It ought to crush your heart if you do not have a deep love for God and His people. Ask God to give you a burden for revival. If you already have such a concern, then keep that burden ever before you until you see God answer your prayers.

3. People Committed to God's Word

God revives people who believe and obey His Word. Revival comes to those who trust God to keep His promises. Whether a member of the church, like Evan Roberts, who urged fellow members to obey God's Word, or a pastor like Jonathan Edwards who faithfully taught and preached God's Word every week, Scripture is always the foundation for revival. In Scotland at the beginning of the 1800s, "the people were very generally as ignorant of the Scriptures and spiritual truth as the inhabitants of Hindostan."[11] Yet William McCulloch, the minister at Cambuslang, faithfully taught the Scriptures to his people. Although he did not at first realize it, the steady diet of biblical teaching was laying a solid foundation for the great revival that would soon come. While God has used traumatic events, natural disasters, and personal testimonies to spark revival, the greatest movements of God have always come on the foundation of Scripture and biblical preaching. While Jonathan Edwards's famous sermon, "Sinners in the Hands of an Angry God" is best known for the stunning effect it had on listeners, Edwards was helping his people clearly understand the truth of the Scriptures, as found in Deuteronomy 32:35. Less known is that another season of revival came under Edwards's tenure in 1740 after he preached a series of sermons on the love of Christ from 1 Corinthians 13.[12] The dramatic nature of the Scripture passage did less to lift the people out of their spiritual lethargy than the careful exposition and *application* of God's Word.

Obviously a pastor is in a strategic position to bring Scripture to bear on people, but laypeople can also lay a biblical foundation for revival in their church. We have seen God powerfully use Bible teachers to refresh adults spiritually in their church. Home Bible studies throughout the week have played key roles in subsequent revivals. Youth ministers have led teenagers into an encounter with God that eventually brought renewal to the entire church. At times small groups have studied the Bible and as participants became convicted over their sin, or they received God's guidance, or they were inspired to strive for holiness, the rest of the church felt the impact.

Henry once received a phone call late one Sunday evening from a church member in Texas. The congregation had been going through a tumultuous, divided time. Members were angry at one another, and business meetings usually degenerated into shouting matches. During this time a small group of members were meeting on Sunday evenings before the evening service to study *Experiencing God.* This group was burdened over the spiritual condition of their church but did not know what to do.

A special business meeting was called for a Sunday evening to deliberate over a contentious issue. People became angry and began to threaten and accuse one another. One member who attended the *Experiencing God* study felt deeply convicted about how the church was behaving. During that evening's lesson Henry spoke on the DVD, sharing what God's Word says about how a church body should function. This man told people in the business meeting he thought they should pause their business meeting and watch the DVD together. As they listened to the biblical teaching, the Holy Spirit descended on the congregation. People began to weep as they realized how far they had departed from God's standard. Members left their seats and began to reconcile with one another. Men and women approached the microphones and began publicly to confess their sins. Revival had come! The person calling Henry that evening excitedly told him the meeting was still going on late into the evening as people were getting right with God and with one another. A small group of laypeople studied God's teaching on the church and God used those truths to revive His people.

4. People Committed to Prayer

Duncan Campbell once said, "The early Church put power before influence . . . power, not influence, was the watchword of the early Church."[13] Not everyone is equipped to preach stirring revival sermons to their congregation, nor is everyone in a position of leadership to make decisions for the church. But everyone can pray. It is the greatest way to serve as a catalyst for revival. Along with interceding individually, pray also with others. Don't use your prayer meetings to discuss the church's problems or the pastor's shortcomings. Simply intercede for your church with all your heart. Allow God to lay His broken heart for your church over your heart so you begin to see your church's problems from God's eternal perspective. Praying regularly and fervently with a growing number of people within your church, denomination, or nation cannot help but make a difference in what God does in your midst.

5. People Committed to Working with Others

Some people feel called to be prophets. They fearlessly denounce people's sins. Yet biblically the prophet's arrival meant God was using His last resort before judgment. By the time a prophet arrived on the scene, the people were usually so far gone they murdered God's messenger, and judgment eventually fell. While someone needs to call sin what it is, some loners feel their role is to be a voice crying in the wilderness. Yet, as Brian Edwards has said, "Rarely will revival come as a result of one man's praying."[14] Loners are rarely catalysts for revival. Those who stand outside the church shouting condemnation rarely bring the church back into a loving relationship with God. Those who stand *inside* loving and praying for one another fill the need.

Nehemiah was used to bring revival to the people of Jerusalem. When he saw the pitiful condition of God's people, he immediately took action and drew them together. As a catalyst among God's people, Nehemiah never condoned the current practices or conditions he found. Nevertheless, he found a way to take God's people from where they were to where God wanted them to be. He worked with others, and soon a host of God's people were revived and serving the Lord.

Jeremiah Lanphier knew how to work with others. He could have stood outside the New York Stock Exchange condemning the vice and greed of his day. He could have entered the churches and denounced the materialism that had overtaken them. Instead he called people of all denominations to pray. He helped people see that God had something better for them than the mere pursuit of wealth. As a result, when the stock market crashed, God's people were already regularly meeting to pray and were poised to help turn their nation back to God in revival.

If you find yourself constantly battling with others and being the lone critic of your church and its leaders, return to God and ask Him to examine your heart. Critics may highlight weaknesses, but they are seldom used as instruments of revival.

6. People Willing to Pay the Price

When Evan Roberts heard Seth Joshua pray and ask God to "bend" the church, Roberts cried out, "Bend me!"[15] Roberts understood that for him to be involved in revival, he would have to be a pliable instrument in God's hands. Revival is costly. That is why so few people are involved in it. Once the revival has come and the crowds are excitedly gathering, many people are willing to participate and to preach. The work of spiritual ploughing and seeding for revival is laborious and demanding, and many lose heart before the sought-after revival comes. The saintly Robert Murray McCheyne observed, "There is a great want about all Christians who have not suffered."[16] Many modern ministers are appalled at George Whitefield's quip that he'd rather "burn out than rust out." Today's seminaries emphasize balance and health for church ministers. While people must obviously be good stewards of their bodies and health, little is taught today concerning what price must be paid for God to work mightily in revival. In George Whitefield's era many people were used powerfully by God in revival, and regular periods of renewal and awakening resulted. During seasons of revival in American history, God has called a series of godly leaders in succession. For example, as Charles Finney was approaching the end of his career, D. L. Moody was being raised up. Yet there has been a long drought since the last great awakening occurred in America. While many wonderful ministries and churches are active today, America's last great awakening is a distant memory. God's people must ask what is needed for God to revive His people once again. What price must be paid for the Holy Spirit to turn the nations back to Him? Where are the people willing to pay the price for revival?

7. People Filled with the Holy Spirit

From the moment Pentecost occurred, the church was never the same (Acts 2). The preaching on the day of Pentecost was so compelling that three thousand people believed the message and were baptized. The city could not ignore the early Christians because the power of the Holy Spirit was so evident in all they did. Being filled with the Holy Spirit, ordinary Christians had great boldness and exerted enormous influence on the city (Acts 4:31). That is why the apostle Paul exhorted the Ephesians to be continually filled with the Holy Spirit (Eph. 5:18). When people are filled with the Spirit, God's hand is on everything they do. They preach in power. Their testimonies bring great conviction. Their service builds up the church body. Conversely, years of toil, without the Holy Spirit's filling, is futile.

That was the story of Duncan Campbell. He served as a respected pastor for seventeen years but saw minimal spiritual fruit. Finally, when he could stand it no longer, he cried out to God and begged for His manifest presence in his life. After crying out to God for hours, God suddenly answered his prayer at five o'clock in the morning. Campbell later recalled: "As I lay there, God the Holy Ghost came upon me. Wave after wave came rolling over me until the love of God swept through me like a mighty river."[17] From that point onward God used Campbell in revival wherever he went. Only after he became desperate to be filled with the Spirit did he see his walk with God raised to an entirely new level.

When you read the transcripts of the sermons preached in many of the great revivals, you might be amazed at the lack of oratorical skill. Knowing that hundreds and even thousands of people were spiritually awakened when the sermon was originally preached, one can often be disappointed when reading the transcript of the message because it is so ordinary. However, words on a page cannot convey the supercharged atmosphere people felt as they met that night and the Holy Spirit filled the room. Even the most mundane words and actions become powerful, overwhelming divine instruments when the Holy Spirit chooses to use them.

We must never take the Spirit's filling for granted. All Christians have the Holy Spirit residing within them, but His filling is another matter. Because last week we walked closely with the Lord and were filled powerfully with His Spirit does not mean the same is true today. God's anointing must be constantly renewed. Those who have been used mightily in revival have been filled with the Spirit. Those who have maintained a state of renewal have heeded Paul's injunction to be daily filled anew with the Spirit's presence.

8. People Who Give God the Glory

Brian Edwards comments that "those whom God uses in leadership in revival are always men who have met with God in a powerfully personal way and have a burning passion for the glory of God and a life of holiness."[18] Revival is about the glory of God. It occurs when people see God as He is and they recognize themselves for what they are. It is recognizing God's proper place in our lives and in the lives of our churches and nation. God uses men and women in revival who readily give all the glory to God.

The Korean revival of 1907 began in large part from missionaries who had heard of the recent outpouring of God's Spirit in India.[19] Church leaders in Korea saw what God was capable of doing, and they wept that He had not done so in their land. They wanted God to be honored in their country in the same way He was being magnified in India. God is pleased to bless those who seek to exalt God in their lives and churches. However, when people begin to covet what belongs to God alone, the Holy Spirit will withdraw His power. James Davenport cherished the limelight great men such as Whitefield and Edwards enjoyed during the First Great Awakening. As a result the Spirit withdrew from his efforts, and Davenport experienced humiliation. David Matthews suggested that Evan Roberts became such a celebrity during the Welsh Revival that when people began to worship him, it was time for Roberts to step aside.[20] While Roberts never desired to rob God of His honor, times of revival bring temptations to leaders as well as to people in the congregation. A priority for anyone involved in revival is diligently and fervently to keep their efforts God focused and God honoring. Those who are effective catalysts for revival bring glory to God in all they do.

Conclusion

One of the greatest callings anyone could have is to be a catalyst for reviving God's people. God is looking for those who will stand in the gap on behalf of others. This is a high calling. Such an assignment demands exacting qualifications. We pray a growing number of people will be willing to pay any price to be used in whatever way God chooses so revival will come. God's people cannot continue doing business as usual and expect something extraordinary to occur. For an extraordinary work to happen, our commitment and the caliber of our walk with God must also be extraordinary. Oh that it would be so!

QUESTIONS FOR REFLECTION AND DISCUSSION

1. In what ways may God be calling you as a catalyst for revival?
2. What does God want to change in your life to make you a catalyst for revival?
3. Have you grown frustrated with the condition of your church? How might God want to use you to build up God's people rather than to criticize them?

CHAPTER 19

Maintaining Revival

One of the most agonizing decisions revival leaders must make is choosing when to bring an end to revival meetings. The Saskatoon revival lasted seven weeks. Others have lasted six months or longer. When a church is experiencing cleansing, salvation, reconciliation, and genuine brokenness before the Lord, most church leaders will be wary of cutting short the divine work they prayed would come. Yet every revival in history, no matter how powerful or dramatic, eventually came to an end. The key is for leaders to recognize when the season of revival has drawn to a close.

Brian Edwards noted that revival doesn't outlast one generation because it is not intended to be normative.[1] He wrote, "Revival pulls the church out of its rut, awakens it from its sleep and sets inertia in motion."[2] Revival is restorative not normative. Once revival has done its work, it is no longer necessary. The new, vibrant walk with God revival produces, however, ought to be carefully nurtured and zealously protected.

Revival is God's means for bringing His people back into an intimate, loving fellowship with Him. Once people have returned to God, the key is to maintain the relationship God has restored. While people can enjoy gathering with their church family night after night and having emotional experiences during the services, returning to God must lead to nurturing the newly experienced, intimate walk with God.

One might view this process in a similar way to the return of the prodigal son (Luke 15:11–32). Revival occurred when the prodigal son came to his senses and recognized how grievously he had sinned against his father. He abandoned his wretched lifestyle and returned home. When the father saw his wayward son coming home, he knew revival had occurred. The father threw a great party. Crowds gathered to celebrate. It was an exciting time to be in that household. Yet as glorious as the festivities were, the next day the party was over. The fattened calf had been eaten. The invited guests departed. The work of farming had to continue. The normalcy of life returned. But had it? Life was not the same afterward. Likewise, periods of revival are but the journey home of prodigals and the subsequent welcome home celebration. The goal is not to maintain the returning, for eventually you will reach your destination. The new relationship must be nurtured and grown.

We offer several general cautions for those who want to maintain the renewed, fresh walk with God they experienced in revival:

First, be sure you do not attempt to take over the work God accomplished. As Octavius Winslow warns, "The work is all His; beware of taking it out of His hands."[3] Once you have returned to an intimate walk with God, allow Him to continue to set the agenda for your relationship with Him. Just as you depended on the Spirit's work in your return to God, so you must rely on the Spirit for your ongoing relationship with Him. The danger is assuming, now that we have returned to God, we can take the reins of our life back into our hands.

Second, beware of excesses. Jonathan Edwards was keenly aware that the greatest danger to revival was when people took the work of God to extremes God never intended. Edwards believed that continuance of revival depended on the vigilance with which excesses were kept in check.[4] He knew some were always enthralled with pushing the limits farther and farther. A simple return to the Lord was not enough for them. They wanted to experience the miraculous, the emotional, the spectacular, or the demonic. While many unusual things can occur during revival, the essence of revival is returning to God in repentance. When that has happened, revival has occurred. We have known many, however, who were dissatisfied with merely returning to an intimate relationship with Him. They continued to experiment with various manifestations of the Spirit, expressions of worship, or demonstrations of God's power as if an intimate relationship with God was not enough.

Third, beware of opposition. Some people will misunderstand and oppose revival. Do not allow those who do not recognize what an intimate walk with God looks like to minimize your renewed relationship with Him. We have encountered many people who have criticized those who claimed God spoke to them because they never had that experience.[5] You do not need to defend yourself against critics of revival. You need only live out the renewed walk with God you are enjoying and let your relationship with God provide its own evidence of the reality of what God has done in your life. Edwards's friend, George Whitefield, prayed: "God give me a deep humility, a well-guided zeal, a burning love and a single eye, and then let men or devils do their worst."[6]

One of Jonathan Edwards's chief critics in his church was a man named Joseph Hawley. A vocal opponent, he ultimately had Edwards forced out of the church as its pastor. Edwards never expressed bitterness toward those who mistreated him. Instead, he accepted a humble pastorate on the American frontier and tried faithfully to serve his Lord in the midst of his reduced circumstances. During that period of exile, Edwards wrote some of his greatest books that are still studied today. Hawley later retracted his vicious comments about his former pastor and repented of his actions. He ultimately committed suicide.[7] Every servant of God needs to be keenly aware that opposition is inevitable to the Lord's work. Those experiencing revival must keep their eyes fixed on Jesus and not on their detractors if they are to continue to enjoy intimate communion with their Savior.

Fourth, to maintain the work of revival in your life, you must diligently guard your heart and mind so sins such as pride and unbelief do not enter. Jonathan Goforth once said of the work of revival, "But will it last? How constantly unbelief puts this question! Of course it will last—if man is faithful. . . . Can we imagine anyone who is determined to co-work with God to the limit of his being asking 'will it last?'"[8] Goforth adds, "But let us be sure that if we are to retain His presence we must walk very carefully."[9] What a tragedy for God to do a marvelous work of renewal and restoration in our lives and then for us to forfeit all we have gained because of spiritual carelessness and neglect. When God does a work in our lives or in our church, we need to be careful, faithful stewards of all God has placed in our lives. If we will nurture the renewed walk with God He has granted us, we can experience no limit of Him in ensuing days.[10]

Fifth, keep your heart receptive. The prophet Hosea urged God's people to "break up the fallow ground" (Hos. 10:12). Our hearts naturally become hardened over time due to the traffic of the world and the cares of life. We must remain sensitive to the Lord. Our hearts need not depart from our Savior if we will carefully guard them. No one else is responsible for guarding our hearts. That is our responsibility, and we must do it diligently (Prov. 4:23).

Conclusion

God desires an intimate, growing, vibrant, fresh walk with each of His children. If we depart from Him, He will do whatever is necessary to bring us back to Himself.

If you sense you are in need of revival, do as the prodigal son did and consider how far you have departed from your loving Father. Ask the Holy Spirit to help you make your way home. You may face many challenges. Sin may have entangled you. Pride may urge you to deny any wrongdoing. Others may try to convince you nothing is wrong and you are a fine Christian. Yet in your heart you may sense you are missing much. Your soul may long for a closer walk with God. That is the work of the Holy Spirit drawing you back to your Father. Listen to His voice. Return in His strength and experience the joy of your Father.

QUESTIONS FOR REFLECTION AND DISCUSSION

1. Have you previously experienced a time of personal or corporate revival? If so, how long did it last?
2. Why do times of spiritual renewal inevitably seem to wane in your life? What might you do to enlarge and support the work God has done previously in your life?
3. Take time to reflect on what God has said to you in the past. Have you been careful to do everything you promised Him? Have you left some promises to God unfulfilled?
4. Make specific plans right now to follow through with any commitment you previously made to God.

Appendix A
Spiritual Leaders and Revival

Introduction

The following material is written especially for pastors and church leaders.[1] It consists of counsel and suggestions for ways to lead your congregation into revival and how to maintain the effects of revival once it occurs. We have witnessed God's activity around the world and the following suggestions come from both our study of Scripture and church history, as well as visiting numerous churches and pastors where God has worked powerfully. You can use no set pattern or formula in revival. The following are simply suggestions for you to consider as you seek to be God's instrument of revival for the people entrusted to your care. Work through this material slowly and prayerfully while inviting the Holy Spirit to help you process what He would have you do in your own life and church.

The Role of Spiritual Leaders

Serving as a leader of God's people is a privilege and an awesome responsibility. Though every believer has direct access and accountability to God, spiritual leaders bear unique responsibility for the condition of God's people. Leaders are also judged more severely if they lead God's people astray (James 3:1). Spiritual leadership is not limited to pastors. Spiritual leaders may include parents, church staff, deacons, elders, teachers, board or committee chairpersons, denominational leaders, heads of para-church ministries, and many others. Anytime you have an assignment from God that places you in a teaching or leadership position over others, you are in a position of spiritual leadership.

God works through leaders to call people back to Himself. Tragically, today many people in positions of spiritual leadership are failing to guide people to return to the Lord. Who is a spiritual leader from God's perspective?

When God established a people for Himself, He called on Moses to lead them. Moses was described as "the servant of the LORD" (Deut. 34:5). Moses was the servant and God was King. Joshua succeeded Moses, and he, too, was known as "the servant of the LORD" (Josh. 24:29). During the period of the Judges, God chose servants to guide the people to return to the Lord and follow Him. One day, however, Israel made a significant departure from the Lord's pattern for leadership:

> All the elders of Israel gathered together and came to Samuel at Ramah, and said to him, "Look, you are old, and your sons do not walk in your ways. Now make us a king to judge us like all the nations."
>
> But the thing displeased Samuel when they said, "Give us a king to judge us." So Samuel prayed to the LORD. And the LORD said to Samuel, "Heed the voice of the people in all that they say to you; for they have not rejected you, but they have rejected Me, that I should not reign over them. According to all the works which they have done since the day that I brought them up out of Egypt, even to this day—with which they have forsaken Me and served other gods—so they are doing to you also. Now therefore, heed their voice. However, you shall solemnly forewarn them, and show them the behavior of the king who will reign over them."
> (I Sam. 8:4–9)

God's people longed to be like the nations around them. They wanted to be like the world. In turning to a person for their direction, they were rejecting God's sovereign rule. Samuel delivered God's warning that the king would take the best of everything they had. The people would be forced to serve the king and to meet his needs. "Nevertheless the people refused to obey the voice of Samuel; and they said, 'No, but we will have a king over us, that we also may be like all the nations, and that our king may judge us and go out before us and fight our battles'" (I Sam. 8:19–20).

We see many similarities today. The reason the world is so obsessed with leadership is because it does not acknowledge God. A plethora of books and theories offer advice to lead people and organizations. Leaders turn to leadership resources, gurus, and trends because they are not turning to God for direction. Human leaders become substitutes for God, and their methods become an alternative for God's ways.

Incredibly many churches have turned to the world for direction as well. We take the world's books on leadership and incorporate them into our books for Christian leaders. Now we have Christian leaders trying to follow substitutes rather than obey God. On the one hand, we know God is our Lord, but we have numerous books and seminars that tell pastors and church leaders what they should be doing and what results they should strive to attain. By following the world's ways, a pastor may function more like a chief executive officer or a chairman of the board instead of pointing the people to the Lord. Churches contribute to the problem by primarily seeking leaders with the qualities admired in business.

As an example, look at what we are doing with the word *vision*. We look for leaders with vision. When we interview a prospective pastor for our church, we enquire about what his vision is for our congregation. We have visioning conferences and do our best demographic research to determine what our vision ought to be. We look at world trends to help guide our future planning. We develop vision statements to guide our churches' activities.

God's people are to function by revelation, not vision (Prov. 29:18). God alone knows the future. He intends to build His church (Matt. 16:18). He can guide our church to be in the center of His will every time. God reveals Himself and what He is doing so we can be involved in His work. You cannot administrate your church into revival. God must show you how He intends to bring your people back to Himself.

God may first reveal His will to the pastor or other church leaders. But once He does, the leaders' job is to guide people to follow the Lord, not their leadership. Jesus told us what kingdom leaders were like: "You know that the rulers of the Gentiles lord it over them, and those who are great exercise authority over them. Yet it shall not be so among you; but whoever desires to become great among you, let him be your servant. And whoever desires to be first among you, let him be your slave—just as the Son of Man did not come to be served, but to serve, and to give His life a ransom for many" (Matt. 20:25–28).

God's chosen leaders don't function the way the world does. They don't rule as dictators or autocrats based on their position or political power. God's leaders are servants. They are first servants of God and then servants to God's people. Jesus provided a model of spiritual leadership by serving rather than by demanding to be treated like a human despot.

Christ as Our Leader

God the Father placed His Son Jesus Christ as Head over the church. Christ, by His Spirit, guides His church to be on mission with Him. But we run into the same problem Israel encountered. We know that Christ is to be our leader, but we tend to treat Him like a figurehead and look instead for a person to be our chief executive officer.

God looks for people whose hearts are right toward Him and who will look to Him for guidance. Spiritual leaders point people to Christ for leadership. Then, as they listen together to the Lord, Christ guides His church to build the kingdom of God. Christ empowers His people to do everything He calls them to do; a watching world sees an exalted Christ and is drawn to Him.

Pointing People to God

Certain spiritual leaders are remembered for the way they carefully guided people to follow Him. Others are notorious for leading God's people astray. Notice how Moses, Joshua, Samuel, and David led God's people to follow Him:

Moses

[Moses said:] "Hear, O Israel: The LORD our God, the LORD is one! You shall love the LORD your God with all your heart, with all your soul, and with all your strength.

"And these words which I command you today shall be in your heart. You shall teach them diligently to your children, and shall talk of them when you sit in your house, when you walk by the way, when you lie down, and when you rise up. . . . So it shall be, when the LORD your God brings you into the land of which He swore to your fathers . . . —when you have eaten and are full—then beware, lest you forget the LORD who brought you out of the land of Egypt, from the house of bondage." (Deut. 6:4–12)

Joshua

[Joshua said:] "Fear the LORD, serve Him in sincerity and in truth, and put away the gods which your fathers served. . . . Serve the LORD! And if it seems evil to you to serve the LORD, choose for yourselves this day whom you will serve. . . . But as for me and my house, we will serve the LORD." So the people answered and said: "Far be it from us that we should forsake the LORD to serve other gods." (Josh. 24:14–16)

Samuel

Samuel said to the people, "Do not fear. You have done all this wickedness; yet do not turn aside from following the LORD, but serve the

LORD with all your heart. And do not turn aside; for then you would go after empty things which cannot profit or deliver, for they are nothing. For the LORD will not forsake His people, for His great name's sake, because it has pleased the LORD to make you His people. Moreover, as for me, far be it from me that I should sin against the LORD in ceasing to pray for you; but I will teach you the good and the right way. Only fear the LORD, and serve Him in truth with all your heart; for consider what great things He has done for you." (I Sam. 12:20–24)

David

David first delivered this psalm into the hand of Asaph and his brethren, to thank the LORD:
> Oh, give thanks to the LORD!
> Call upon His name;
> Make known His deeds among the peoples!
> Sing to Him, sing psalms to Him;
> Talk of all His wondrous works!
> Glory in His holy name;
> Let the hearts of those rejoice who seek the LORD!
> Seek the LORD and His strength;
> Seek His face evermore! (1 Chron. 16:7–11)

Early Christian Leaders

In the New Testament the early church's leaders pointed people to the resurrected Lord. They saw themselves as "servants" and "bond-slaves" of Jesus Christ. The apostles knew God was their leader, so they devoted themselves to prayer and the Scriptures (Acts 6:4).

As Goes the Leader

In the Old Testament God's actions toward His people were often affected by their leader's walk with God. Here are some examples:

- When Israel built and worshipped a golden calf, God was prepared to destroy them. Moses begged God not to decimate the people. God punished them but did not obliterate them because of Moses' intercession (Exod. 32).

- During David's reign, a three-year famine plagued the land. David sought the Lord's perspective. God revealed it was because King Saul had broken the covenant Israel had with the Gibeonites by trying to annihilate them (Josh. 9). Saul's sin brought disaster on his people even after his death. David, on behalf of the nation, acknowledged the sins of his predecessor and sought to be reconciled with the Gibeonites. "After that God heeded the prayer for the land" (2 Sam. 21:14).
- David decided to take a census of his fighting men against the counsel of Joab. David recognized his sin and asked God for forgiveness, but God first brought a plague on the land that cost the lives of seventy thousand people (2 Sam. 24).
- Because of their rebellion against God, Israel fell to the Assyrians. Hezekiah, king of Judah, humbly pled with the Lord in prayer on behalf of the people. God sent an angel to destroy 185,000 Assyrian soldiers, and Jerusalem was spared (2 Kings 18–19).
- After Hezekiah, Manasseh became king. He was extremely wicked. God said, "'Because Manasseh king of Judah has done these abominations (he has acted more wickedly than all the Amorites who were before him, and has also made Judah sin with his idols), therefore thus says the LORD God of Israel: "Behold, I am bringing such calamity upon Jerusalem and Judah, that whoever hears of it, both his ears will tingle"'" (2 Kings 21:11–12).
- After God determined to bring destruction on Jerusalem and Judah, King Josiah led his people back to the Lord (2 Chron. 34). Because of Josiah's humility and responsiveness to God, God promised not to judge the people during his lifetime. "All his days they did not depart from following the LORD God of their fathers" (2 Chron. 34:33). Often people followed the Lord as long as their leader did.

Judged More Strictly

Spiritual leadership carries a tremendous accountability to God. In New Testament times a problem arose when people sought to be spiritual leaders for reasons other than God's calling. James warned, "My brethern, let not many of you become teachers, knowing that we shall receive a stricter judgment" (James 3:1).

The apostle Paul gave sober counsel to leaders: "Moreover it is required in stewards that one be found faithful. . . . He who judges me is the Lord. . . . Who will bring to light the hidden things of darkness and reveal the counsels of the hearts" (1 Cor. 4:2, 4–5).

Jesus said, "'Everyone to whom much is given, from him much will be required; and to whom much has been committed, of him they will ask the more'" (Luke 12:48). Spiritual leaders must have holy lives and pure hearts before God. Faithful leaders of God's people may make the difference between revival and judgment.

Spiritual Physicians

Spiritual leaders are to function as spiritual physicians. Pastors ought not to be surprised when God's people act in unchristlike ways. Unchristlike behavior is merely a symptom of spiritual illness. Church leaders are remiss if they treat symptoms in their church as if they are the primary problem. Church conflict is the result of deeper spiritual issues. Outbursts of anger, criticism, unwillingness to serve, and gossip are manifestations of sin. Wise spiritual leaders seek to treat their people's primary issues and assume the symptoms will naturally dissipate.

While Moses was on Mount Sinai to receive the law, Aaron and the people rebelled against the Lord and built a golden calf. God said to Moses, "Let Me alone, that My wrath may burn hot against them and I may consume them. And I will make of you a great nation" (Exod. 32:10).

Moses could have vented his anger at his people's foolish behavior and encouraged God to be as harsh as possible. Then he would have become the father of the nation. But Moses demonstrated the character of a true spiritual leader when he unselfishly prayed: "LORD, why does Your wrath burn hot against Your people whom You have brought out of the land of Egypt with great power and with a mighty hand? Why should the Egyptians speak, and say, 'He brought them out to harm them, to kill them in the mountains, and to consume them from the face of the earth'? Turn from Your fierce wrath, and relent from this harm to Your people." (Exod. 32:11–12)

God heard Moses' plea on behalf of the people, and "the LORD relented from the harm which He said He would do to His people" (Exod. 32:14). After the spies brought back a majority report against entering the promised land, the people rebelled against the Lord. God determined to destroy the people, and Moses once again pled with God to spare them (Num. 14). A spiritual leader must be prepared to stand unselfishly in the gap before the Lord on behalf of the people, even when they are sinful and rebellious. Spiritual leaders don't give up on their people. When the people of God are sin sick, the spiritual character of a leader is put to the test. God never gave Moses permission to abandon the people when they were wicked and rebellious. The people needed spiritual leadership at those times more than ever. When God's people are at their sickest spiritually, they most need a physician.

Spiritual Leadership in Times of Crisis

The crises we face in our churches, in our nation, and in the world today require God-prepared, Christ-centered, Holy Spirit-empowered people of prayer. Spiritual leaders must seek God with all their hearts. They must be God centered. In these unique times God is mightily working worldwide. He is breaking down barriers to the spread of the gospel—political barriers, language barriers, and technological barriers. We are witnessing the beginnings of one of God's greatest moves in bringing a lost world to Himself. Casual leadership will be inadequate. Human-centered leadership will never accomplish God's eternal purposes. God is seeking to raise up spiritual leaders who will effectively lead God's people in these extraordinary times.

A Revived Pastor and Church

Lonnie was pastor of a relatively small church in Ohio. Because of problems and frustrations he had faced, he had written his letter of resignation and prepared a résumé to return to a career in engineering. Later that week he attended a statewide conference where God met him through the Scriptures and godly counsel. Lonnie said, "I spent the next three days on my face, weeping before the Lord." God began to deal with Lonnie and the kind of pastoral leadership he had provided. Over and over he confessed that God was right, and he asked for forgiveness.

God dealt with Lonnie on two particular issues. One was Lonnie's approach to church growth. He was studying and copying the latest methods of church growth in his congregation. During his time before the Lord, God impacted him with Matthew 16:18. Jesus said He would build His church, and the gates of hell would not prevail against it. Lonnie sensed God's saying to him, "Lonnie, you have had My church long enough. I want it back." Lonnie agreed, wept before the Lord, and surrendered his church back to Christ. He asked Christ to build His church any way He wanted to—with or without the pastor's help.

Lonnie claimed to be an evangelistic pastor. He preached evangelistic messages and witnessed to people door-to-door. These activities were not wrong, but as Lonnie prayed, God turned his thoughts to John 10. Lonnie read how the Good Shepherd cared for His sheep. The Lord confronted Lonnie as he prayed by asking, "What are you doing to shepherd My sheep in your church?" Lonnie confessed he was focused on pursuing new sheep. The Lord broke him when He said, "Lonnie, you haven't taken care of the sheep I gave you. Why would I give you new sheep?"

Lonnie surrendered his life to the Good Shepherd and pledged to do whatever God told him to do to care for his church members. Then he sensed God's saying, "Lonnie, you take care of my sheep. When they are healthy, well-fed, and contented, I will work through them to produce new sheep."

That three days of returning to the Lord had a profound impact on Lonnie, his family, and his church. He began guiding his family into an intimate relationship with the Lord. God reconciled him with a wayward son. His daughter saw God begin to work through her at her high school. Lonnie's wife took some steps of faith as she experienced God's guidance and power to provide for their family in a fresh new way.

As this revived pastor began guiding God's people back to the Lord, God changed situations in the church. During the following eight months, the church began to see and know the power of God as never before.

- One member was delivered from addiction to pornography and reconciled with his family.
- Ten couples whose marriages were headed for divorce were reconciled, and the church did not experience a divorce during the following year.
- God added a lay leader to the church and led the congregation to begin ministries in an apartment community in a high crime area. The chief of police reported that 911 calls from that area decreased by 30 percent.
- The lay leader quit his job in obedience and faith so he could do the Lord's work full-time. When the church began praying, God provided the necessary money for him to serve in the ministry. A church of an entirely different denomination donated $12,000 and explained, "We believe God wants us to have a part in the apartment ministry." The church was amazed at what God did.
- God led them to begin work with Russian emigrants. Then God called a Russian-speaking college professor to work with them. He, too, sensed God's leading him to quit his job, and God provided for his salary. This led to the establishment of a mission partnership with a city in Russia.
- When Lonnie reported on God's activity eight months after his personal revival, he said, "Our people are experiencing the mighty power and

presence of God, and they can't help telling people about it. Last Sunday we had seven professions of faith, and I only knew one of those people previously."

Once the pastor allowed God to set the agenda for His church, amazing things immediately began to happen. Jesus demonstrated what He could do to build His church when He had people willing to follow Him. God began His work by reviving a discouraged and self-centered pastor, transforming him into a spiritual leader who pointed his people to follow their Good Shepherd.

Qualities of a Spiritual Leader

In Matthew 10, Jesus prepared His twelve disciples for their mission. This set the pattern for those who would serve Christ in the future. He gave His twelve disciples guidelines on the cost of spiritual leadership. Those instructions are just as powerful and relevant today. Here are thirteen qualities God looks for in spiritual leaders:

A Sense of Urgency

The context for chapter 10 is found in the last verses of Matthew 9: "Jesus went about all the cities and villages, teaching in their synagogues, preaching the gospel of the kingdom, and healing every sickness and every disease among the people. But when He saw the multitudes, He was moved with compassion for them, because they were weary and scattered, like sheep having no shepherd. Then He said to His disciples, 'The harvest truly is plentiful, but the laborers are few'" (Matt. 9:35–37).

Jesus expressed a sense of urgency over the condition of God's people. Spiritual leaders must have a godly, Godlike sense of urgency. Jesus was burdened and had compassion for God's people "because they were weary and scattered, like sheep having no shepherd." Those who serve as spiritual leaders must care deeply for God's people.

A Person of Fervent Prayer

When faced with such a desperate need, Jesus told His disciples to pray: "'Therefore pray the Lord of the harvest to send out laborers into His harvest'" (Matt. 9:38). In times of need, spiritual leaders must be intercessors who know what it means to labor before God in prayer for their people. Even though you may not know what to pray, the Holy Spirit will guide your praying according to the will of God as He intercedes with us (Rom. 8:26–27). Prayer must be the leader's first priority.

A Church That Prays

A church in Alaska was studying *Experiencing God: Knowing and Doing the Will of God.* The pastor became convicted that the church had manipulated people into taking leadership positions that God had not called them to do. He knew the church could not function as a healthy body of Christ unless it was organized and led by Christ. One Sunday the pastor preached on the need for God-called leaders. For his invitation the pastor asked all leaders to pray during the week about their leadership positions. He asked leaders who did not sense God had called them to their current positions to resign the following week. Then the church would pray for God to call forth the necessary laborers.

The next Sunday every leader in the church resigned with the exception of two Sunday school teachers. The church began to pray with confidence that God would call forth the needed laborers. Within two weeks every position in the church was filled by people who sensed God wanted them to serve in that position.

This kind of bold action required great faith and confidence in the One who said, "Pray the Lord of the harvest to send out laborers into His harvest" (Matt. 9:38). Prayer is not preparation for the work; it is the work! Spiritual leaders must not be people who pray but people of prayer.

People Who Radiate Christ's Presence

Jesus "had called His twelve disciples to Him" (Matt. 10:1). Jesus' primary invitation to His disciples was not to serve Him but to be with Him. Out of their intimate relationship with Him and the quality time they spent with Him, they knew what to do and had the power to accomplish what Jesus asked. Leaders whose ministry flows out of their walk with God experience the truth that "He who calls you is faithful, who also will do it" (1 Thess. 5:24).

Profound Sense of Accountability to God

You did not choose God as your Master. He chose you as His servant. As a God-called leader you are accountable to Him for your leadership. Your primary accountability is to the God who called you. Spiritual leaders cannot compromise God's call and direction in order to please or placate people.

Demonstrating Spiritual Authority

In Matthew 10 Jesus commissioned spiritual leaders and sent them out. "He gave them power over unclean spirits, to cast them out, and to heal all kinds of sickness and all kinds of disease. . . . 'Heal the sick, cleanse the lepers, raise the dead, cast out demons. Freely you have received, freely give'" (Matt. 10:1, 8).

Spiritual authority comes from Christ. Christ does not give His royal prerogative away to others. He always retains His authority. However, He takes up residence within believers to work through them to accomplish His purposes (Col. 2:9–10). Christ exercises His power and authority through spiritual leaders.

The term *spiritual authority* has been terribly abused in the church. True spiritual leaders serve in humility. They do not have to insist on others' respect or acquiescence because they know they are bond slaves of the One who has all authority (Matt. 28:18). Others will see when the risen Christ is working in and through someone's life.

Spiritual leaders function with God's presence in all they do for Him. No crisis catches God unprepared by surprise. You can face any challenge knowing that God will exercise His power and authority through you on behalf of His people. God's power and authority ought to be evident to all those who observe your ministry. You can humbly trust God to always work through you. You do not need to pressure God's people to follow. Resorting to pressure tactics with God's people reveals your lack of faith in the power of God.

Absolute Faith, Trust, and Confidence in God

Jesus explained to His disciples that they did not need to worry about resources for their ministry because all of heaven was at their disposal. Jesus instructed them saying, "'Provide neither gold nor silver nor copper in your money belts, nor bag for your journey, nor two tunics, nor sandals, nor staffs; for a worker is worthy of his food'" (Matt. 10:9–10).

Spiritual leaders must exercise a profound faith, trust, and confidence in God and in His provision. The God who calls and sends you is also the One who will always provide for you. Spiritual leaders ought to exude the same confidence as Paul who claimed: "God is able to make all grace abound toward you, that you, always having all sufficiency in all things, may have an abundance for every good work" (2 Cor. 9:8). You dare not face the crises of your world without that kind of confidence in the God you serve. A God-called leader ought never be tentative, hopeless, or despairing. Spiritual leaders understand like David: "He only is my rock and my salvation; He is my defense; I shall not be greatly moved" (Ps. 62:2).

God-Given Sense of Direction

God appoints leaders intentionally and strategically. He also commissions them on His terms:

> "Do not go into the way of the Gentiles, and do not enter a city of the Samaritans. But go rather to the lost sheep of the house of Israel. And as you go, preach, saying, 'The kingdom of heaven is at hand'. . . . 'Now whatever city or town you enter, inquire who in it is worthy, and stay there till you go out. And when you go into a household, greet it. If the household is worthy, let your peace come upon it. But if it is not worthy, let your peace return to you. And whoever will not receive you nor hear your words, when you depart from that house or city, shake off the dust from your feet. Assuredly, I say to you, it will be more tolerable for the land of Sodom and Gomorrah in the day of judgment than for that city! Behold, I send you out as sheep in the midst of wolves. Therefore be wise as serpents and harmless as doves.'" (Matt. 10:5–7, 11–16)

Spiritual leaders are under no misconception of what is involved in following Christ. Jesus warned the disciples they would face great distress in their service of Him. If you have grown discouraged at the problems, criticisms, opposition, or disappointments you are facing in ministry, you need to review the nature of your call. You must have a God-given sense that God has sent you; that He knows where He is sending you; that He knows what you will face; and He will be present to guide, direct, and enable you to complete what He asked you to do.

Willingness to Suffer Any Cost

Jesus explained the cost of following Him:

> "But beware of men, for they will deliver you up to councils and scourge you in their synagogues. You will be brought before governors and kings for My sake, as a testimony to them and to the Gentiles. But when they deliver you up, do not worry about how or what you should speak. For it will be given to you in that hour what you should speak; for it is not you who speak, but the Spirit of your Father who speaks in you.
>
> "Now brother will deliver up brother to death, and a father his child; and children will rise up against parents and cause them to be put to death. And you will be hated by all for My name's sake. But he who

endures to the end will be saved. When they persecute you in this city, flee to another. For assuredly, I say to you, you will not have gone through the cities of Israel before the Son of Man comes." (Matt. 10:17–23)

Spiritual leaders ought not be surprised when they encounter opposition. Jesus assured us this would occur. Yet spiritual leaders shouldn't worry about what to do. Jesus reminded His servants that the Holy Spirit was present in every circumstance to guide them.

You must be acutely aware of the great cost in being a spiritual leader. Spiritual leadership is not for the fainthearted, nor is it for those who crave constant appreciation and affirmation. Spiritual leaders are not motivated by the desire to be popular with people but by an earnest desire to faithfully deliver the message God gave them. Spiritual leaders understand that calling people to repent of their sin will inevitably invite opposition. At times such opposition can be painful and relentless.

Christlike

Jesus told His disciples to pattern their lives after Him. He was their Master. They were His servants. Spiritual leaders function using kingdom methodology. "A disciple is not above his teacher, nor a servant above his master. It is enough for a disciple that he be like his teacher, and a servant like his master. If they have called the master of the house Beelzebub, how much more will they call those of his household! Therefore do not fear them" (Matt. 10:24–26).

Do not pattern your ministry after megachurch pastors or corporate business leaders. Pattern your life and ministry after Jesus. He is your Master. You are His servant. The longer you serve Him the more like Him you should become. God's ways are not the world's ways (Isa. 55:8–9). Spiritual leaders follow kingdom principles and methods, not the latest fad. In order to pattern your life after Him, however, you must thoroughly study His life. You must seek His counsel for every decision and direction as He lives out His life in you.

Spiritual leaders do not have the option to pick and choose the characteristics of Jesus they are willing to imitate. Spiritual leaders must be prepared to carry their cross just as Paul said: "I may know Him . . . and the fellowship of His sufferings, being conformed to His death" (Phil. 3:10). Isaiah 53 provides a graphic portrait of what it looks like to serve like Jesus. This is the standard God uses for His servants. When God the Father sent Jesus to earth, He did not spare His Son any discomfort or sacrifice (Rom. 8:32). Many of those who have followed Jesus have lost their lives.

The requirements for following and serving Jesus have not lessened over time. In a day when many are violently opposing God's kingdom, a high-calibre spiritual leader is needed among God's people.

An Open Witness to Jesus as Lord

Spiritual leaders demonstrate an unmistakable witness to Jesus as Lord. This is especially critical at a time when the world is filled with people who do not believe in God or His lordship. Jesus declared: "Whoever confesses Me before men, him I will also confess before My Father who is in heaven. But whoever denies Me before men, him I will also deny before My Father who is in heaven" (Matt. 10:32–33).

Jesus was not looking for lip service. Spiritual leaders must live authentically for Christ before a watching world. They must have a lifestyle in which Christ openly displays Himself through them. Paul had such a lifestyle. He said to the church at Corinth: "For I determined not to know anything among you except Jesus Christ and Him crucified. . . . And my speech and my preaching were not with persuasive words of human wisdom, but in demonstration of the Spirit and of power, that your faith should not be in the wisdom of men but in the power of God" (1 Cor. 2:2, 4–5).

Spiritual leaders ought to live lives that are a clear "demonstration of the Spirit's power." They ought not to lead in a manner that is a tribute to their ingenuity or dynamic ability but to the undeniable power and wisdom of God.

Willing to Risk for the Kingdom

Spiritual leaders are willing to risk everything for God's kingdom. They are prepared for spiritual warfare, wherever it may come. "Do not think that I came to bring peace on earth. I did not come to bring peace but a sword. For I have come to 'set a man against his father, a daughter against her mother, and a daughter-in-law against her mother-in-law'; and 'a man's enemies will be those of his own household'" (Matt. 10:34–36).

Not everyone will support you as you follow God. Your enemies may even be within your own household. You must be prepared for an intensity of spiritual warfare that may test every close relationship you have. If you are motivated by saving and protecting your life, you will not be used mightily by God.

Jesus said, "'For judgment I have come into this world'" (John 9:39). When Jesus sends you with such a message, He does not bring peace but a sword. You will face spiritual warfare. Will you be willing to risk all, including your reputation, security, friendships, and even your life to deliver that message?

Wholehearted Love for Jesus

Jesus knew full well the world into which He was appointing spiritual leaders. Jesus deliberately called them to a lifestyle that required a cross. He knew the future of the kingdom of God rested on the quality of the love relationship His disciples had with Him. Jesus demanded absolute surrender to Him—nothing withheld. "He who loves father or mother more than Me is not worthy of Me. And he who loves son or daughter more than Me is not worthy of Me. And he who does not take his cross and follow after Me is not worthy of Me. He who finds his life will lose it, and he who loses his life for My sake will find it" (Matt. 10:37–39).

Jesus hid nothing from His followers. For on them, as they guided God's people, rested the redemption of the world.

Spiritual leaders demonstrate a wholehearted love for God that exceeds every other affection. That is the only relationship worthy of Christ. The love of Christ will compel you to serve Him. But that love relationship will inevitably require a cross. Be careful that you do not turn aside from the will of God when the demands for a cross become real. This will be reflected in your total abandonment to God's will. The calibre of your love relationship with Him will determine your obedience to what He commands (John 14:21, 23–27; 15:1–17).

Unmistakably Identified with Christ

Jesus called His disciples to identify themselves completely with Him and His purposes. They would be in union with Him, taking on the nature, pattern, and lifestyle of their Lord. They knew, however, that this would bring them into conflict with the prevailing attitudes and even the religious practices of their day. They also knew that a day of accountability was coming. "He who receives you receives Me, and he who receives Me receives Him who sent Me. He who receives a prophet in the name of a prophet shall receive a prophet's reward. And he who receives a righteous man in the name of a righteous man shall receive a righteous man's reward. And whoever gives one of these little ones only a cup of cold water in the name of a disciple, assuredly, I say to you, he shall by no means lose his reward" (Matt. 10:40–42).

Spiritual leaders will do everything with a clear anticipation of accountability before their Lord. The consuming passion of their heart should be to long for the day they hear, "Well done, good and faithful servant" (Matt. 25:21).

Appendix B
Personal Revival for Spiritual Leaders

In the Bible revivals were led by spiritual leaders. If you are a spiritual leader of a family, a church, a denomination, or another group, our prayer is that you will experience a personal revival in preparation for leading others to return to the Lord. Perhaps God has already prepared your life. Let this chapter point you to the Lord for fine-tuning your personal preparation so you will be the kind of servant God will be pleased to use to revive His people.

Allow God to Shape Your Life

God is continually wanting to draw you into a closer walk with Him. As He begins His work of revival in you, guide other church or group leaders to respond to the Lord as you have been. Biblical revivals generally began with the leaders and spread to the people. You may want to consider some of the following suggestions.

- Find a godly pastor or other leaders that you respect for their spiritual maturity. Put your life alongside them as prayer partners and counselors. Help one another lead your churches or groups to encounter God. God created us for interdependence.
- Work diligently to expunge pride from your life. The hour is late. Time is short. Live with a sense of urgency and humble yourself before God. Don't allow pride to keep you from fully participating in God's activity.
- Determine from the outset that you are more concerned with pleasing God than yourself or others. If you struggle with that commitment, stay before God until He gives you that desire. "It is God who works in you both to will and to do for His good pleasure" (Phil. 2:13).
- Surrender your will and every aspect of your life to God. Ask Him to reveal any sin or impurity that is keeping you from greater kingdom usefulness. Ask God to make your life a "highway of holiness" over which others may travel in coming to the Lord (Isa. 35).

- Take a personal prayer retreat. Get away from your busy home and church routines to spend time with your heavenly Father. Jesus often did this. Focus on your love relationship with God. Let Him guide the agenda of your praying because "the Spirit also helps in our weaknesses. For we do not know what we should pray for as we ought, but the Spirit Himself makes intercession for us with groanings which cannot be uttered. Now He who searches the hearts knows what the mind of the Spirit is, because He makes intercession for the saints according to the will of God" (Rom. 8:26–27).
- Like Paul, ask people to pray for you at every opportunity.
- If you have not already done so, consider studying *Experiencing God*. It may help you learn to hear God's voice more clearly and to understand ways to guide God's people into deeper intimacy with God.

A Plumb Line for Shepherds

Pastors, church staff members, Sunday school teachers, deacons, elders, Bible study teachers, and other leaders in a church have a crucial role in shepherding the people they serve. The following passage describes the kind of shepherd God desires and the kind he despises. Take time to read carefully the following and consider how God would evaluate your leadership of God's people: "Let the LORD, the God of the spirits of all flesh, set a man over the congregation, who may go out before them and go in before them, who may lead them out and bring them in, that the congregation of the LORD may not be like sheep which have no shepherd" (Num. 27:16–17).

- Are you guiding God's people to be what God wants them to be?

  "So Samuel grew, and the LORD was with him and let none of his words fall to the ground. . . . Then the LORD appeared again in Shiloh. For the LORD revealed Himself to Samuel in Shiloh by the word of the LORD." (I Sam. 3:19, 21)

- Do your words come from God, and is He obviously blessing what you teach and preach?

  The LORD is my shepherd;
  I shall not want.
  He makes me to lie down in green pastures;

He leads me beside the still waters.
He restores my soul;
He leads me in the paths of righteousness
For His name's sake.
Yea, though I walk through the valley of the shadow of death,
I will fear no evil;
For You are with me;
Your rod and Your staff, they comfort me.
You prepare a table before me in the presence of my enemies;
You anoint my head with oil;
My cup runs over.
Surely goodness and mercy shall follow me
All the days of my life;
And I will dwell in the house of the LORD
Forever. (Ps. 23:1–6)

- Do you guide people to Christ and His Word in such a way that their hunger is satisfied with the bread of life and their thirst with the living water?
- Are you guiding people into paths of righteousness through the model of your own life? Are you modeling unrighteousness in any way?
- Do you help people find comfort in God even in the shadow of death?
- Are you guiding people into God's presence in such a way that He overflows their spiritual cup?

He also chose David His servant,
And took him from the sheepfolds;
From following the ewes that had young He brought him,
To shepherd Jacob His people,
And Israel His inheritance.
So he shepherded them according to the integrity of his heart,
And guided them by the skillfulness of his hands. (Ps. 78:70–72)

- Are you shepherding God's people with integrity and skillful hands?

He will feed His flock like a shepherd;
He will gather the lambs with His arm,

And carry them in His bosom,
And gently lead those who are with young. (Isa. 40:11)

- Do you love people and gently lead them? Or do you have hard feelings toward them and treat them harshly?

His watchmen are blind,
They are all ignorant;
They are all dumb dogs,
They cannot bark;
Sleeping, lying down, loving to slumber.
Yes, they are greedy dogs
Which never have enough.
And they are shepherds
Who cannot understand;
They all look to their own way,
Every one for his own gain,
From his own territory. (Isa. 56:10–11)

- Are you a faithful watchman alerting God's people to any impending danger?
- Do you lack a knowledge of God's ways or requirements?
- Do you waste your time?
- Do you have a strong appetite for personal gain that is never satisfied?
- Are you consumed with your goals or God's will?

The priests did not say, "Where is the LORD?"
And those who handle the law did not know Me;
The rulers also transgressed against Me;
The prophets prophesied by Baal,
And walked after things that do not profit. (Jer. 2:8)

- Do you long for God's presence?
- Do you know God by experience in an intimate and personal way?
- Have you rebelled against God's lordship over you or His people?
- Have you pursued worthless idols, especially idols of the heart?

"Return, O backsliding children," says the LORD; "for I am married to you. I will take you, one from a city and two from a family, and I will bring you to Zion." (Jer. 3:14)

- Will you allow God to make you a shepherd after His own heart? Will you lead with knowledge and understanding of God, His purposes, and His ways?

> For the shepherds have become dull-hearted,
> And have not sought the LORD;
> Therefore they shall not prosper,
> And all their flocks shall be scattered. (Jer. 10:21)

- Is prayer your primary planning strategy whereby you ask God for every direction and patiently wait until He shows you?
- Is your flock failing to prosper? Are the people being scattered?

> "Many rulers have destroyed My vineyard,
> They have trodden My portion underfoot;
> They have made My pleasant portion a desolate wilderness.
> They have made it desolate;
> Desolate, it mourns to Me;
> The whole land is made desolate,
> Because no one takes it to heart." (Jer. 12:10–11)

- Have your actions built up God's people or torn them down? Are they stronger or weaker because of your leadership? Do you care?

> "Woe to the shepherds who destroy and scatter the sheep of My pasture!" says the LORD. Therefore thus says the LORD God of Israel against the shepherds who feed My people: "You have scattered My flock, driven them away, and not attended to them. Behold, I will attend to you for the evil of your doings," says the LORD. "But I will gather the remnant of My flock out of all countries where I have driven them, and bring them back to their folds; and they shall be fruitful and increase. I will set up shepherds over them who will feed them; and they shall fear no more, nor be dismayed, nor shall they be lacking," says the LORD. (Jer. 23:1–4)

- Are you destroying or strengthening the sheep God entrusted to you?
- Are you scattering or gathering God's sheep?
- Are any of your sheep afraid? Intimidated? Missing?
- How well are you caring for the sheep God has given you?
- Will you be a shepherd who feeds the sheep and is loved by them?

> "Wail, shepherds, and cry!
> Roll about in the ashes,
> You leaders of the flock!
> For the days of your slaughter and your dispersions are fulfilled;
> You shall fall like a precious vessel.
> And the shepherds will have no way to flee,
> Nor the leaders of the flock to escape.
> A voice of the cry of the shepherds,
> And a wailing of the leaders to the flock will be heard.
> For the LORD has plundered their pasture." (Jer. 25:34–36)

- How aware are you of your accountability to God for the sheep entrusted to you?
- Are you concerned about how God punishes unfaithful shepherds?
- Do you fear God?

> "My people have been lost sheep.
> Their shepherds have led them astray;
> They have turned them away on the mountains.
> They have gone from mountain to hill;
> They have forgotten their resting place.
> All who found them have devoured them;
> And their adversaries said, 'We have not offended,
> Because they have sinned against the LORD, the habitation of justice,
> The LORD, the hope of their fathers.'" (Jer. 50:6–7)

- Have you led anyone astray? Have you guided people to do things that are not in God's will?
- Have the people forgotten their calling?
- Have the people forgotten their resting place? Have they strayed from an intimate and personal relationship with God?

- Are your sheep being devoured by enemies like crime, abuse, bankruptcy, or sin's consequences?

> "Son of man, prophesy against the shepherds of Israel, prophesy and say to them, 'Thus says the Lord GOD to the shepherds: "Woe to the shepherds of Israel who feed themselves! Should not the shepherds feed the flocks? You eat the fat and clothe yourselves with the wool; you slaughter the fatlings, but you do not feed the flock. The weak you have not strengthened, nor have you healed those who were sick, nor bound up the broken, nor brought back what was driven away, nor sought what was lost; but with force and cruelty you have ruled them. So they were scattered because there was no shepherd; and they became food for all the beasts of the field when they were scattered. My sheep wandered through all the mountains, and on every high hill; yes, My flock was scattered over the whole face of the earth, and no one was seeking or searching for them.""" (Ezek. 34:2–6)

- Are you more concerned about taking care of yourself than tending God's sheep?
- Have you strengthened the weak? Healed the sick? Cared for the injured?
- Have you brought back the strays or searched for the lost?
- Have you ruled your sheep harshly or tenderly?
- Are your sheep being devoured by wild animals like divorce, adultery, greed, materialism, envy, and strife? Or, are they standing strong against the world?

> "'Therefore, you shepherds, hear the word of the LORD: "As I live," says the Lord GOD, "surely because My flock became a prey, and My flock became food for every beast of the field, because there was no shepherd, nor did My shepherds search for My flock, but the shepherds fed themselves and did not feed My flock"—therefore, O shepherds, hear the word of the LORD! Thus says the Lord GOD: "Behold, I am against the shepherds, and I will require My flock at their hand; I will cause them to cease feeding the sheep, and the shepherds shall feed themselves no more; for I will deliver My flock from their mouths, that they may no longer be food for them.""" (Ezek. 34:7–10)

- How has God held you accountable for the condition of His sheep?
- Have you experienced attempts to remove you from your leadership role? If so, could it be because of God's discipline?
- Are personal financial problems God's discipline for unfaithfulness?

> "'For thus says the Lord GOD: "Indeed I Myself will search for My sheep and seek them out. As a shepherd seeks out his flock on the day he is among his scattered sheep, so will I seek out My sheep and deliver them from all the places where they were scattered on a cloudy and dark day. And I will bring them out from the peoples and gather them from the countries, and will bring them to their own land; I will feed them on the mountains of Israel, in the valleys and in all the inhabited places of the country. I will feed them in good pasture, and their fold shall be on the high mountains of Israel. There they shall lie down in a good fold and feed in rich pasture on the mountains of Israel. I will feed My flock, and I will make them lie down," says the Lord GOD. "I will seek what was lost and bring back what was driven away, bind up the broken and strengthen what was sick; but I will destroy the fat and the strong, and feed them in judgment.""" (Ezek. 34:11–16)

- What kind of shepherd does God want for His sheep? What will a godly shepherd do for the flock?

> For the idols speak delusion;
> The diviners envision lies,
> And tell false dreams;
> They comfort in vain.
> Therefore the people wend their way like sheep;
> They are in trouble because there is no shepherd.
> "My anger is kindled against the shepherds,
> And I will punish the goatherds.
> For the LORD of hosts will visit His flock,
> The house of Judah,
> And will make them as His royal horse in the battle."
> (Zech. 10:2–3)

- Have your people been deceived by false teaching?

- Have your people turned to false gods and come into bondage and oppression for their sins?

  "For indeed I will raise up a shepherd in the land who will not care for those who are cut off, nor seek the young, nor heal those that are broken, nor feed those that still stand. But he will eat the flesh of the fat and tear their hooves in pieces." (Zech. 11:16)

- Has God raised up an ungodly leader over your people to discipline and judge them for their sins?

  Jesus, when He came out, saw a great multitude and was moved with compassion for them, because they were like sheep not having a shepherd. So He began to teach them many things. (Mark 6:34)

- Do you have compassion for scattered sheep?
- Are you faithfully teaching your people about God's ways?

  "What man of you, having a hundred sheep, if he loses one of them, does not leave the ninety-nine in the wilderness, and go after the one which is lost until he finds it? And when he has found it, he lays it on his shoulders, rejoicing. And when he comes home, he calls together his friends and neighbors, saying to them, 'Rejoice with me, for I have found my sheep which was lost!' I say to you that likewise there will be more joy in heaven over one sinner who repents than over ninety-nine just persons who need no repentance." (Luke 15:4–7)

- Are you willing to leave the sheep that are safe to go after the ones that have gone astray?
- Have you shown concern for the non-resident members in your church who may need to transfer to another flock so they can be cared for?

  "But he who enters by the door is the shepherd of the sheep. To him the doorkeeper opens, and the sheep hear his voice; and he calls his own sheep by name and leads them out. And when he brings out his own sheep, he goes before them; and the sheep follow him, for they know his voice. Yet they will by no means follow a stranger, but will flee from him, for they do not know the voice of strangers." . . . "I am the good shepherd. The good shepherd gives

His life for the sheep. But a hireling, he who is not the shepherd, one who does not own the sheep, sees the wolf coming and leaves the sheep and flees; and the wolf catches the sheep and scatters them. The hireling flees because he is a hireling and does not care about the sheep. I am the good shepherd; and I know My sheep, and am known by My own. As the Father knows Me, even so I know the Father; and I lay down My life for the sheep." (John 10:2–5, 11–15)

- Do you love the sheep enough that you are willing to give your life away in service to them? Or do you focus more on how your sheep are caring for you?

The following Scriptures are especially directed to the pastors or overseers of the flock.

So when they had eaten breakfast, Jesus said to Simon Peter, "Simon, son of Jonah, do you love Me more than these?" He said to Him, "Yes, Lord; You know that I love You." He said to him, "Feed My lambs." (John 21:15)

- How does the way you are loving your people reflect your love for Jesus?

"Therefore take heed to yourselves and to all the flock, among which the Holy Spirit has made you overseers, to shepherd the church of God which He purchased with His own blood. For I know this, that after my departure savage wolves will come in among you, not sparing the flock. Also from among yourselves men will rise up, speaking perverse things, to draw away the disciples after themselves." (Acts 20:28–30)

- How are you keeping watch over the flock and protecting them from enemies that destroy and false teachers that lead astray?

If a man desires the position of a bishop, he desires a good work. A bishop then must be blameless, the husband of one wife, temperate, sober-minded, of good behavior, hospitable, able to teach; not given to wine, not violent, not greedy for money, but gentle, not quarrelsome, not covetous; one who rules his own house well, having his children in submission with all reverence (for if a man does not know how to rule his own house, how will he take care of the church of God?); not a novice, lest being puffed up with pride he fall into the same condemnation as the devil. Moreover he must have a good testimony among those who are outside, lest he fall into reproach and the snare of the devil. (I Tim. 3:1–7)

- Are you above reproach inside and outside the church?
- How faithful are you to your spouse?
- Are you temperate, self-controlled, respectable, hospitable, able to teach, and not given to drunkenness?
- Are you gentle?
- Are you managing your family well? Do your children obey and respect you?
- Are you spiritually mature?

> If a man is blameless, the husband of one wife, having faithful children not accused of dissipation or insubordination. For a bishop must be blameless, as a steward of God, not self-willed, not quick-tempered, not given to wine, not violent, not greedy for money, but hospitable, a lover of what is good, sober-minded, just, holy, self-controlled, holding fast the faithful word as he has been taught, that he may be able, by sound doctrine, both to exhort and convict those who contradict. For there are many insubordinate, both idle talkers and deceivers, especially those of the circumcision, whose mouths must be stopped, who subvert whole households, teaching things which they ought not, for the sake of dishonest gain. (Titus 1:6–11)

- Are you blameless?
- Are you opinionated and overbearing?
- Are you patient or quick-tempered?
- Are you holy and disciplined?
- Do you encourage others with sound doctrine?
- Are you rebellious or deceitful?
- Do you serve in order to profit?

> The elders who are among you I exhort, I who am a fellow elder and a witness of the sufferings of Christ, and also a partaker of the glory that will be revealed: Shepherd the flock of God which is

among you, serving as overseers, not by compulsion but willingly, not for dishonest gain but eagerly; nor as being lords over those entrusted to you, but being examples to the flock; and when the Chief Shepherd appears, you will receive the crown of glory that does not fade away. Likewise you younger people, submit yourselves to your elders. Yes, all of you be submissive to one another, and be clothed with humility, for "God resists the proud, but gives grace to the humble." Therefore humble yourselves under the mighty hand of God, that He may exalt you in due time, casting all your care upon Him, for He cares for you. (I Pet. 5:1–7)

- Are you serving out of duty or love?
- Are you ministering more for money or the pleasure of service?
- Do you lead by your position and authority or by your example?
- Are you proud and arrogant or humble and submissive?
- Are you casting your burdens and anxiety on the Lord?

The Vine and the Branches

If you are like most shepherds of God's people, the plumb line may have left you feeling incapable as a spiritual leader. The truth is that you are inadequate apart from the Lord. The good news is that God has a remedy. Jesus said:

"I am the true vine, and My Father is the vinedresser. Every branch in Me that does not bear fruit He takes away; and every branch that bears fruit He prunes, that it may bear more fruit. You are already clean because of the word which I have spoken to you. Abide in Me, and I in you. As the branch cannot bear fruit of itself, unless it abides in the vine, neither can you, unless you abide in Me.

I am the vine, you are the branches. He who abides in Me, and I in him, bears much fruit; for without Me you can do nothing." (John 15:1–5)

Jesus said you can do nothing apart from your relationship with Him. However, when you have His life flowing through you, He produces much fruit. God will prune your life of things that keep you from being as productive as He wants you to be. He will remove things from your life that are good in order to produce what is best. The word that God may have spoken to you through the plumb line may be His invitation to come to Him for cleansing. Let Him thoroughly rid your life of every impurity.

> "'If you abide in Me, and My words abide in you, you will ask
> what you desire, and it shall be done for you. By this My Father is
> glorified, that you bear much fruit; so you will be My disciples.'"
> (John 15:7–8)

After reading the plumb line for shepherds, are there things you want to ask the Father to do so He may be glorified in and through your life? Ask Him first to enable you to abide in Him. Ask Him to teach you to let Christ's words abide in you. Then ask Him for the desires you have as a shepherd.

> "'As the Father loved Me, I also have loved you; abide in My love.
> If you keep My commandments, you will abide in My love, just as
> I have kept My Father's commandments and abide in His love.
> These things I have spoken to you, that My joy may remain in you,
> and that your joy may be full.'" (John 15:9–11)

Jesus loves you with an eternal love. If you do as He commands, you will experience a profound assurance that God loves you. Your ministry will also be characterized by an irrepressible joy!

> "No longer do I call you servants, for a servant does not know what
> his master is doing; but I have called you friends, for all things that
> I heard from My Father I have made known to you. You did not
> choose Me, but I chose you and appointed you that you should go
> and bear fruit, and that your fruit should remain, that whatever you
> ask the Father in My name He may give you." (John 15:15–16)

As a shepherd of God's flock, you must remember that you did not choose Him. He chose you. He gave you an assignment. He is the One who enables you to bear fruit, and that fruit will last. Jesus has chosen you to be His friend if you obey His commands. This kind of abiding relationship with God leads to this promise: "Whatever you ask the Father in My name He may give you" (John 15:16). Don't let any failures of your past keep you from your future in Christ. Learn to abide and experience His love, joy, and life flowing through you.

Christ's Yoke

Perhaps you have served for some time as a shepherd of God's people. You may be weary and considering giving up. You may be longing for retirement or hoping another job opportunity comes along. Jesus has another invitation for you: "Come to Me, all you who labor and are heavy laden, and I will give you rest. Take My yoke upon you and learn from Me, for I am gentle and lowly in heart, and you will find rest for your souls. For My yoke is easy and My burden is light" (Matt. 11:28–30).

This invitation is for you. Jesus has a yoke built for two. He is already going about His Father's work. His invitation is for you to get into the yoke with Him. Learn from Him. Experience His gentleness, lowliness, meekness, and humility. Put away any pride you may have about your ministry and join Him in His work. You will find that the yoke is perfectly designed for you. The burden is light because He carries the greater load. You get to experience working with God as He completes His work in God-sized dimensions.

Appendix C
Preparing the Way for the Lord

When God sent His Son to earth, He commissioned John the Baptist to prepare the way for His coming. When Jesus returns to take His bride (the churches) to heaven for His wedding, the bride will have prepared herself.

> "Alleluia! For the Lord God Omnipotent reigns! Let us be glad and rejoice and give Him glory, for the marriage of the Lamb has come, and His wife has made herself ready." And to her it was granted to be arrayed in fine linen, clean and bright, for the fine linen is the righteous acts of the saints. (Rev. 19:6–8)

We, too, need to prepare ourselves for the coming of the Lord, for His coming in revival and awakening, and for His return to take His bride away. The place for revival to begin is in your heart and life. Whether you are the pastor, an elder or a deacon, or a member without elected responsibilities, you can allow God to prepare your heart for revival.

Jesus often said that every word He spoke was not His but the Father's. For example, Jesus said: "I have not spoken on My own authority; but the Father who sent Me gave Me a command, what I should say and what I should speak. And I know that His command is everlasting life. Therefore, whatever I speak, just as the Father has told Me, so I speak" (John 12:49–50).

Is that your pattern of ministry? As Christ's servant you must be so acquainted with God that when you speak, people know they have heard a word from God. Your people don't need sermons or lessons; they need a word from God.

Prepare the Way

God's people need to be taught how to respond to God as a corporate body. For instance, they need to know guidelines for confession—when it should be private and when it should be public. People need to know how to confess moral failure without damaging others and without inviting lustful or sinful thoughts as a result of the confession. They need to know how to share in such a way that God receives the glory.

Here is a list of things you may want to deal with in preparing your people for a fresh encounter with God:

- Preach on revivals in Scripture.
- Teach on fasting and prayer.
- Teach about confession and repentance.
- Discuss the need to quit clock watching. Time is required for returning to God. If God does not finish His work in an hour, we don't need to start making plans to leave.
- Explain how to prepare to meet God. In Exodus 19:9–15 Moses told people to spend three days preparing to meet God. People need clean hands and pure hearts to enter God's presence.
- Focus people's attention on the nature of God and how He works with His people.
- Preach about the corporate nature of the church. Emphasize the importance of every member's response.
- Point people to an intimate, real, personal love relationship with God.
- Pray for the demolishing of strongholds due to bondage to the past (2 Cor. 10:3–5).
- Help people recognize the difference between spiritual warfare and God's discipline.
- Teach believers to deny self.
- Help people to develop a servant heart for others.
- Teach people to fear God and to dread offending Him.
- Help people make an absolute surrender to Christ's lordship.
- Develop a readiness in your people to release everything to Him: resources, schedule, programs, positions of leadership, calendar of activities, conflicting involvement in secular pursuits, plans, goals, and so forth.
- Prepare for brokenness before restoration. Help people understand the process of moving toward spiritual health.
- Help your church look beyond the brokenness of repentance to the joy and fruits of revival.

Pray for Revival

Second Chronicles 7:14 instructs God's people to humble ourselves, pray, and seek His face. United, visible, and extraordinary prayer has preceded every great revival in history. Some have concluded that prayer is the secret to compel God to act. Many pray, however, and never experience revival.

Prayer is not merely a religious activity. Prayer is a relationship between people and God. Prayer alone does not cause revival. We pray because God initiates a relationship with us. He invites us into His presence. When we pray, we enter into the throne room of the universe. There we learn the heart and will of our heavenly Father. In His presence, through prayer, we recognize our sinful condition. We cry out to God with a broken and contrite heart, and He calls us to repent.

Prayer alone is not the key to revival. Humility is not enough. Seeking God's face is inadequate. While these are important, repentance is the ultimate requirement. Without repentance no revival will take place. We must turn from our wicked ways. When we return to God, He has promised He will return to us (James 4:8). He is a covenant-keeping God; He keeps His promises.

Prayer for revival is not a tool for manipulating God. It is not a magic formula or a religious task to complete. Prayer is a relationship with God where we respond to Him, draw near to Him, and find Him. Prayer that results in genuine repentance is our part of the process. Then God keeps His promises. As people enter His presence in prayer, they cannot help but be confronted by their sinfulness. That can lead to the repentance required for revival.

Gather the People

Ask the Lord to guide you to gather your people together. Because many church members have lost their sense of corporate identity, many do not sense any accountability to their church. Yet all members need to be involved when their church returns to God. The sin of one or a few can affect the entire body. When one member is sick, the whole body is affected.

Emphasize the importance of coming together before God to respond to His summons. Help people understand that God Himself is issuing the call to return. Remember, however, that God is the One who does the convincing. Your job is to bear witness to what you sense God is saying.

Recite God's Activity In Your Church

In Deuteronomy 29, Moses gathered the people to renew their covenant with God. He began by reviewing the nation's spiritual history to remind the people of God's faithfulness and His covenant love. Remembering the mighty activity of God in the past also strengthens faith for the present. Psalm 105 was used to help Israel remember God's great works. Reciting God's past activity among His people played a prominent part in the sacred assemblies in Israel's history.

In Psalm 78, history is recalled to remind God's people how seriously He treats their sin. The psalmist said, "We will not hide them from their children, telling to the generation to come the praises of the LORD, and His strength and His wonderful works that He has done" (Ps. 78:4).

In the revival under Ezra and Nehemiah, the leaders called people to celebrate their past relationship with God and to worship Him before they moved on to repentance. Nehemiah said, "'Do not sorrow, for the joy of the LORD is your strength'" (Neh. 8:10).

The church at Ephesus in Revelation 2 had left its first love. Christ commanded them to "'remember therefore from where you have fallen'" (Rev. 2:5). Remembering where we have been with God, remembering the mountaintop experiences, will better prepare us for repentance and revival.

Plan on a special service for your church to recite God's activity among His people. Celebrate what God did in the past. Allow members who remember the "good old days" to tell stories of what God did in earlier days. Don't hide God's activity from His people. Magnify it! Take time to praise and thank the Lord for all He has done.

Keep the focus on God's activity and not on human accomplishments. These are some things that may help you celebrate:

- Ask someone to read through or research your church's history and prepare a report on what God did.
- Report on missions started, people called into ministry, and significant salvation experiences.
- Remember God's guidance at crucial decision times.
- Ask for testimonies of where God did a special work in answer to prayer.
- Allow time for testimonies of ways people experienced God at work in the past.
- Report on previous significant revival experiences.
- Invite testimonies of ways God has worked in individual lives.

Help your congregation remember where they have been with God. This will prepare them for the next steps of returning to the Lord. This will also orient a new generation of members to what God has already done in your church.

Identify Corporate Sins

Ask people to identify anything that may be a sin your church has committed. Help people understand that this is a positive process that can restore church health.

Collect a list of possible sins the church has committed. As the pastor, gather church leaders together. Pray and discuss the issues that have surfaced. Compile a list of things the people believe are sins of the church. You will want to deal with this list in a time of corporate worship. You might ask one or more leaders to read through the list of corporate sins. Call the church to confess their sins. Guide the people in corporate prayer for repentance like that in Daniel 9, Ezra 9, or Nehemiah 9.

What are corporate sins? Any occasion the church sinned by its action or lack of action is a corporate sin. Corporate sins might also include an individual sin that is common to a large number of your people (for example, the intermarriage dealt with by Ezra in Ezra 9–10 might be similar to a church with widespread sexual immorality or divorce). Churches need to deal with all sin for which they have not repented—including past sins. Examples of corporate sins might include such things as:

- participating in a church split
- adopting the world's ways
- allowing an ungodly person (or persons) to "run off" an innocent pastor or staff person, especially if your church has a pattern of doing so
- choosing to do good things instead of God's will
- beginning a church, group, or denomination in a sinful way, such as a split, envy, controversy, or pride
- covering up past sins
- defaulting on a debt
- disgracing God's name in the eyes of the community (for example, a leader or member experiences moral failure that became known in the community with no response by the church)
- failing to care for the needs of members, families, or couples
- failing to take a strong stand on God's standards for family and marriage and failing to support those needing help
- forcing agreement or compromise on a decision with no unity of mind, heart, or spirit

- isolating yourself from other believers, churches, denominations in your community or state; doing your own thing when others needed your help, encouragement, or leadership
- lacking faith when confronted with a God-sized assignment and deciding not to trust God with your limited resources
- leaving a field of ministry to take an easier path (like leaving the inner city for the suburbs rather than dealing with the problems of the people in the inner city)
- making a decision contrary to God's guidance
- mistreating a pastor, staff member, or family member
- permitting controversy, strife, or dissension
- practicing prejudice or discrimination
- refusing to follow God's commands related to church discipline of sinful members
- refusing to pursue stray members who have become inactive
- refusing to obey God because it would "cost" too much
- shifting control of the church from Christ as its Head to anyone else: pastor, deacons, elders, board, or power block in church
- tolerating evil in the congregation
- trying to save your life rather than give it away in service and ministry
- selfishly using resources for personal comforts and not responding to the needy or missions opportunities

This is by no means a comprehensive list. Perhaps it has given you an idea of what we mean by corporate sin. Pay attention to what God brings to the minds of your members. Take every suggestion seriously.

Identify Departure Markers

Corporate sin may include things that took place many years ago. A small, struggling, declining church, for instance, invited a guest speaker to talk about the new church planting work being done in the area. Two different members spoke to him later, and each said something like this: "Our pastor tried to lead us to start a new church years ago, but we refused to do it. I believe God has been punishing us for that decision ever since."

Such an event may be a "departure marker." If your church members believe your church has departed from God, ask them to try to identify those points of departure.

Was an event or decision the beginning of the departure? When and how did the first signs of departing from God begin to surface? What was happening during that time that may have been a cause of the departure? If something surfaces during this search, it may help you understand what you need to do to repent, make restitution, and be restored. Typically the point of departure needs to be the initial point of return.

Prepare for Spiritual Awakening

When revival comes, a natural result that follows is spiritual awakening of unbelievers. Revival is for God's people. Spiritual awakening is for unbelievers at large. Churches need always to be prepared for a spiritual awakening. However, you cannot simply wait for God to revive your church so your people are prepared for a subsequent spiritual awakening. You must prepare for it in advance. Here are some suggestions to help your church prepare for a spiritual awakening that will turn your community and nation back to God in large numbers.

- Provide extensive discipleship training at all levels of spiritual growth for your church members. Remember that the Great Commission task is not complete until you have taught your people to obey *all* that Christ commanded (Matt. 28:19–20).
- Develop leaders and teachers who can instruct new believers. Every member of the church needs to be equipped for the work of ministry, for building up the body (Eph. 4:11–13).
- Pray that the Lord of the harvest will thrust forth laborers into the harvest (Matt. 9:37–38). Now is the time to pray for leaders and to prepare them for service. If you wait until awakening comes, you will be behind schedule.
- Prepare counselors for those who will be coming to Christ in large numbers during the awakening. These counselors need to be spiritual physicians who can guide people to repent of their sins, place their faith in Christ, and surrender to His lordship.
- Train members to help new believers mature as disciples of Christ.
- Prepare for an avalanche of ministry needs. The world is filled with brokenness. Families are fractured and hurting. Often in awakening, the poor and needy respond in great numbers. People will be brought into the kingdom and into your church with significant needs. They need to experience the healing power of Christ at work reconciling relationships,

restoring families, healing the pains of the past, and setting them free from bondage. Many will have tangible needs for food, clothing, jobs, health care, and housing. The model in the New Testament church is that church members gave sacrificially to provide for the needs of others "nor was there anyone among them who lacked" (Acts 4:34).

- Prepare your people to make major adjustments. Any time God invites you to become involved in His activity, you must change your schedule and activities. Prepare your church to accept any cost or adjustment involved in seeing the kingdom advance in your community.

- Be prepared to give all the glory to God. A sure way to quench revival and spiritual awakening is to grasp God's glory for yourself or your church. Recognize that revival and spiritual awakening are things only God can do. When God accomplishes a great work, magnify God in the eyes of His people. Don't take any of the credit.

- Prepare yourself and God's people to surrender control to Christ. Another way to shut down God's work is to succumb to the temptation to try to organize or control God's activity. For spiritual awakening to come, pastors must be willing to lose control!

- Allow the Holy Spirit to set the agenda each day. Adjust your plans and agenda to what God is doing. If you don't know what to do next, ask for the counsel of others in your church. God will lead His church. You can depend on Him.

Prepare to Lead

God wants to guide you and your church in revival. Many people will offer you advice on what you should do. Beware. If you are always turning to people for all guidance, you are relying on substitutes for God. That could indicate you have departed from God. Don't hesitate, however, to seek God's counsel through other believers and particularly other leaders in your church. But let God be your first and primary source, not your last resort.

Every member of your congregation is a royal priest. Seek the counsel of other leaders about what they sense God is saying to your church. The "eye" and the "ear" both need to be heard as the body seeks to discern God's will (1 Cor. 12; Rom. 12).

Trust God. What needs to take place in your church cannot happen unless God does it. Yes, a human response is required; but God is the One who initiates, guides, and completes His work. "Trust in the LORD with all your heart, and lean not on your own understanding; in all your ways acknowledge Him, and He shall direct your paths" (Prov. 3:5–6).

In Revelation 2–3, Christ stands in the midst of His churches. He holds the stars (pastors) in His hand. He is present to help and to guide the response of His people. Trust Him to be present and at work in your midst.

Trust God to enable you to do His work. You may feel like Moses and tell God, "I can't do this. Find someone else." The truth is, apart from Him you can't bring revival or spiritual awakening, but with Him all things are possible (Luke 1:37). God is far more interested in bringing revival than you are. He will be present to fill you with His power and authority, working through you to accomplish what you cannot (Col. 1–2).

When you feel overwhelmed by your weakness, remember the words of Paul: "'My grace is sufficient for you, for My strength is made perfect in weakness'" (2 Cor. 12:9).

Don't trust in a method, but rely on God. A method or program is not the answer to your needs. You do not have to know the right words to say or the correct things to do. You need God's presence and guidance. Obey Him each step of the way, and you will find yourself and your church in the center of His activity and mighty power.

Don't substitute an outside leader for God's leadership in times of revival. At some point, God may guide you to invite someone from outside your church to help you in revival or spiritual awakening. However, this may be far more appropriate after revival when your church is prepared to be part of an evangelistic harvest.

Don't be discouraged by the failure of others. Keep your eyes on God and not on people's response.

Develop and display a spirit of humility. Your dependence on God and your humility will set the tone for the response of others. The first requirement of revival is to humble yourself (2 Chron. 7:14).

Guiding God's People to Return to Him

The time to guide God's people to return to Him commences the moment the Holy Spirit begins to convict your people of their sin. Like peeling layers from an onion, God will cleanse one "layer" of sin away at a time until a person and church are thoroughly clean. Then a church and individuals should be encouraged to keep "short accounts" with the Lord. Daily times for personal cleansing should limit the need for dealing with sin as thoroughly as is generally done during times of revival.

Obedience to the conviction of the Holy Spirit ought to be immediate. Regardless of the times you may have planned for revival experiences, leaders should be prepared to call for confession and repentance anytime they sense God is bringing people under conviction for sin. This may mean canceling a sermon or class session and giving an invitation. It might mean calling a special service tomorrow night because of what you see God doing. If God decides to bring revival, let Him do it His way! Agree with your people that you will drop your agenda and adjust to God's schedule if He chooses to bring revival. God's timing will always be perfect.

Not Methods but a Person

One factor in biblical times of revival ought to encourage you. None of those leaders had a manual on how to guide people to return to the Lord. You don't need one either. All you need is the Lord. He will guide you in practical ways to lead your people to return to Him. He is the One most interested in their return. Trust the Lord uniquely to guide you and His people to return to Him.

One advantage biblical leaders had was that they grew up in the middle of a people who knew how to respond to the Lord corporately. Today's Christians have lost the understanding of how groups of people respond to the Lord. The following are some suggestions that may help you lead your people corporately to respond to God in revival. Prayerfully ask the Lord to guide, teach, and prepare you for leading His people. Don't attempt anything He doesn't guide you to do.

Involve Multiple Leaders

In biblical times the king, governor, prophet, scribe, or priest led their nation in revival. Often national revivals included two or more of these leaders. In Nineveh the king led his city to repent. Jacob (as father) led his family to repent. We sense that the established leaders of a group need to lead their people to respond to God. Trust the Lord to guide you to lead His people. Multiple leadership is the primary model. Seldom did one person carry the burden alone.

Pastors may want to involve church staff or other church leaders to act as a leadership team for guiding the people to return to the Lord. The pastor should provide the primary leadership. He also should lead in discerning when and how to guide the church in repentance. A wise pastor, however, will listen carefully to suggestions that come from the Lord through other people. This may require the pastor and people to pray intensely as they seek God's directions for their church.

Mobilize Prayer

Because you need to be sensitive to the Spirit's leadership, you must always be in a Spirit of prayer. Make prayer your primary revival strategy. Like the apostles in Acts 6, devote yourself to prayer and the ministry of the Word:

> The twelve summoned the multitude of the disciples and said, "It is not desirable that we should leave the word of God and serve tables. Therefore, brethren, seek out from among you seven men of good reputation, full of the Holy Spirit and wisdom, whom we may appoint over this business; but we will give ourselves continually to prayer and to the ministry of the word.' And the saying pleased the whole multitude. (Acts 6:2–5)

Perhaps you cannot imagine asking your church to allow you the freedom to devote yourself to prayer and the ministry of the Word. Some pastors would not dare suggest such a thing. However, something about the spiritual character of the apostles and the leadership of the Holy Spirit caused the whole church to be pleased with this suggestion. They chose seven men to help carry the load so their spiritual leaders could spend sufficient time with the Lord in prayer and in His Word.

Don't allow anything to rob you of your time with God. Revival is such a crucial need in the life of your church that you cannot afford to miss what God wants to do through you. Don't always pray alone. Jesus said, "If two of you agree on earth concerning anything that they ask, it will be done for them by My Father in heaven. For where two or three are gathered together in My name, I am there in the midst of them" (Matt. 18:19–20).

Jesus promised a greater authority to united prayer and a powerful experience of God's power when you pray and agree with others. Pray with other leaders in your church. Pray with and for other churches and Christian denominations. Pray with other pastors. Imagine the kind of unity that might develop in the Christian community if you were to say to other pastors, "We are praying for God's blessing on your church and ministry. How can we pray for you and your church?" One common factor where God is sending community-wide revivals is that pastors and groups are already meeting together across denominational lines to pray.

Prayer should also be a major emphasis in all you do as a church. God is interested in your being a "house of prayer for all nations" (Isa. 56:7). Consider some of the following suggestions to increase corporate praying and thus enhance the frequency of encounters with God:

- Provide a prayer room with people who intercede for the services while they are going on. Give your people permission to leave the service at any time and move to the prayer room to meet with God. Prayer counselors should be ready to pray with those who come.
- Encourage people to come to the front of the auditorium to pray. This will give people a tangible way to respond to the Lord. It may give others a needed opportunity to humble themselves. Dealing with pride often requires a public response.
- Encourage small-group prayer. Whether in classes, in special prayer meetings, or at other times, encourage members to pray together and for one another. Encourage people to pray for spiritual concerns, not just for physical problems.
- Plan times of corporate prayer just as carefully as you do the music or sermon. Guide the church in praying together in worship. Allow time for corporate prayer.
- Some churches offer opportunities for persons to seek out someone to pray with them about a specific need. One pastor called these times "set-free services." Following his Wednesday evening service, he would extend an invitation to those who needed prayer to remain in the sanctuary. He encouraged mature disciples to linger and to be available to pray with those with burdens. Those needing prayer would seek out one person, share his or her burden, and receive prayer. The Scripture says, "The effective, fervent prayer of a righteous man avails much" (James 5:16). The church found this time of prayer to be life changing. The pastor noticed his counseling load dropped significantly after they began these weekly prayer times.

Clear the Calendar of Competition

Activity, even religious activity, can crowd God out of people's lives. Members need to focus their attention on God and His call. Satan will resort to every distraction he can to keep Christians from dealing with the sin in their lives. Do everything possible as a church to remove activities that distract your people from a fresh encounter with God.

A church in Austin, Texas, sensed God was calling them to repent for a variety of sins. The church decided that what God was asking them to do was far too important to try and squeeze into an already full church schedule. The leaders decided to cancel all unrelated church programming for the summer months and devote time to prayer, fasting, and repentance.

They had two things on the calendar each week: Sunday morning services and a Wednesday evening church assembly. They spent Wednesday evenings standing before God's Word focusing on one theme or subject each week. After a time of reading the Word and some brief exposition by the pastor, the people responded to God in prayer, confession, and repentance. They spent the entire summer returning to God.

God did some wonderful things in the lives of individuals and families. By summer's end the leaders sensed God was saying to them, "I'm not finished with you yet, but you may return to your regular schedule."

That may seem like a radical adjustment. As church leaders, however, you will have to determine how important revival is for your church. Revival comes at a cost. Your church's willingness to make adjustments may be a good indicator of how serious it is about its relationship to God. You will be wise to clear the church calendar of conflicting events. Sometimes so many other church activities are scheduled at the same time as the prayer meting that the church inadvertently tells its people that prayer is just one of many options they can choose. Prayer must be the priority.

Hold the Plumb Line before People

God calls His people to revival, because they have departed and need to return. God's people, however, do not always realize they have strayed from God's standards. God's Word serves as a plumb line to reveal God's ideal for the church and for Christian living. As God's people clearly understand His standards, the Holy Spirit brings conviction of sin. Godly sorrow over sin should lead to repentance (2 Cor. 7:10).

- Use God's Word in services, Bible studies, handouts, and in other ways to set forth God's plumb line beside His people.
- Preach on a particular topic or theme that uses God's Word as a plumb line. Help people measure themselves and the church by God's standards.
- Go beyond being Word centered to being Christ centered. The Word is not an end in itself. It points to a relationship with a person

(John 5:39–40). The Word helps identify places where people may have departed from God. The next step is to go to God and seek to be restored to a right relationship with Him. Once people are in a right relationship with God, they can seek God's help in reordering their behavior to be obedient to God's expectations.

Respond to God's Activity in a Group

One of the lessons leaders must understand is how God's people respond to God corporately. We have not generally been taught how to respond when God interrupts our worship services, group activities, plans, or programs. This is something God can and will teach you. God cares far more about your people than you do. However, you must make some prior commitments in the way you function as a spiritual leader. You must surrender your plans and agenda to God. If He interrupts what you had planned, cancel your agenda and watch to see what God wants to do. If you have not decided beforehand to do this, you may fail to make the adjustment in the middle of a service when God tries to interrupt you and take over the agenda.

Henry and Claude were leading a conference together for 150 people. Small groups were completing a sharing and prayer time. Henry was scheduled to speak next. A woman stood and explained that someone in her group needed us to pray for her. The woman had been abused as a young child, and now her father was at home dying from cancer. She was struggling to come to terms with her father's impending death.

We have often seen God bring dramatic emotional and spiritual healing to people in conditions such as this. We had to decide whether to pray briefly and then go on with our teaching agenda or to turn the session over to God. We had already agreed before the conference that if God interrupted us, we would cancel our agenda and give Him freedom to work. That is what we did.

We knew that God had entrusted that woman's needs to the particular small group she was in, so we assumed He also had placed people in that group who could best minister to her. We asked those who could identify with her need to stand around her and pray with her. Eight or ten women came to minister to her in prayer. We then gave an invitation for others to come for prayer if they had deep needs that only God could meet. Then people came to pray with those who responded.

As God completed His work in people's lives, we gave them an opportunity to share with the group what God had done. Often the testimony would be used by God to invite someone with a similar problem also to be set free. For the rest of the hour, God used members of that group to minister to other members. People who had been in spiritual bondage for decades found freedom in Christ. Others experienced the comfort, healing, and peace that only God can give. Some, for the first time in their lives, experienced the unconditional love of a father—a heavenly Father. Those who were used by God in ministry to others experienced God working through them in dramatic ways they had never before experienced. We discovered more about God in that hour than we could have learned in a week of lectures.

Here are some suggestions for responding to God's activity in your group:

- Spend much time in developing your personal relationship with God so you learn to recognize God's voice when He is speaking to you. You must always be right with God when you stand before His people. Any impurity in your life could cost the whole group a fresh encounter with God.
- Trust God to guide you when He wants to work in your group setting.
- Decide beforehand that you will cancel your agenda and give God freedom to move anytime He shows you He wants to do a special work. When you see God at work in your group, that is your invitation to join Him.
- Watch for things like tears of joy or conviction, emotional or spiritual brokenness, the thrill of a newfound insight, or an urgency for prayer in response to a need. These things are sometimes seen only in a facial expression or quiet sigh. Determine whether you need to talk to the person in front of the group or later in private. You must depend on the Holy Spirit for such guidance. Don't be afraid of making a mistake.
- Respond by asking probing questions like one of these: Is something happening in your life right now that you would share with us? How can we pray for you? Would you share with us what God is doing in your life? What can we do to help you?
- If a person responds by sharing, then provide ministry based on the need. If he or she does not appear ready to respond, don't pressure the individual. Give God time to work in people's lives.
- When appropriate, invite members to minister to one another. This may be to pray, to comfort, to counsel privately, or to rejoice with the person.

When you do not feel equipped to deal with a problem that surfaces, ask the group if someone feels led to help. You will be amazed at how God works to provide the right person to provide the needed ministry.

- When one person shares with the group, prayerfully consider an appropriate response. You need not respond after each person shares. However, you might:

  —Ask them to pray aloud and respond to the Lord.

  —Ask others with the same burden or sin to pray together.

  —Invite those who want this person to pray for them about a similar matter.

  —Ask others to come and pray for this person out of their personal victory.

  —Invite those with common sin to stand and have people around them pray, or have someone lead in prayer.

  —Read a Scripture as a promise, instruction, or correction.

  —Redefine sin as sin. There are no minor sins. Do not dismiss a lie as a "white lie." Do not dismiss adultery as an "affair."

  —Encourage members to form accountability groups where they meet together for prayer and sharing to help one another obey what God told them.

- Give people opportunities to testify about what God is doing. This is a critical point. Often God may use one person's testimony to help others with identical problems or challenges. This is also one of the best ways for people to experience God—by hearing testimonies of His wonderful work in the lives of other people. Don't hide God's glory from His people.
- When you do not sense a clear direction about what to do next, ask the group. Say something like this: "I do not have a clear sense of what we need to do next. Does anyone have a sense of what God wants us to do?"
- Continue on God's agenda until you sense He is finished with you.

We cannot give you directions for handling every situation. But we can speak from experience: when God wants to work in a group, He can and will give the guidance needed. Your job is to recognize His voice or His activity and then do everything He asks you to do. At the same time, trust Him to work through His body, the church. He has placed members in your congregation and gifted them to build up the body of Christ. Acknowledge and use all of the resources God has given you.

Guide Corporate Responses

During times of corporate worship, you will need to guide people's responses. Follow the basic guideline that the circle of confession should be as large as the circle of offense. Public confession normally should be limited to public sin.

Remind members that confession is not the same as repentance. It is merely the beginning of a process of repentance. When appropriate, remind members of the need to be reconciled to offended persons and to make restitution when tangible damage has been done. At times people who come under conviction should be encouraged to take the individual aside privately to confess and be reconciled first, before announcing anything to the church at large. For example, husbands who confess infidelity to their wives, or wives who confess abortions to their husbands ought first to confess to their spouses in private.

Claim and confess the sins of those who have gone before you. If the church becomes aware of sins that occurred years ago but have never been dealt with, guide a time of confession for the sins of your predecessors. Daniel 9 provides a sample prayer of confession for the sins of ancestors. In confessing their sins, you agree with God that what they did was wrong. You agree to make whatever restitution is necessary. Then you pledge to correct your ways and not sin as your spiritual ancestors did.

Lists of corporate sins could be read, followed by prayers of confession. A time of covenant renewal might follow. Then seek God's direction on what to do with any idols or false gods that your church may have discovered. Some suggestions for a corporate response include:

- Ask key people to stand, read, confess, or pray.
- Write sins on paper and nail them to a cross or burn them in a basket.
- Prepare and read a corporate written prayer and/or a written covenant.
- Provide for times of silent prayer.
- Provide for times of small- and large-group prayer.
- Offer times for simultaneous prayer.
- Invite people to come for prayer at the front of the church auditorium.
- Allow members to request prayer and then immediately get an individual or group to pray for them. Use the members of the body.
- Don't prematurely assure people of forgiveness. Allow God to bring conviction until the person realizes God is the only hope of cleansing and restoration.

Lead Times of Testimony (contributed by Bill Elliff, pastor, Little Rock, Arkansas)

Historically one of the primary ingredients for the spread of revivals has been personal testimonies. The accounting of the work of God in individual hearts can prove a powerful tool in the hands of God to inspire, encourage, and convict others.

Often pastors are fearful of public testimony times for the following reasons:

- embarrassing "dry" testimonies
- excessively long or emotional testimonies
- testimonies that step over lines of propriety
- nonspecific, generalized testimonies that appear useless and unedifying
- immature or attention-seeking people monopolizing time at the microphone

Testimonies can provide freedom for God to accomplish considerable good in the following ways:

- Give God the glory due Him as He transforms lives.
- Help believers confirm and verbalize what God is doing in their lives.
- Allow specific testimonies to inspire, convict, encourage, teach, and train other believers.
- Grow the church through a fresh sense of the magnitude of God's work in their church.
- Give the pastor an opportunity to identify and "preach" on certain themes that are repeatedly mentioned during testimonies.
- Provide a spiritual "thermometer" by giving church leaders an increased understanding of where God is at work and by identifying primary areas of need.
- Give opportunity for public confession and corporate forgiveness.

The following are hints on how to lead an effective testimony time. The average lay person may be as fearful regarding these times as a pastor, often because of bad experiences in the past. Carefully explaining how the sharing time will be conducted can pave the way for a fresh release of God's Spirit through His people in the body.

Pray! Spend time privately and publicly praying for:

- God to bring the right people to share.
- protection from the enemy.

- wisdom, as the pastor, to know how to lead the time—particularly how to be sensitive to key points of conviction.

Take time to educate the congregation on how to give a testimony. The following model might be used.

1. Share how each person has a unique spiritual pilgrimage that can encourage others. Learning to articulate and transparently communicate God's activity in your life is one of the great keys to usefulness for God's kingdom.
2. Describe how to share a testimony.
    - Share where God found you. Be specific regarding areas of sin and need.
    - Share what you were experiencing as a result of controlling your own life.
    - Share what God said to you.
    - Share how you responded. You may have reacted negatively at first. Be honest.
    - Share what you are now experiencing as a result of obedience to God's truth. What benefits of obedience are you experiencing?
3. Describe simple ground rules.
    - Be brief.
    - Be specific.
    - Be current.
    - Bring all the glory to God.
    - Don't reflect negatively on others.
    - Use the term *moral failure* for any moral sins.
4. Invite the congregation to think of one area where God has been working in recent days (you may want to identify this as the past week, month, six months, etc.). Then ask members to turn to one other person and, using the above method, share a three-minute testimony.
5. Spend a moment in prayer. Let members ask God whether He wants them to share a public testimony. Invite those who feel led to share to come and be seated on the front row. Indicate that you may or may not get to all those who came forward. This gives the pastor the discretion to choose those he feels led to call upon.

6. As they come, the pastor can stand by the microphone with those who are sharing. Feel free to interrupt and help them clarify or give further specifics if needed. Offer encouragement and love. At times you may have to shut down a testimony that is entirely off-track or disruptive to what God is doing. Make sure you always keep control of the microphone!

7. Lead in ministering to people after they have shared.
   - Give a word of encouragement or affirmation, if appropriate.
   - If someone asks for the church's forgiveness, lead the church in corporately verbalizing forgiveness to the individual.
   - Invite people to give a hug, a word of encouragement, or a blessing to those testifying as they head back to their seats.
   - If anyone still has needs or burdens, invite a group of concerned people to gather around or take them to a side room for prayer, encouragement, counsel, or other needed help.

8. Be sensitive not only to the person testifying but also to what God is saying to the church through the testimony. Remind people that they are not spectators but participants. God may be speaking directly to them about related issues. When a similar testimony is repeated several times, recognize this as God speaking to the church.

9. Be sensitive to opportunities to preach based on the testimonies. Don't feel the need to speak after every testimony. If God brings to your mind key thoughts that help crystallize and convict through the testimonies, seize the opportunity, perhaps even stopping to give people an opportunity to respond to what has just been said.

Other helpful hints include:

1. Don't worry about excesses. If someone seems to step over the line in some way, discreetly take control of the microphone and thank God publicly that people feel the freedom to share. Then gently remind folks of the boundaries for the testimonies.

2. When people share things that should have been related in private, ask them to go to that individual immediately, if possible, to clear their conscience.

3. Don't feel you must have everyone share publicly. It is often better to stop on a significant note instead of dragging it out. If you extend the sharing time too long, some people may feel they need to say something even

though God has not been doing a special work in their life. This will also leave the congregation eager to hear more from God the next time they meet. Inform those who did not get to share that they will have other opportunities and affirm that they have been obedient to God by being willing to share.

4. Remind people that every testimony is significant.

Although the above suggestions may seem mechanical, they have proven helpful to many. Trust God to use you to open the way of blessing to others through this biblical practice.

APPENDIX D
TIMES FOR CONTINUING RENEWAL

One of the reasons many churches are so far from what God intends is that they have failed to renew their love relationship with God on a regular basis. We may have made attempts at renewal or gone through the motions of revival services, but our current state indicates we have failed to help our people maintain and nurture their love relationship with God.

Because of our commitment to evangelism, we have often placed the primary emphasis of our services on evangelistic messages to unbelievers. In doing so, we have neglected the spiritual renewal of God's people.

Regular Times for Renewal

We pray that the *Fresh Encounter* message will be a tool God uses to bring you and your church through genuine revival. Revival, however, will be a recurring need for God's people. We tend to depart from God habitually. You must intentionally plan for regular times of spiritual renewal. When God brings revival, don't allow the flames to die out. Guide God's people to return regularly to the Lord. The following suggestions may give you some help in planning and conducting regular times for renewing your people's love relationship with God.

Holy Days

Christian holy days (holidays) like Christmas and Easter ought to be special times of renewal. On these days and during the related seasons, place your focus on both celebration and renewal of our relationship with God. These are days to remember the love God lavished on us by sending His Son. Rather than going through time-honored traditions as mere ritual, these can be unique opportunities to remember and respond to God's love.

Help people understand what God has done that affects their lives practically. Holy days are good times to give special offerings for mission causes as an expression of thanksgiving and gratitude to the Lord for all He has done. They also can be opportunities to call for repentance when people realize they have broken fellowship with God because of their sin.

Pre-Communion Meetings

In the past, pre-Communion meetings were used as a powerful time for repentance. On the Saturday before the Sunday observance of the Lord's Supper, the entire congregation would set aside all regular work and come together for a time of personal examination and reflection. This time was used for people to repent of all known sin and to reconcile broken relationships lest they partake of the Lord's Supper unworthily (I Cor. 11:27–32). This allowed people to have clean hands, pure hearts, and clear consciences before God as they approached the Lord's table.

Sometimes this pre-Communion time lasted a week or two. Andrew Murray wrote a book in the nineteenth century in South Africa called *The Lord's Table*.[1] It was used as a daily study one week before the Lord's Supper to help people focus their attention on Jesus. Readers went through a careful time of self-examination prior to the Sunday observance. The focus during the Lord's Supper was on Christ's sacrifice on the cross. This guided people to remember the Lord's death and also anticipate His future return. The book then provided a daily study for the coming week to reflect on the difference the Lord's provision makes in daily life related to power, sanctification, obedience, work, and fellowship with Jesus.

Pentecost Prayer Meetings

In *The Prayer Life*, Andrew Murray describes the beginning of Pentecost prayer meetings.[2] The revival of 1857–1858 in America spread to South Africa by 1860. In 1861 the pastors decided to hold prayer meetings in the afternoons one week prior to the annual observance of Pentecost. Many hearts were warmed and deeply touched during this time.

Since Pentecost has special significance for the historic coming of the Holy Spirit, churches decided to spend the ten days between ascension and Pentecost praying daily like the disciples in the upper room. Over the next fifty years, the Pentecost prayer meetings were observed. According to Murray, these prayer meetings frequently erupted into times of revival. He claimed they were often followed by fruitful evangelistic harvests.

Pilgrim Prayer Meetings

In 1816 in Wales, William Williams was preaching about the work of the Holy Spirit. He offered this suggestion to the parish: "What if you were to consent to have Him to save the whole of this parish? 'Ah, but how can we have Him?' Well, hold prayer-meetings through the whole parish; go from house to house—every house that will open its door. Make it the burden of every prayer that God should come here to save. If God has not come by the time you have gone through the parish once, go through it again; but if you are in earnest in your prayers, you shall not go through half the parish before God has come to you."[3]

In that service was a lonely old woman with little religious background. Though extremely poor, she splurged and bought two wax candles to be ready for the pilgrim prayer meeting when it came to her house. Almost a year later the discouraged woman went to the shop where she had bought the candles. She asked the owner when the prayer meeting was coming to her house. The owner felt instantly rebuked, for none of the church members had taken the suggestion seriously. He reported the incident to the church, and the congregation began to pray from home to home throughout their community. On a Sunday evening in August 1817, the Holy Spirit descended in power and revival swept through that area.

Body Life Meetings

The church is described as the body of Christ. Every member has an important role in helping the body function properly. A "body life" meeting is a time for members of the body to care for and strengthen one another. It can be a time for testimonies, sharing special prayer requests, praying for one another, rejoicing with those who rejoice, and weeping with those who weep. It can be a time for members to share faults, weaknesses, or needs and have the rest of the body minister to them.

A body life meeting is a time of corporate worship and sharing that is more informal and intimate than a traditional service. Consider planning a service around the idea of body life. Ask members to study Romans 12 and 1 Corinthians 12, making a list of ways the members of the body of Christ relate to one another. Encourage members to share needs, request prayer, testify to God's goodness, remember God's blessings in the past, and discuss ways to help and encourage one another. Ask members to think about and share how they can "stur up love and good works" (Heb. 10:24).

Cleansing by Washing with the Water of the Word

Present Scriptures related to a particular theme in a bulletin insert or in some other publication. Read the Scripture from the pulpit or guide the congregation in a responsive reading. Present a choral reading of Scriptures.

Scriptures are not an end in themselves. They should always be pointing people to a relationship. Ask people to reflect on those Scriptures or respond to God in some way:

- Suggest that people pray and ask God what He wants them to do in response to this truth. Point people to the Lord so He speaks directly to His people.
- Ask, "Is God convicting you of any sin? Then confess it and return to Him." Notice the emphasis on what God is doing rather than what people are thinking or saying. In using questions like this, you encourage people to be God centered.
- Request that people gather in groups of four or five and pray sentence prayers of response to the Lord. Sometimes this is the point where a person may allow the dam of resistance to break. Then God floods in, and their lives are radically changed. When this happens, others in the group encounter God too. Testimonies from these kinds of experiences can lead to a major breakthrough in God's work among His people.

Preparing Plumb Line Messages

Pastors and other spiritual leaders need to allow God to identify a subject that He wants to deal with in their congregation. Provide a list of Scriptures with appropriate questions or activities to help people evaluate their lives against God's plumb line. Preach or teach on the subject and then call people to respond to God and return in any area where they recognize they have departed from Him. During many of the revivals in history, sermons focused on one specific sin. As the preacher dealt thoroughly with that one sin, God dealt deeply with His people. Messages might include such sins as pride, bitterness, gossip, divisiveness, greed, adultery, theft, or deceit.

Church Discipline

God holds every individual accountable for his or her own sin. He expects us to respond to the conviction of the Holy Spirit in dealing with it. If Christians refuse to deal with their own sin, God intends for the church to address it. A church is made up of many members, but they are one body. If one member is living in rebellion, the whole body is accountable.

Church discipline must be undertaken in a careful, loving, and God-directed manner. When the early church disciplined wayward members, great fear came on all the people, and that fear increased the level of everyone's faithfulness (Acts 11). God commanded the church to deal with sin in its midst (Matt. 18:15–18). When we fail to take God-prescribed action, the church sins and invites God's discipline.

You probably will need to prepare your church for such a step. Because of former abuses of church discipline, we have departed from the clear commands of the Lord. Careful teaching and much prayer are required for a church to let God guide it in this practice.

What does God's Word say about church discipline?

So then each of us shall give account of himself to God. (Rom. 14:12)

There should be no schism in the body, but that the members should have the same care for one another. And if one member suffers, all the members suffer with it; or if one member is honored, all the members rejoice with it. (I Cor. 12:25–26)

Brethren, if a man is overtaken in any trespass, you who are spiritual restore such a one in a spirit of gentleness, considering yourself lest you also be tempted. Bear one another's burdens, and so fulfill the law of Christ. (Gal. 6:1–2)

Brethren, if anyone among you wanders from the truth, and someone turns him back, let him know that he who turns a sinner from the error of his way will save a soul from death and cover a multitude of sins. (James 5:19–20)

Do not receive an accusation against an elder except from two or three witnesses. Those who are sinning rebuke in the presence of all, that the rest also may fear. I charge you before God and the Lord Jesus Christ and the elect angels that you observe these things without prejudice, doing nothing with partiality. (I Tim. 5:19–21)

Reject a divisive man after the first and second admonition. (Titus 3:10)

Preach the word! Be ready in season and out of season. Convince, rebuke, exhort, with all longsuffering and teaching. (2 Tim. 4:2)

If anyone does not obey our word in this epistle, note that person and do not keep company with him, that he may be ashamed. Yet do not count him as an enemy, but admonish him as a brother. (2 Thess. 3:14–15)

Warn those who are unruly, comfort the fainthearted, uphold the weak, be patient with all. See that no one renders evil for evil to anyone, but always pursue what is good both for yourselves and for all. Rejoice always, pray without ceasing, in everything give thanks; for this is the will of God in Christ Jesus for you. (I Thess. 5:14–18)

Your glorying is not good. Do you not know that a little leaven leavens the whole lump? Therefore purge out the old leaven, that you may be a new lump, since you truly are unleavened. For indeed Christ, our Passover, was sacrificed for us. . . . I wrote to you in my epistle not to keep company with sexually immoral people. Yet I certainly did not mean with the sexually immoral people of this world, or with the covetous, or extortioners, or idolaters, since then you would need to go out of the world. But now I have written to you not to keep company with anyone named a brother, who is sexually immoral, or covetous, or an idolater, or a reviler, or a drunkard, or an extortioner—not even to eat with such a person. For what have I to do with judging those also who are outside? Do you not judge those who are inside? But those who are outside God judges. Therefore "put away from yourselves the evil person." (I Cor. 5:6–7, 9–13)

For even if I made you sorry with my letter, I do not regret it; though I did regret it. For I perceive that the same epistle made you sorry, though only for a while. Now I rejoice, not that you were made sorry, but that your sorrow led to repentance. For you were made sorry in a godly manner, that you might suffer loss from us in nothing. For godly sorrow produces repentance leading to salvation, not to be regretted; but the sorrow of the world produces death. For observe this very thing, that you sorrowed in a godly manner: What diligence it produced in you, what clearing of yourselves, what indignation, what fear, what vehement desire, what zeal, what vindication! In all things you proved yourselves to be clear in this matter. Therefore, although I wrote to you, I did not do it for the sake of him who had done the wrong, nor for the sake of him who suffered wrong, but that our care for you in the sight of God might appear to you. (2 Cor. 7:8–12)

"By the mouth of two or three witnesses every word shall be established." (2 Cor. 13:1)

Some ministries you may want to consider developing include:

- God watch—Encourage people to watch for God's activity around your church and community and then report to the body.
- Discipleship training—When a life is swept clean and yet not filled with a new way of living, old patterns may return (Matt. 12:43–45). Provide training in Christian living to fill the void left in a cleansed life.
- House of prayer—Make every effort to develop a praying church. Don't focus on the activity of prayer but on the relationship to the Lord.
- Restore meaning to worship—Many practices of worship have lost their significance. We tend to treat worship as common or as mere ritual. Baptism and the Lord's Supper ought to be significant times of worship.

Pentecost Prayer Meetings

Wellington, Texas, is a rural community with about thirty-five hundred people in the county. First Baptist Church had been through a time of renewal. The pastor couldn't explain what had happened, but he said: "This church is different. We are not the same church we were three years ago. We have a spirit of unity. The people love each other. They love the Lord and are seeking to obey Him. They have a burden to pray and a concern to see unbelievers come to saving faith in Christ."

During 1993 and 1994, the church had not held the traditional spring and fall revival services. They had focused their attention on seeking the Lord. They had prepared to follow the Lord as soon as He let them know what they should do. Early in 1995, as groups and individuals were praying, they began to sense a burden to give themselves more fully to prayer. Since they realized God had changed them, they anticipated they would begin to see a harvest of people becoming Christians. As they prayed and sought the counsel of others, they sensed God leading them to a particular approach.

They learned from a study of the Jewish festivals that the Jewish people had a family emphasis counting up the fifty days to Pentecost. The emphasis in Scripture on Pentecost is firstfruits, and the early church experienced the fulfillment of the firstfruits on the Day of Pentecost when three thousand were converted. They also heard about Andrew Murray's testimony regarding Pentecost prayer meetings the ten days between ascension and Pentecost. As a congregation they committed the spring of 1995 to an emphasis on prayer, especially prayer for a spiritual harvest.

Beginning the day after Passover, families met daily to read a portion of Scripture and to pray. Families began to list all the non-Christians they knew personally and to pray for their salvation. This continued for the fifty days leading up to Pentecost.

For six weeks prior to Pentecost Sunday, the entire church studied the discipleship material *In God's Presence*, a study on prayer. Each Sunday every adult and youth Sunday school class spent an hour praying together and practicing what they had learned. During their worship services volunteers spent time in a prayer room praying for special requests submitted by members. They also began to pray through a growing list of names of non-Christians in their community.

On each of the ten days prior to Pentecost, they met nightly to pray together. One evening they invited all the other churches in the community to join them in prayer for their county. Some nights they divided and went to homes to pray in small groups. Some small groups went on prayer walks throughout the town; still others went on prayer drives throughout the county, praying for a spiritual harvest. One night the church commissioned a team of members who were leaving on a mission trip to Russia; together they prayed for a spiritual harvest. By the time Pentecost Sunday came, God had prepared this church as a house of prayer for the nations.

Pentecost Sunday's service became a time of testimony and sharing about what God had done in recent months. Some who had never given a public testimony told of how they came to know Christ. Four people made public commitments to the Lord that day. These were viewed as firstfruits in Wellington. Then the church held a dinner on the grounds to celebrate God's bounty and the provision for the physical needs of His people. Another person was born again that afternoon.

During the coming months they began to see the power of the Lord released in bringing people to Christ. Their Russian mission trip saw four hundred people come to Christ. Their church was already participating in a variety of prison ministries. They saw more than three hundred prisoners come to saving faith in Christ. Members began to disciple the new converts in the prison, and they saw lives radically changed. Twenty-five people they had been praying for in their small community placed their faith in Christ. This ordinary church saw what Almighty God could do when they surrendered themselves to God's agenda.

Conclusion

These appendixes are a resource for pastors and church leaders as they seek to be an instrument in God's hands to bring revival to their church and community. These are only examples. The key is not to copy them but to seek the same God who guided these people and to see what God wants you to do for your church. God loves you, and He loves your church. God knows what to do to bring your people back to Him. Don't grow discouraged if you have not yet seen God bring your people back to Him. Trust Him and follow Him. Then watch to see the mighty work God does through you to revive God's people.

NOTES

Foreword

1. Anne Graham Lotz, *I Saw the LORD* (Grand Rapids, MI: Zondervan, 2006), 27, 29.

Preface

1. Brian Edwards, *Revival! A People Saturated with God* (Durham, England: Evangelical Press, 1990; reprint ed., 1994), 22.

Chapter I, The Normal Christian Life

1. Martin Lloyd Jones, *Revival* (Weschester, IL: Crossway Books, 1987), 93.
2. Duncan Campbell, *The Price and Power of Revival* (n.p.: The Faith Mission, n.d.), 7.
3. Octavius Winslow, *Personal Declension and Revival of Religion in the Soul* (n.p.: n.p., 1841; reprint ed., Eugene, OR: Wipf and Stock Publishers, n.d.), 15.
4. Henry Scougal, *The Life of God in the Soul of Man* (n.p.: n.p, 1741; reprint ed., New York: Cosimo Classics, 2007), 48-49.
5. Duncan Campbell, *The Price and Power of Revival*, 21.
6. Ibid., 27.
7. David Matthews, *I Saw the Welsh Revival* (Belfast: Ambassador Publications, 2004), 122.

Chapter 2, What Is Revival

1. Stephen Olford, *Heartcry for Revival* (Memphis: EMI Books, 1962; reprinted ed., 1980), 26.
2. Malcom McDow and Alvin Reid, *Firefall: How God Has Shaped History through Revivals* (Nashville, TN: Broadman & Holman, 1997), 7.
3. Francois Carr, *Revival: The Glory of God* (Pretoria, South Africa: Anker Printers, 2004), 17.
4. Duncan Campbell, *The Price and Power of Revival*, 33.
5. Richard Owen Roberts, *Revival* (Carol Stream, IL: Tyndale House Publishers, 1982), 16.
6. Martin Lloyd Jones, *Revival* (Weschester, IL: Crossway Books, 1987), 47.
7. Brian Edwards, *Revival! A People Saturated with God*, 28.
8. Arthur Wallis, *In the Day of Your Power: A Picture of Revival from Scripture and History* (Columbia, MO: City Hill Publishing, 1956; reprint ed., 1990), 22.

9. Elmer Towns describes "nine faces of revival" with "repentance revival" being one of those nine in his book with Neil Anderson, *Rivers of Revival* (Ventura, CA: Regal Books, 1998) and in his book with Douglas Porter, *The Ten Greatest Revivals Ever* (Ann Arbor, MI: Vine Books, 2000).

10. Richard Owen Roberts, *Repentance: The First Word of the Gospel* (Wheaton, IL: Crossway Books, 2002).

11. Jonathan Edwards, "A Narrative of Surprising Conversions" in *Jonathan Edwards on Revival* (Carlisle, PA: The Banner of Truth Trust, 1984), 33.

12. Ibid., 31.

13. Helen Wessel, ed., *The Autobiography of Charles G. Finney* (Minneapolis: Bethany House, 1977), 57.

14. Jonathan Goforth, *By My Spirit* (Grand Rapids, MI: Zondervan, 1942), 101.

15. Ibid., 9.

16. John Avant, Malcom McDow, and Alvin Reid, *Revival!: The Story of the Current Awakening in Brownwood, Fort Worth, Wheaton, and Beyond* (Nashville, TN: Broadman & Holman, 1996), 157.

17. Brian Edwards, *Revival! A People Saturated with God*, 212.

18. Ibid., 30.

19. Ibid., 47.

20. W. J. Couper, James Burns, and Mary Duncan, *Scotland Saw Her His Glory: A History of Revivals in Scotland* (Wheaton, IL: International Awakening Press, 1995), Richard Owen Roberts, ed., 128.

21. H. Elvet Lewis, G. Campbell Morgan, and I. V. Neprash, *Glory Filled the Land: A Trilogy of the Welsh Revival* (1904–1905) (Wheaton, IL: International Awakening Press, 1989), Richard Owen Roberts, ed., 186.

22. John Greenfield, *Power from on High: The Story of the Great Moravian Revival of 1727* (Bethlehem, PA: The Moravian Church of America, 1928), 19.

23. Brian Edwards, *Revival! A People Saturated with God*, 230.

24. J. Edwin Orr, *The Event of the Century: The 1857–1858 Awakening* (Wheaton, IL: International Awakening Press, 1989), Richard Owen Roberts, ed., 23–38.

25. George Marsden, *Jonathan Edwards: A Life* (New Haven, CT: Yale University Press, 2003), 163.

26. J. Edwin Orr, *Campus Aflame: A History of Evangelical Awakenings in Collegiate Communities* (Wheaton, IL: International Awakening Press, 1994), Richard Owen Roberts, ed.

27. George Marsden, *Jonathan Edwards: A Life*, 150.

28. J. Edwin Orr, *My All His All* (Wheaton, IL: International Awakening Press, 1989), Richard Owen Roberts, ed., 19.

29. Ibid., 23.

Chapter 3, Current Status of the Church and the World

1. "Willow Creek Repents?" 18 October 2007, *Christianity Today* http://blog. christianitytoday.com/outofur/archives/2007/10/willow_creek_re.html.

Chapter 5, God's Plumb Line

1. Jonathan Goforth, *When the Spirit's Fire Swept Korea* (Elkhart, IN: Bethel Publishing, 1984), 8.

2. C. L. Culpepper, *The Shantung Revival* (n.p.: Crescendo Book Publications, 1971; reprint ed., Atlanta: Home Mission Board, SBC, 1982; reprint ed., 1986), 9.

3. Adapted from C. L. Culpepper, *The Shantung Revival* and Bertha Smith, *Go Home and Tell* (Nashville, TN: Broadman & Holman, 1995).

4. Stephen F. Olford, *Heartcry for Revival*, 34.

5. Martin Lloyd Jones, *Revival*, 35.

6. Brian Edwards, *Revival!*, 64.

7. Octavius Winslow, *Personal Declension*, 17.

8. Martin Lloyd Jones, *Revival*, 47.

9. Jonathan Goforth, *By My Spirit*, 136.

10. Thomas Phillips, *The Welsh Revival: Its Origin and Development* (Carlisle, PA: The Banner of Truth Trust, 1989), 51.

11. Ibid., 23.

12. Erwin Lutzer, *Flames of Freedom: A Penetrating, behind the Scenes Report of a Recent Spiritual Movement Carried Worldwide by Laymen* (Chicago: Moody Press, 1976), 35.

13. James Alexander Stewart, *William Chambers Burns and Robert Murray McCheyne: Biographical Sketches by James Alexander Stewart* (Asheville, NC: Revival Literature, 1963), 14.

14. John Avant, Malcom McDow, and Alvin Reid, *Revival! The Story of the Current Awakening in Brownwood, Fort Worth, Wheaton, and Beyond* (Nashville, TN: Broadman & Holman, 1996).

15. Erwin Lutzer, *Flames of Freedom*.

16. James Alexander Stewart, *William Chambers Burns and Robert Murray McCheyne: Biographical Sketches by James Alexander Stewart*, 80.

Chapter 6, The Biblical Record of Revival

1. See for example, C. E. Autrey, *Revivals of the Old Testament* (Grand Rapids, MI: Zondervan Publishing, 1960).

2. Malcom McDow and Alvin Reid, *Firefall*, 45.

Chapter 7, Biblical Foundations for Revival

1. T. W. Hunt, "Christ-centered Revival," *National Prayer Conference Notebook* (June 1990), 9–12.

Chapter 9, God Disciplines His People

1. Ann Graham Lotz, *I Saw the LORD*, 19–20.

2. Henry Scougal, *The Life of God in the Soul of Man*, 95.

3. Octavius Winslow, *Personal Declension*, 176.

4. Jonathan Goforth, *By My Spirit*, 131.

Chapter 10, God's People Cry Out in Repentance

1. J. Edwin Orr, *My All His All*, 19.

2. Details for this revival are taken from the unpublished work: Mark D. Partin, *The 40 Day Reign of God: The Life-Changing Revival in Which God Rained Down and Reigned Over a Small Church in Rural Tennessee for 40 Days* (LaFollette, TN: 2008).

3. Richard Owen Roberts, *Revival*, 16.

4. Henry Scougal, *The Life of God in the Soul of Man*, 69.

5. Nancy Leigh DeMoss, *Holiness: The Heart God Purifies* (Chicago, IL: Moody Press, 2004), 83.

6. Henry Scougal, *The Life of God in the Soul of Man*, 73.

7. C. L. Culpepper, *The Shantung Revival*, 31-32.

8. J. Edwin Orr, *Revival Is like Judgment Day* (Atlanta, GA: Home Mission Board, 1987).

9. J. Edwin Orr, *My All His All*, 41.

10. Richard Owen Roberts, *Repentance: The First Word of the Gospel*, 23.

11. Arthur Wallis, *In the Day of Your Power*, 26.

12. For a more extensive report see John Avant, Malcom McDow and Alvin Reid, *Revival! The Story of the Current Awakening in Brownwood, Fort Worth, Wheaton, and Beyond* (Nashville, TN: Broadman & Holman, 1996).

13. Andrew Bonar, *Robert Murray M'Cheyne: Memoirs and Remains* (Carlisle, PA: Banner of Truth, 1960), 42.

Chapter 11, Responding to Revival

1. Jonathan Goforth, *When the Spirit's Fire Swept Korea*, 6–8.

2. Ibid., 8.

3. Arthur Wallis, *In the Day of Your Power*, 22.

4. Jonathan Goforth, *By My Spirit*, 9.

5. Richard Owen Roberts, *Revival*, 16.

6. Duncan Campbell, *The Nature of a God-Sent Revival* (Vinton, VA: Christ Life Publications, 1993), 19.

7. Robert E. Coleman, *One Divine Moment: The Asbury Revival* (New York, NY: Fleming H. Revell Company, 1970; revised ed., 1995), 10.

8. Iain Murray, *Jonathan Edwards: A New Biography* (Carlisle, PA: Banner of Truth, 2003), 130.

9. Helen Wessel, ed., *The Autobiography of Charles G. Finney* (Minneapolis, MN: Bethany House, 1977), 115.

10. Duncan Campbell, *The Nature of a God-Sent Revival*, 22.

11. John Pollock, *Moody: A Biography* (Grand Rapids, MI: Baker Books, 1963; reprint ed., 1995), 85.

12. Ibid., 89.

13. Helen Wessel ed., *The Autobiography of Charles G. Finney*, 137.

14. Henry Scougal, *The Life of God in the Soul of Man*, 81.

15. Ibid., 79.

16. John Pollock, *Moody*, 163.

17. For an account of this event see John Avant, Malcom McDow, and Alvin Reid, *Revival!*, 104–139.

Chapter 12, Great Awakenings

1. Adapted from Claude King, *Come to the Lord's Table* (Nashville, TN: LifeWay Press, 2006), 11–15.

2. Andrew Murray, *The Key to the Missionary Problem* (New York, NY: American Tract Society, 1901), 47, 49.

3. Arthur Wallis, *In the Day of Your Power*, 49.

4. Brian Edwards, *Revival!*, 30.

5. Arthur Wallis, *In the Day of Your Power*, 28, 47.

6. H. H. Osborn, *Fire in the Hills: The Revival Which Spread from Ruanda* (East Sussex, Great Britain: Highland Books, 1991).

7. J. Edwin Orr, *Campus Aflame: A History of Evangelical Awakenings in Collegiate Communities*, 33.

8. George M. Marsden, *Jonathan Edwards: A Life*, 150.

9. J. Edwin Orr, *Campus Aflame*, 39.

10. Malcom McDow and Alvin Reid, *Firefall*, 229.

11. Ibid. See *Firefall* for more extensive treatment of the results of the awakening, 247–49.

12. Lewis Drummond, *Eight Keys to Biblical Revival* (Minneapolis, MN: Bethany House, 1994), 35.

13. Duncan Campbell, *The Nature of God-Sent Revival*, 15.

14. Thomas Phillips, *The Welsh Revival*, 7.

15. Ibid., 8.

16. Ibid., 10.

17. Ibid., 20, 36, 43.

18. Ibid., 72, 106.

19. David Matthews, *I Saw the Welsh Revival*, 52–55.

20. J. Edwin Orr, *My All His All*, 7.

Chapter 13, The Role of Prayer in Revival

1. Richard Owen Roberts, ed., *Scotland Saw His Glory* (Somerville, MA: International Press, 1995), 128.

2. D. Macfarlan, *The Revivals of the Eighteenth Century* (Wheaton, IL: Richard Owen Roberts Publishers, 1980), 35.

3. Richard Owen Roberts, ed., *Scotland Saw His Glory*, 132.

4. Ibid., 137.

5. Jonathan Goforth, *By My Spirit*, 132.

6. Arthur Wallis, *In the Day of Your Power*, 211.

7. E. M. Bounds, *Power through Prayer* (Grand Rapids, MI: Baker Books, 1972; reprint ed., 1982), 31.

8. Brian Edwards, *Revival!*, 84.

9. Jonathan Goforth, *When the Spirit's Fire Swept Korea*, 17.

10. Octavius Winslow, *Personal Declension*, 18–19.

11. Helen Wessel, *Charles G. Finney*, 39.

12. Ibid., 59.

13. Arthur Wallis, *In the Day of Your Power*, 172.

14. Ibid., 188.

15. Ibid., 50.

16. James Alexander Stewart, *William Chambers Burns and Robert Murray McCheyne: Biographical Sketches by James Alexander Stewart*, 21.

17. Ibid., 44.

18. This account found in Collin and Mary Peckham, *Sounds from Heaven: The Revival on the Isle of Lewis, 1949–1952* (Ross-shire, Scotland: Christian Focus Publications, 2004), 113.

19. Duncan Campbell, *The Price and Power of Revival*, 35.

20. Ibid., 18.

21. Arthur Wallis, *In the Day of Your Power*, 118.

22. John Pollock, *Moody*, 96–97.

23. Thomas Phillips, *The Welsh Revival*, 21.

24. Ibid., 49.

25. Jonathan Goforth, *When the Spirit's Fire Swept Korea*, 8.

26. Jonathan Goforth, *By My Spirit*, 34.

27. J. Edwin Orr, *The Event of the Century: The 1857–1858 Awakening*.

28. See also Samuel I. Prime, *The Power of Prayer: Illustrated in the Wonderful Displays of Divine Grace at the Fulton Street and Other Meetings in New York and Elsewhere, in 1857 and 1858* (n.p: n.p., 1859; reprint ed., Carlisle, PA: Banner of Truth Trust, 1991).

29. Ibid., 52.

30. Frank Grenville Beardsley, *A History of American Revivals* (Boston, MA: American Tract Society, 1904), 216.

Chapter 14, Corporate Hindrances to Revival

1. Octavius Winslow, *Personal Declension*, 27.

Chaper 15, Worship and Revival

1. Henry Scougal, *The Life of God in the Soul of Man*, 81.

2. David Matthews, *I Saw the Welsh Revival*, 44.

3. Jonathan Goforth, *By My Spirit*, 46.

4. Octavius Winslow, *Personal Declension*, 16.

5. C. L. Culpepper, *The Shantung Revival*, 13.

6. Erwin W. Lutzer, *Flames of Freedom*, 39.

7. A. Daniel Frankforter, *Stones for Bread* (Louisville, KY: Westminster John Knox Press, 2001), 133.

8. Ibid., 158.

9. Ibid., 19.

10. Ibid., 134.

11. Stephen Olford, *Heartcry for Revival*, 19.

12. Lewis Drummond, *Eight Keys to Biblical Revival*, 125.

13. Francois Carr, *Revival: The Glory of God*, 40.

14. Robert E. Coleman, ed., *One Divine Moment: The Asbury Revival*, 32.

15. Ibid., 34.

16. Duncan Campbell, *The Nature of God-Sent Revival*, 11.

17. Thomas Phillips, *The Welsh Revival*, 41.

18. C. L. Culpepper, *The Shantung Revival*, 36.

19. Ibid., 37.

20. A. Daniel Frankforter, *Stones for Bread*, 13.

21. Henry and Richard Blackaby, *Spiritual Leadership: Moving People on to God's Agenda* (Nashville, TN: Broadman & Holman, 2001).

22. Brian Edwards, *Revival!*, 31.

23. Jonathan Edwards, *Jonathan Edwards on Revival*, 44.

24. Brian Edwards, *Revival!*, 212.

25. Jonathan Goforth, *By My Spirit*, 9.

26. Martin Lloyd Jones, *Revival*, 99.

27. Robert Coleman, *One Divine Moment*, 14.

28. Jonathan Goforth, *By My Spirit*, 113.

29. Thomas Phillips, *The Welsh Revival*, 18.

30. C. L. Culpepper, *The Shantung Revival*, 33.

31. A. Daniel Frankforter, *Stones for Bread*, 12.

32. Ibid.

Chapter 16, Counterfeits to Revival

1. Arthur Wallis, *In the Day of Your Power*, 167.

2. Arnold Dallimore, *George Whitefield: God's Anointed Servant in the Great Revival of the Eighteenth Century* (Wheaton, IL: Crossway Books, 1990), 142.

3. Iain Murray, *Jonathan Edwards*, 225.

4. Arnold Dallimore, *George Whitefield*, 143.

5. Iain Murray, *Jonathan Edwards*, 225.

6. Ibid., 227.

7. Jonathan Edwards, "The Distinguishing Marks of a Work of the Spirit of God" in *Jonathan Edwards on Revival*, 86.

8. Ibid., 89.

9. Ibid., 142.

10. C. L. Culpepper, *The Shantung Revival*, 67.

11. Thomas Phillips, *The Welsh Revival*, 54.

12. Arthur Wallis, *In the Day of Your Power*, 91.

13. Duncan Campbell, *The Price and Power of Revival*, 37.

14. Jonathan Goforth, *By My Spirit*, 28.

15. Henry Scougal, *The Life of God in the Soul of Man*, 86.

16. Ibid., 129.

17. Francois Carr, *Revival: The Glory of God*, 61.

18. James Alexander Stewart, *William Chambers Burns and Robert Murray McCheyne: Biographical Sketches by James Alexander Stewart*, 23.

19. Jonathan Goforth, *By My Spirit*, 135.

20. I. V. Neprash, "The Spirituality of the Welsh Revival" in *Glory Filled the Land: A Trilogy of the Welsh Revival* (1904–1905) (Wheaton, IL: International Awakening Press, 1989), Richard Owen Roberts, ed., 187.

21. Ibid., 188.

22. Ibid., 188–89.

Chapter 17, Why Revival Tarries

1. Leonard Ravenhill, *Why Revival Tarries* (Minneapolis, MN: Bethany House, 1979).

2. Richard Owen Roberts, *Repentance*, 101.

3. Arthur Wallis, *In the Day of Your Power*, 205.

4. Ibid., 60.

5. Martin Lloyd Jones, *Revival*, 21–22.

6. Arthur Wallis, *In the Day of Your Power*, 204.

Chapter 18, Becoming a Catalyst for Revival

1. Brian Edwards, *Revival!*, 50.

2. Thomas Phillips, *The Welsh Revival*, 132.

3. Brian Edwards, *Revival!*, 48.

4. Richard Owen Roberts, ed., *Scotland Saw His Glory*, 115.

5. Ibid.

6. James Alexander Stewart, *William Chambers Burns and Robert Murray McCheyne: Biographical Sketches by James Alexander Stewart*, 19.

7. Ibid.

8. Arthur Wallis, *In the Day of Your Power*, xi.

9. James Alexander Stewart, *Robert Murray McCheyne*, 12.

10. Malcom McDow and Alvin Reid, *Firefall*, 278.

11. D. Macfarlan, *Revivals in the Eighteenth Century*, 11.

12. Malcom McDow and Alvin Reid, *Firefall*, 212.

13. Duncan Campbell, *The Price and Power of Revival*, 23.

14. Brian Edwards, *Revival!*, 50.

15. David Matthews, *I Saw the Welsh Revival*, 19.

16. Andrew Bonar, *Robert Murray M'Cheyne: Memoirs and Remains*, 143.

17. Duncan Campbell, *The Nature of a God-Sent Revival*, 25.

18. Brian Edwards, *Revival!*, 48.

19. Jonathan Goforth, *When the Spirit Swept Korea*, 6.

20. David Matthews, *I Saw the Welsh Revival*, 74.

Chapter 19, Maintaining Revival

1. Brian Edwards, *Revival!*, 230.

2. Ibid.

3. Octavius Winslow, *Personal Declension*, 62.

4. Iain Murray, *Jonathan Edwards*, 238.

5. Henry Blackaby and Richard Blackaby, *Hearing God's Voice* (Nashville, TN: Broadman & Holman, 2002).

6. Arnold Dallimore, *George Whitefield*, 30.

7. Iain Murray, *Jonathan Edwards*, 348.

8. Jonathan Goforth, *By My Spirit*, 11.

9. Ibid., 21.

10. For a challenge on how Christians tend to limit what God does in their life, see Richard Blackaby, *Unlimitng God: Increasing Your Capacity to Experience the Divine* (Colorado Springs, CO: Multnomah, 2008).

Appendix A

1. Two helpful resources on spiritual leadership are: Henry Blackaby and Richard Blackaby, *Spiritual Leadership: Moving People on to God's Agenda* (Nashville, TN: Broadman & Holman, 2001), and Henry Blackaby and Richard Blackaby, *Called to Be God's Leader: Lessons from the Life of Joshua* (Nashville, TN: Thomas Nelson, 2004).

Appendix D

1. Andrew Murray, *The Lord's Table: A Help to the Right Observance of the Lord's Supper* (Fort Washington, PA.: Christian Literature Crusade, 1985).

2. Andrew Murray, *The Prayer Life* (Springdale, PA: Whitaker House, 1981).

3. Lewis H. Elvet, "With Christ Among the Miners," *Glory Filled the Land*, ed., Richard Owen Roberts (Wheaton, IL: International Awakening Press, 1989), 20.

Scripture Index